The American Presidency

Compton's by Britannica®

ENCYCLOPÆDIA
Britannica®

CHICAGO   LONDON   NEW DELHI   PARIS   SEOUL   SYDNEY   TAIPEI   TOKYO

Learn & Explore series
The American Presidency
Compton's by Britannica

Library of Congress Control Number: 2007908762
International Standard Book Number: 978-1-59339-843-9

Printed in China

Britannica may be accessed at http://www.britannica.com on the Internet.

www.britannica.com

EDITOR'S PREFACE

The 2008 U.S. presidential election was one with several historic implications. During the Democratic primaries Senator Barack Obama became the first African American to be nominated for the presidency by either major party. His closest rival was Senator Hillary Rodham Clinton who, if she had won the nomination, would have made history as well by becoming the first woman nominated by either major party. The Republicans nominated Senator John McCain who, if elected, would have become the oldest candidate to have entered the office. His choice of Governor Sarah Palin as his vice-presidential running mate was yet another historic milestone in that she was the first woman nominated for that office by the Republican party. In the end more history was made by Barack Obama when on Nov. 4, 2008, he was elected 44th president of the United States, the first African American to hold the office.

The American Presidency is a review of the people who have held the office from George Washington to Barack Obama. Each profile is presented in a format that is either two, three, or four pages and includes each president's signature, who served as vice president, a profile of the first ladies, and timelines. The introduction was written by author Thomas J. Craughwell who has written books on a variety of subjects including politics. *Failures of the Presidents: From the Whiskey Rebellion and War of 1812 to the Bay of Pigs and War in Iraq* (2008) and *Stealing Lincoln's Body* (2007) are among his best-sellers. His introduction for this volume can be found on page *vi*. What follows is an overview article titled Office of the President which outlines presidential duties. Articles on the presidents are then presented in the order of their service. There is, however, only one entry for Grover Cleveland who served both as 22nd and 24th president. Following the final profile are articles on the Presidential Election Process, Cabinet, White House, a table of election results, and capsules on the presidential flag and the presidential seal history. A bibliography and two-page index complete the volume.

Over the years it has been the Compton's tradition to inspire ambition, to stimulate the imagination, and to provide the inquiring mind with accurate information. With over 175 images, 43 timelines, and 33 world events maps, *The American Presidency* joins the family of *Compton's by Britannica* products that have been designed to do just that.

TABLE OF CONTENTS

THE AMERICAN PRESIDENCY

This introduction was contributed by Thomas J. Craughwell, author of Stealing Lincoln's Body *(Harvard University Press, 2007) and* Failures of the Presidents *(Fair Winds Press, 2008). He has written articles on history, politics, religion, and popular culture for* The Wall Street Journal, The New York Times, U.S. News and World Report, The American Spectator, Emmy magazine, *and* Inside the Vatican.

INTRODUCTION

In 1789 the world was ruled by kings and queens, emperors and empresses, sultans and rajahs. No nation had ever been governed by a president, so when George Washington was elected first president of the United States he had to invent the job. Some of Washington's ideas about the presidency have not survived—for example, today no one addresses the president as "Your High Mightiness." But the idea that the members of the president's Cabinet answer to him, that he has final say over the policy decisions of his administration, originated with George Washington. As commander in chief of the Continental Army during the American Revolution he often turned to his officers for advice, but Washington regarded the ultimate decision-making authority as his alone. Washington's model ensured that the president of the United States would not be a figurehead, but someone with real political power.

Foreign observers wondered, if Washington was not a king, would he be a dictator and remain president for life? Once again our first president set the pattern for all the presidents who would follow him: when his two terms were up, he left office and went home to Mount Vernon. The two-term precedent has been honored by every president except Franklin D. Roosevelt, who broke with tradition and served for four terms. (After his death in 1945, Congress passed a law limiting the president to two terms.)

Over the years other presidents learned how to increase the power of their office. Andrew Jackson used his political capital as a war hero and a "man of the people" to influence legislation on Capitol Hill. The crisis of the Civil War led Abraham Lincoln to exercise power in ways earlier presidents could only dream of. In addition to acting as commander in chief, he suspended the right of habeas corpus, arresting anyone who was suspected of disloyalty to the Union, and even ignored the decisions of the Supreme Court when it suited him. Theodore Roosevelt declared that the presidency was a "bully pulpit" from which he could speak directly to the American people and persuade them to support his programs. And Roosevelt's programs were ambitious: he insisted on national standards for food and drugs sold to the American public; he broke up big corporate monopolies known as "trusts" because they stymied competition; and he convinced Congress to set aside millions of acres of wilderness as national parks.

After World War II the president took on a greater role in defining America's foreign policy. Harry S. Truman directed the Marshall Plan to rebuild war-torn Europe and ordered U.S. troops to Korea without going to Congress for a declaration of war. Some critics, believing that the president's power was becoming too broad, spoke of "an imperial presidency." If there was an imperial presidency, much of the steam went out of it in the 1970s, the decade of the Watergate scandal and resignation of Richard M. Nixon, America's defeat in Vietnam, and the humiliating hostage crisis in Iran.

The power of the office is not the only aspect of the American presidency that has evolved over time. One of the first changes was how the vice president was selected. Initially the candidate who received the greatest number of electoral votes became president, and the runner-up became vice president. This was an idea doomed to failure, as the country witnessed when President John Adams was saddled with his political enemy, Thomas Jefferson, as his vice president. Congress settled the matter in 1803 when it passed the Twelfth Amendment to the U.S. Constitution, which called for the vice president to be elected in his own right. The first vice president to be elected was George Clinton in 1804.

Just as no one knew what to call the president, no one knew what to call his wife, either. Martha Washington was generally addressed as "Lady Washington," as if she were an aristocrat. In 1863 Mary Todd Lincoln was referred to as "the First Lady in the Land," but the title did not catch on until Lucy Webb Hayes moved into the White House in 1877; she was very popular, and the title "First Lady" was as much a token of affection as it was of respect.

Finally, everyone wants to know about the president's salary. George Washington was paid $25,000 a year; his vice president, John Adams, received $5,000. Over the years the amount paid to the president steadily increased: $50,000 in 1873; $75,000 in 1909; $100,000 in 1949; and $200,000 in 1969. In addition, from 1949 through 1994 both the president and vice president had expense accounts. Beginning in 2001 the president's salary was raised to $400,000, and in 2005 the vice president's salary was $208,100.

OFFICE OF THE PRESIDENT

The founders of the United States originally intended the presidency to be a narrowly restricted office. Newly independent of Great Britain, they distrusted executive authority because of their experience with British King George III and his governors in the American Colonies. Yet from the start, the office of the president—as defined through the practice of George Washington and his successors—was vested with great authority. Today, the president of the United States is arguably the most powerful elected official in the world.

Although Washington and future presidents would put their own stamp on the office, they all worked within the basic framework laid out during the Constitutional Convention in 1787. The delegates had sharp disagreements on the nature of the office. Should there be one president or three? Should he serve for life or for a limited term? Was he eligible for reelection? Should he be elected by the people, by the governors of the states, or by Congress?

The outcome of the debates was Article II of the Constitution, outlining the office of the president. The presidency would consist of one individual holding office for four years but eligible for reelection. To be eligible for the presidency a person must be a native-born citizen, must be at least 35 years of age, and must have lived in the United States for at least 14 years.

Based on the example set by George Washington, successive presidents did not seek more than a second term until Franklin D. Roosevelt ran for office and was elected four times, beginning in 1932. The 22nd Amendment, ratified in 1951, limits presidents to two terms of office.

The Constitution gives many specific powers to the president. Other powers have accrued to the office through laws passed by Congress, through interpretations of laws by the courts, and through the president's position as leader of his party.

The president's chief duty is to make sure that the laws are faithfully executed, and this duty is performed through a system of executive agencies that includes Cabinet-level departments. Presidents appoint all Cabinet heads and most other high-ranking officials of the executive branch of the federal government. They also nominate all judges of the federal judiciary, including the members of the Supreme Court. Their appointments to executive and judicial posts must be approved by a majority of the Senate, the upper house of Congress.

The president exercises far-reaching powers in the conduct of foreign policy. In most cases he acts through the secretary of state and the Department of State. The president negotiates treaties, mostly through subordinates. These are subject to confirmation by a two-thirds vote in the Senate. He nominates ambassadors, ministers, and consuls to represent the United States abroad. He takes the lead in recognizing new regimes or withholding official recognition.

Closely related to his foreign policy authority is the president's role as commander in chief of all the armed forces. He appoints all commissioned officers of the Army, Navy, Air Force, and Marines. During wartime he may become involved in planning strategy.

Proper functioning of the government depends in great measure on the president's relations with Congress. It is his responsibility to keep Congress informed of the need for new legislation. He must also submit an annual budget for all government expenditures. The departments and agencies are required to send Congress periodic reports of their activities, and members of departments and agencies are often required to testify before Congressional committees on matters of pending legislation or other issues.

In times of war or other national crisis, Congress usually grants the president emergency powers. These powers include the authority to issue orders regulating most phases of national life and the war effort, to organize special agencies of government, and to make appointments without confirmation.

In normal times, as well as during emergencies, Congress may pass laws establishing a policy but leaving the details to be worked out by the executive office. The president then publishes an executive order that has the force of law. The president has the power to approve or reject (veto) bills passed by Congress, though Congress can override the president's veto by summoning a two-thirds majority in favor of the measure.

The only official duty of the vice president is to preside over the Senate, though he does not take part in its deliberations. He casts a deciding vote in case of a tie. In the president's absence he presides over meetings of the Cabinet. Article II of the Constitution provides for the succession of the vice president to the presidency in case of the death, resignation, or removal of the president. The 25th Amendment, ratified in 1967, provides that he also serve as acting president if the president is temporarily incapacitated.

GEORGE WASHINGTON

**1st President of the United States
(1732–99; president 1789–97)**

Vice President: John Adams (1735–1826)

Remembered as the Father of His Country, George Washington stands alone in American history. He was commander in chief of the Continental Army during the American Revolution, chairman of the convention that wrote the U.S. Constitution, and the first president of the United States. He led the people who transformed the United States from a British colony into a self-governing nation. His ideals of liberty and democracy set a standard for future presidents and for the entire country.

Early Life

The eldest child of Augustine and Mary Ball Washington, George Washington was born on Feb. 22, 1732, on the Wakefield plantation in Westmoreland County, Va. His father was a prosperous landowner who managed farms, businesses, and mines. Later the family moved to Ferry Farm on the Rappahannock River, opposite Fredericksburg, Va. Ferry Farm was the setting of George's boyhood adventures as described by Mason Locke Weems in his book *The Life and Memorable Actions of George Washington* (1800). In perhaps the most famous of these stories, George chops down a cherry tree with a hatchet and later admits it to his father, stating that he cannot tell a lie. Today the stories are thought to be fiction rather than fact.

After his father's death in 1743, George lived with his half brother Augustine at Wakefield and attended Henry William's school, one of the best schools in Virginia. By age 15 George was skilled in mathematics and mapmaking and had developed an interest in surveying.

In 1748 George went to live with his other half brother, Lawrence, at an estate on the Potomac River named Mount Vernon. There he met a wealthy landowner who hired him to help survey his holdings in Virginia. George excelled at his new profession. In July 1749 he was appointed surveyor of Culpeper County, his first public office. When Lawrence died in 1752, Washington inherited Mount Vernon, thus becoming a landowner.

French and Indian War

Inspired by his brother's experiences in the British Navy, Washington pursued a military career. He was made a lieutenant colonel in 1754, as tensions rose between the British and the French over control of the Ohio River valley. Washington was sent with nearly 200 troops to take possession of Fort Duquesne, at the site of present-day Pittsburgh, Pa., but he found that the French had claimed it first. Washington built Fort Necessity nearby. From there, his troops and their Native American allies ambushed a French scouting party, killing the commander and nine others. The French and Indian War had begun.

First Lady Martha Washington (1731–1802)

Martha Washington set many of the standards for the proper behavior and treatment of the president's wife. Born Martha Dandridge, she grew up among the wealthy plantation families of eastern Virginia. Her education, traditional for young women of her class and time, emphasized domestic skills and the arts. At age 18 she married Daniel Parke Custis, an heir to a neighboring plantation. His death in 1757 made her wealthy. Two years later she married George Washington and moved with her children to Mount Vernon, where she became known for her graciousness and hospitality. By nature a private person, Martha reluctantly assumed a public role after George became president. In doing so, she contributed to the eventual strength and influence of the position of first lady.

George Washington Timeline

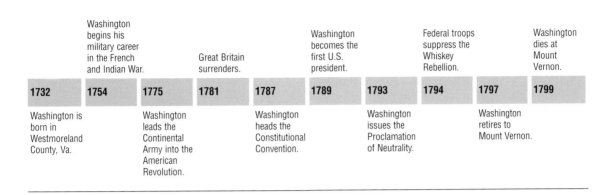

1732	1754	1775	1781	1787	1789	1793	1794	1797	1799

Washington begins his military career in the French and Indian War. (1754)

Great Britain surrenders. (1781)

Washington becomes the first U.S. president. (1789)

Federal troops suppress the Whiskey Rebellion. (1794)

Washington dies at Mount Vernon. (1799)

Washington is born in Westmoreland County, Va. (1732)

Washington leads the Continental Army into the American Revolution. (1775)

Washington heads the Constitutional Convention. (1787)

Washington issues the Proclamation of Neutrality. (1793)

Washington retires to Mount Vernon. (1797)

Washington was promoted to colonel and given command of a small army of Virginia and North Carolina troops and Native American allies. In July 1754 Washington's troops attacked the French forces at Fort Duquesne, but the French and their Native American allies outnumbered them and forced Washington to surrender. In February 1755 Washington was sent to serve as aide to British Maj. Gen. Edward Braddock in another offensive against Fort Duquesne. On July 9, 1755, French forces ambushed and defeated Braddock's forces, and Braddock was killed in the battle. Washington assembled the remaining troops and led them back to Virginia.

In August 1755 Washington was appointed commander of all Virginia's troops. In 1758 he accompanied British Gen. John Forbes and finally defeated the French at Fort Duquesne, which was burned to the ground by the retreating French troops. Washington then resigned from the army with the honorary rank of brigadier general. While serving in the final campaign against Fort Duquesne, Washington was elected to the Virginia House of Burgesses.

Entry into Politics

On Jan. 6, 1759, Washington married a young widow, Martha Dandridge Custis. Martha had two children from her previous marriage—a son named John and a daughter, Martha, who was called Patsy. From the time of his marriage, Washington supervised both Mount Vernon and the large Custis estate, thus becoming one of the wealthiest and most industrious landowners in Virginia. In addition to overseeing the farming, planting, and industry on his estates, Washington continued to serve in the Virginia House of Burgesses.

Washington's happy life was interrupted by deteriorating relations between Great Britain and the colonies. After the French and Indian War ended in 1763, Britain faced a heavy debt as well as continued military costs to protect the land it acquired during the war. As the British government imposed new taxes to generate revenue from the colonies, the colonists protested. Some demanded independence at once.

A loyal British subject, Washington was not yet in favor of separation from Great Britain. However, he

General George Washington and the marquis de Lafayette survey the troops camped at Valley Forge, Pa., during the harsh winter of 1777–78.

The Granger Collection

believed that the British had attacked the rights of the colonists, and he was ready to defend these rights. By the late 1760s he was calling for boycotts of British-made goods. In 1774 Washington and other Virginia legislators signed the resolutions calling for a Continental Congress. He was elected to the Virginia delegation that attended the First Continental Congress in Philadelphia on Sept. 5, 1774. He also attended the Second Continental Congress in 1775.

American Revolution

In April 1775 skirmishes between British troops and the colonists at Lexington and Concord intensified colonial hostility toward Great Britain. Though still not in favor of independence, Washington was prepared to support armed resistance against the British.

Recognizing Washington's military experience and leadership, the Continental Congress made him commander in chief of all colonial military forces in June 1775. Reports of how courageously the colonial militia fought against British soldiers at Bunker Hill in June 1775 gave Washington confidence about the impending war. However, he faced a multitude of hardships as he assembled the Continental Army. His recruits were untrained and poorly paid, terms of army enlistment were short, and his officers frequently quarreled among themselves.

Washington commanded the respect of his troops through his confidence, poise, and determination as a general. In March 1776 his army staged a siege and eventually expelled British troops from Boston. Washington also instilled a sense of national pride in his troops. He maintained discipline within his army by punishing dishonest soldiers and deserters. At the same time, he attended to their welfare by petitioning to the Continental Congress for better rations and pay.

On July 4, 1776, the Continental Congress adopted the Declaration of Independence. Congress wrote the Articles of Confederation, the first constitution in the United States, to implement a national government.

In December 1776 Washington's forces crossed the Delaware River from Pennsylvania to New Jersey and won battles at Trenton and Princeton. The Continental Army gained an advantage in the war with Gen. Horatio Gates's victory in New York at the battle of Saratoga in October 1777. However, Washington's army suffered losses against the British forces in Pennsylvania at the battles of Brandywine and Germantown in the fall of 1777. In December 1777 Washington withdrew to Valley Forge, Pa., where he set up winter quarters. Enduring months of bitter cold and some 2,000 desertions, Washington managed to reorganize his army for the ongoing fight.

The decisive stroke of the war came under Washington's leadership in 1781. His army, with the help of French allies, staged a siege at Yorktown, Va. The commander of the British Army, Gen. Charles Cornwallis, was forced to surrender. The Treaty of Paris was signed on Sept. 3, 1783, officially ending the American Revolution. Washington remained with the Continental Congress until December 1783, when he resigned his commission and returned to his home at Mount Vernon.

Washington's stepdaughter, Patsy, died in 1773, and his stepson, John, died in 1781. George and Martha Washington adopted John's two children, George and Eleanor Custis. Washington acquired more than 50,000 acres (20,000 hectares) in the western territories, and his farms continued to thrive. He worked to develop the Potomac River as a thoroughfare for settlers and trade goods.

Washington's retreat to private life did not last long, however. Concerned with the chaotic political situation of the young country, Washington became a leader in the movement that led to the Constitutional Convention of 1787. For four months he presided over the convention as it drafted a new constitution to replace the ineffective Articles of Confederation. After ratification by the states, the U.S. Constitution became the supreme law of the land.

Presidency

On Feb. 4, 1789, the electoral college unanimously chose George Washington as the first president of the United States. Washington took the oath of office in New York City on April 30, 1789. He was elected to a second term in 1792. John Adams was his vice president.

Washington was committed to a strong federal government. He also believed that the United States should remain neutral in foreign affairs. When war

Washington is inaugurated as the first president of the United States at Federal Hall in New York City on April 30, 1789.

The Granger Collection, New York

broke out between France and Great Britain in 1793, Washington decided that the United States should not interfere because the United States was not prepared to enter another war so soon. Accordingly, he issued the Proclamation of Neutrality, which stated that the United States must maintain a sense of national identity, independent from any other country's influence. Washington's successors continued his neutrality policy.

Disagreements over foreign policy and the powers of the national government led to the emergence of political parties during Washington's presidency. Alexander Hamilton, Washington's secretary of the treasury, became leader of the Federalist party. The Federalists advocated a strong central government and wanted to maintain close ties with Great Britain. Thomas Jefferson, the secretary of state, led the Republican (later Democratic-Republican) party. The Republicans wanted to limit the authority of the national government and defended the power of state and local governments. Washington favored Federalist ideas but worked to sustain a balance between the two parties.

Washington spent many contented years overseeing his Mount Vernon estate. Though he disapproved of slavery, he depended on slaves to do the work of the plantation.

Nathaniel Currier—The Bridgeman Art Library/Getty Images

The U.S. government met its first serious domestic challenge with the Whiskey Rebellion in 1794. Washington set a tax on whiskey to help pay down the national debt. Farmers in western Pennsylvania who relied on income from selling whiskey resisted the tax by assaulting federal revenue officers. After negotiations failed, Washington dispatched 13,000 federal troops to quell the rebellion. The event reinforced the authority of the federal government and further aligned Washington with the Federalists.

Washington's administration faced boundary disputes with Native Americans, Great Britain, and Spain. On the western frontier, Native Americans were fighting settlers who tried to move onto their land. Washington sent an army under the command of Gen. Anthony Wayne, who defeated the Native Americans at the battle of Fallen Timbers. Washington addressed grievances with Great Britain by sending John Jay, chief justice of the Supreme Court, abroad for negotiations. In the Jay Treaty, Great Britain and the United States agreed to the boundaries between the United States and British North America. In Spain, the American diplomat Thomas Pinckney signed a treaty that set the southern boundary of the United States at 31° N latitude and opened the Mississippi River to U.S. trade through Spanish territories.

Retirement

When Washington's second term ended in 1796, he refused to run for a third. He considered it unwise for one person to hold such a powerful position for so long. The precedent he set was maintained until the 20th century, when Franklin D. Roosevelt served four terms as president.

Washington retired to Mount Vernon, where he spent time with his family and resumed the management of his farms and estates. On Dec. 12, 1799, he returned home from a horseback ride in cold, snowy weather. He developed laryngitis and became weak and ill. He died two days later, on Dec. 14, 1799, and was buried in the family vault at Mount Vernon.

JOHN ADAMS

AP

**2nd President of the United States
(1735–1826; president 1797–1801)**

Vice President: Thomas Jefferson (1743–1826)

As a lawyer in the American colonies, John Adams fought for independence from Great Britain. As a diplomat, he helped to secure the peace. His prominent role in the Revolutionary era led to his election as first vice president and second president of the United States.

Early Life

John Adams was born on Oct. 30, 1735, in Braintree (now Quincy), Mass. His parents, John and Susanna Boylston Adams, were descendants of the first generation of Puritan settlers in New England. The elder Adams was a farmer, businessman, lieutenant of a militia, and a deacon in Braintree's Congregational church.

Adams enrolled at Harvard College in Cambridge, Mass., in 1751. He graduated in 1755 and then taught grade school for three years in Worcester, Mass. During this period Adams developed an interest in law and studied in his spare time under one of Boston's most prominent lawyers.

Adams was admitted to the Massachusetts bar in 1758 and established his own law practice in Braintree. On Oct. 25, 1764, Adams married Abigail Smith, a Congregational minister's daughter from Weymouth, Mass. The couple had four children: Abigail Amelia, John Quincy, Charles, and Thomas Boylston.

Entry into Politics

Adams' political career began in Boston in 1765 when he was appointed as a town attorney to challenge the legality of British taxation in the colonies. The British Parliament had instituted the Stamp Act in 1765, which levied a tax on all publications and legal documents in the colonies. The act enraged the colonists, inspiring riots and a boycott of goods that required stamped papers. The widespread protests coupled with the impassioned legal arguments of Adams and his colleagues forced Parliament to repeal the act in 1766. Adams also led the opposition against the Townshend Acts of 1767, which imposed taxes on imported British goods.

Although hostile toward the British government, Adams used his legal skills to defend British soldiers who killed five colonists in the Boston Massacre of 1770. He attested that the crowd had provoked the soldiers by taunting and threatening them. Six of the eight British soldiers involved in the incident were acquitted. Adams' insistence on upholding the legal rights of the soldiers made him temporarily unpopular, but it also marked him as one of the most principled radicals in the growing movement for American independence.

First Lady Abigail Adams (1744–1818)

In thousands of letters to family and friends, Abigail Adams left behind an intimate and vivid portrayal of life in the early years of the United States. Born Abigail Smith, she received no formal education but read widely and developed into a learned, witty young woman. She married John Adams in 1764. In the 1770s, as John took part in the colonial struggle for independence, Abigail managed the family farm and her husband's business affairs. As first lady she kept a rigorous daily schedule, managing a busy household, receiving guests, and advising her husband on political matters. She was an early advocate for women's rights, particularly the right to education. Her son John Quincy Adams was the sixth president of the United States.

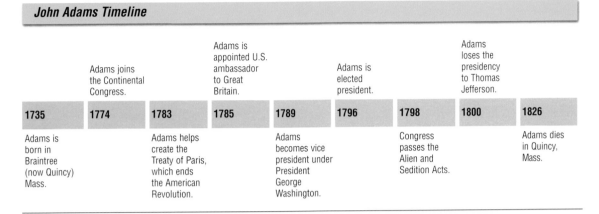

John Adams Timeline

1735	1774	1783	1785	1789	1796	1798	1800	1826

Adams joins the Continental Congress. (1774)

Adams is appointed U.S. ambassador to Great Britain. (1785)

Adams is elected president. (1796)

Adams loses the presidency to Thomas Jefferson. (1800)

Adams is born in Braintree (now Quincy) Mass. (1735)

Adams helps create the Treaty of Paris, which ends the American Revolution. (1783)

Adams becomes vice president under President George Washington. (1789)

Congress passes the Alien and Sedition Acts. (1798)

Adams dies in Quincy, Mass. (1826)

Continental Congress

In 1774 Adams attended the First Continental Congress in Philadelphia as a Massachusetts delegate. Along with the other members, he rejected any further reconciliation with Great Britain. At the Second Continental Congress in 1775, soon after the outbreak of the American Revolution, Adams nominated George Washington as commander in chief of all colonial military forces.

Adams played a major role as the Congress debated independence. He selected Thomas Jefferson to draft the Declaration of Independence and demanded unanimous Congressional support for it. On July 4, 1776, Adams and the rest of the Congress approved the Declaration. The Continental Congress then formulated a plan for a national government with the Articles of Confederation, which served as the first constitution of the United States.

In 1779 Adams participated in the Massachusetts Constitutional Convention. He composed the Massachusetts constitution in 1780; the new document authorized formation of a bicameral, or two-chambered, legislature and the separation of powers within the state government. The Massachusetts constitution provided a foundation for the constitutions of other states and later served as the model for the U.S. Constitution.

Foreign Diplomat

Beginning in 1778 Adams served for a decade as a diplomat in France, the Netherlands, and Great Britain. After the British surrendered to the United States in 1781, Adams joined Benjamin Franklin in Paris to negotiate a peace treaty. The Treaty of Paris, signed in 1783, officially ended the American Revolution. Adams and Franklin, experienced and shrewd foreign diplomats, were credited with achieving favorable terms in the treaty.

In 1785 Adams was appointed the first U.S. ambassador to Great Britain. He spent the next three years in London analyzing the strengths and weaknesses in European politics. His goal was to devise plans for a stable, democratic form of government in the United States, which no major European country had managed to achieve. Adams'

insights into politics and government were published in a massive collection in 1787.

Vice Presidency

Adams returned to the United States in 1788 and was placed on the ballot in the first presidential election in 1789. George Washington was elected president, and Adams became vice president. Adams' primary role as vice president was to cast the deciding vote in the Senate to break a tie. He later described the vice presidency as "the most insignificant office that ever the invention of man contrived or his imagination conceived."

Political parties emerged during Washington's administration, creating dissension within the government. Adams and Alexander Hamilton, the secretary of the treasury, organized the Federalist party. Adams' friend

Adams (second from right) was a member of the committee appointed by the Continental Congress to prepare the Declaration of Independence. The other committee members were (from left to right) Benjamin Franklin, Thomas Jefferson, Robert R. Livingston, and Roger Sherman.

MPI—Hulton Archive/Getty Images

Major World Events During John Adams' Administration

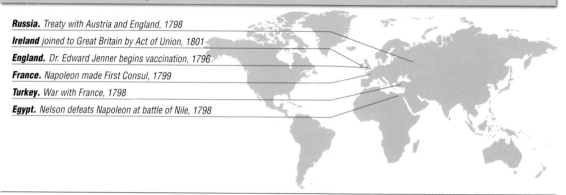

Russia. Treaty with Austria and England, 1798

Ireland joined to Great Britain by Act of Union, 1801

England. Dr. Edward Jenner begins vaccination, 1796

France. Napoleon made First Consul, 1799

Turkey. War with France, 1798

Egypt. Nelson defeats Napoleon at battle of Nile, 1798

and fellow statesman, Thomas Jefferson, created the Republican (later Democratic-Republican) party with the help of James Madison. The Federalists favored a strong central government, while the Republicans preferred the state and local governments to have more power. The opposing viewpoints of their respective parties strained the friendship between Adams and Jefferson.

Presidency

In the presidential election of 1796, Adams ran as the Federalist candidate against Jefferson, the Republican candidate. Adams prevailed by a narrow margin of electoral votes (71–68) and was sworn into office on March 4, 1797. Under the system of the time, the presidential candidate with the second largest number of votes became vice president—thus Jefferson was required to serve as Adams' vice president, even though the two were members of opposing political parties.

When Adams began his presidency, the United States was involved in a naval conflict with France. French

Adams is presented to King George III in 1785 as the first U.S. ambassador to Great Britain.

The Granger Collection, New York

privateers were attacking U.S. merchant vessels in the West Indies. In 1797 Adams sent three delegates to Paris to negotiate a peace settlement. When the U.S. delegates arrived, three French officials demanded a bribe of 250,000 dollars payable to France's foreign minister before any talks could begin. Outraged by France's audacity, Adams ordered his delegates home and began preparing U.S. military forces for war with France. Adams referred to the three French officials as X, Y, and Z in his correspondence to Congress, and the incident became known as the XYZ Affair.

As war continued between Great Britain and France, Federalists and Democratic-Republicans debated over which country to support. The Federalist-controlled Congress was eager for war with France. For the next two years U.S. naval ships battled French forces in the Caribbean Sea. Adams, however, was reluctant to declare war and sent another peace delegation to France in 1799. Although his fellow Federalists opposed this tactic, the negotiations were successful, sparing the United States from engaging in a costly war.

The XYZ Affair incited the Federalists in Congress to issue the Alien and Sedition Acts in 1798. Congress persuaded Adams to sign the acts into law. The acts permitted the government to deport foreign-born residents and indict anyone who published "false, scandalous, and malicious writing or writings against the government of the United States." By 1802, however, these acts had been either repealed or allowed to expire. Their passage was Adams' chief domestic failure.

Adams and Thomas Jefferson, by now bitter political adversaries, ran against each other in the presidential election of 1800. Jefferson won a majority of electoral votes (73–65) and succeeded Adams in 1801.

Retirement

Adams spent his retirement years with his family in Quincy. He read new and classical literature, studied politics, and wrote prolifically. Adams also renewed his friendship with Jefferson, beginning a correspondence around 1812, after Jefferson's presidency had ended. Adams died in Quincy within hours of Jefferson's death on July 4, 1826, the 50th anniversary of the adoption of the Declaration of Independence.

THOMAS JEFFERSON

Rembrandt Peale—The Bridgeman Art Library/Getty Images

3rd President of the United States (1743–1826; president 1801–09)

**Vice Presidents: Aaron Burr (1756–1836; vice president 1801–05)
George Clinton (1739–1812; vice president 1805–09)**

Th Jefferson

Thomas Jefferson was the chief author of the Declaration of Independence and the third president of the United States. His remarkable public career also included service in the Continental Congress, as the country's first secretary of state, and as its second vice president. Among the Founding Fathers, Jefferson was the most eloquent proponent of individual freedom as the core meaning of the American Revolution.

Early Life

Thomas Jefferson was born on April 13, 1743, in Shadwell, Va. His father, Peter Jefferson, was a landowner, surveyor, and public official of Albemarle County. His mother, Jane Randolph Jefferson, was descended from one of the most prominent families in Virginia. In 1745 the family moved to Tuckahoe, the Randolph plantation near Richmond, Va. Thomas was educated by private tutors until 1752, when his family returned to Shadwell. He continued his education at boarding schools and the College of William and Mary

in Williamsburg, Va., where he studied law for five years. He became a lawyer in 1767.

In 1768 Jefferson returned to Shadwell and built a mansion on an 867-foot (264-meter) mountain nearby. He named his new estate Monticello, an Italian word meaning "little mountain." On Jan. 1, 1772, Jefferson married Martha Wayles Skelton, a widow whose estate more than doubled Jefferson's landholdings when the couple combined their properties. The couple had six children, but only two survived childhood: Martha (called Patsy as a girl) and Maria (called Polly).

Jefferson depended on slave labor for the upkeep of Monticello. His ownership of slaves would become perhaps the most controversial aspect of his legacy. Even as he maintained that slavery contradicted the principles of freedom and equality upon which the United States was founded, he insisted that it was wrong for the federal government to end the practice. Further complicating the issue is Jefferson's relationship with Sally Hemings, one of his house slaves. In 1998 DNA evidence revealed that Jefferson fathered at least one child with Hemings.

Declaration of Independence

In 1769 Jefferson was elected to the House of Burgesses, Virginia's representative assembly. He used his law knowledge to support colonial opposition to British legislation and taxation. In 1774 Jefferson wrote the influential essay *A Summary View of the Rights of British America*, which stated that the British Parliament had no authority to legislate for the colonies. After the American Revolution began in 1775, the Virginia legislature

---

First Lady Martha Jefferson (1748–82)

Martha Jefferson, the wife of Thomas Jefferson, never made it to the White House because she died long before her husband became president. Born Martha Wayles, she was a young widow when she married Jefferson in 1772. After giving birth to six children, Martha was weakened by the physical strain. She died at Monticello in 1782. Thomas went into seclusion for weeks following his wife's death, and wanting to keep his memories of Martha private, he burned all their letters to one another and rarely spoke of her after her death. The only surviving image of her is a silhouette. As president, Jefferson often called upon Dolley Madison, wife of Secretary of State James Madison, to handle social events at the White House. On other occasions his daughters Patsy and Polly served as hostesses.

Thomas Jefferson Timeline

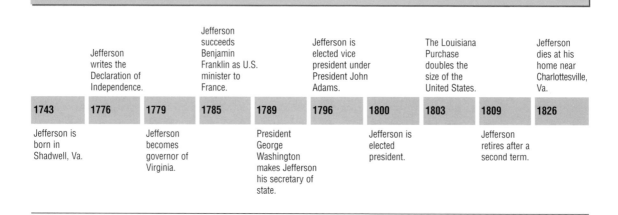

1743	1776	1779	1785	1789	1796	1800	1803	1809	1826

Jefferson writes the Declaration of Independence. *(1776)*

Jefferson succeeds Benjamin Franklin as U.S. minister to France. *(1785)*

Jefferson is elected vice president under President John Adams. *(1796)*

The Louisiana Purchase doubles the size of the United States. *(1803)*

Jefferson dies at his home near Charlottesville, Va. *(1826)*

Jefferson is born in Shadwell, Va. *(1743)*

Jefferson becomes governor of Virginia. *(1779)*

President George Washington makes Jefferson his secretary of state. *(1789)*

Jefferson is elected president. *(1800)*

Jefferson retires after a second term. *(1809)*

appointed Jefferson as a delegate to the Second Continental Congress in Philadelphia. The Congress called for independence from Great Britain.

In 1776 Jefferson was selected to a committee to outline a formal document outlining the reasons for independence. The committee, which also included John Adams and Benjamin Franklin, chose Jefferson to draft the document. He expressed what the majority of the colonists desired when he wrote: "We hold these truths to be self-evident, that all men are created equal, that they are endowed by their Creator with certain unalienable Rights, that among these are Life, Liberty, and the pursuit of Happiness…." On July 4, 1776, the Continental Congress adopted the Declaration of Independence, which officially announced the separation of the colonies from Great Britain.

State Government

Jefferson retired from the Continental Congress in 1776 and returned to the Virginia legislature. With the assistance of his colleague James Madison, Jefferson drafted the Virginia constitution complete with a declaration of rights. The Virginia constitution served as a model for the U.S. Constitution. As a lawmaker he proposed bills to end the privileges of the wealthy, to make education available to everyone, and to separate church and state.

Jefferson was elected governor of Virginia in 1779. The American Revolution reached Virginia in 1780 as British troops invaded Richmond. Jefferson's administration retreated from the capital while he assembled his family at Monticello. The Virginia press labeled him a coward for abandoning his duties as governor. In 1781 he retired from public life and returned to Monticello. His retirement was short-lived, however, as he returned to the Continental Congress in 1782. After the American Revolution ended, the Continental Congress sent Jefferson to Paris to succeed Benjamin Franklin as U.S. ambassador to France.

The U.S. Constitution was ratified while Jefferson was in Paris. When he returned to the United States in 1789, Jefferson criticized the framers of the Constitution for its lack of a bill of rights. He argued that every U.S. citizen was entitled to rights provided by the national

Monticello, Jefferson's home near Charlottesville, Va., is one of the finest examples of the early Classical Revival style in America.
David Muench/Corbis

Major World Events During Jefferson's Administration

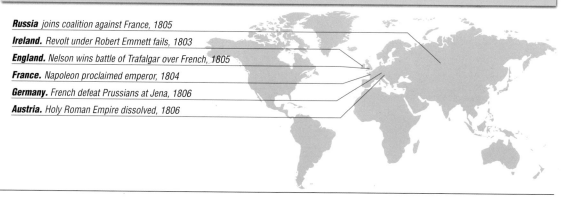

Russia *joins coalition against France, 1805*

Ireland. *Revolt under Robert Emmett fails, 1803*

England. *Nelson wins battle of Trafalgar over French, 1805*

France. *Napoleon proclaimed emperor, 1804*

Germany. *French defeat Prussians at Jena, 1806*

Austria. *Holy Roman Empire dissolved, 1806*

government. He also asserted that the authority of the federal government under the Constitution severely imposed on states' rights.

Party Politics

After George Washington became the first president of the United States in 1789, he appointed Jefferson as U.S. secretary of state. In this role Jefferson's principal responsibility was foreign policy. When the Napoleonic Wars between France and Great Britain began in 1793, Washington issued the Proclamation of Neutrality. However, Jefferson sought to uphold the U.S. alliance with France that had been made during the American Revolution. His political opponents, Vice President John Adams and Treasury Secretary Alexander Hamilton, favored friendship with Britain. The political differences between Jefferson and Adams strained their personal friendship.

Two political parties emerged during Washington's administration, dividing the U.S. government. The Federalist party, led by Adams and Hamilton, promoted a strong central government. Jefferson and his political ally, James Madison, created the Republican party (from 1798, Democratic-Republican party), which favored more autonomy for state governments. The Republicans equated the Federalist plan of government with a monarchy and referred to its pro-British policies as a betrayal of U.S. relations with France. Frustrated by the Federalist-controlled administration, Jefferson retired as secretary of state in 1793 and returned to Monticello.

Jefferson reentered national politics with a more stable Republican party supporting him in the presidential election of 1796. Jefferson was defeated by his political nemesis, John Adams, in a closely contested race (71 electoral votes to 68). Under the system of the time, Jefferson became vice president because he had the second largest number of votes.

In 1798 President Adams passed the Alien and Sedition Acts, which implemented tough standards for citizenship in the United States and incriminated U.S. citizens who printed criticism of the government. Jefferson and Madison responded with the Virginia and Kentucky Resolutions of 1798–99, which protested that these acts were unconstitutional because they violated

the freedom of speech clause in the First Amendment to the Constitution. As dissension between the Federalists and Democratic-Republicans intensified throughout Adams' administration, Jefferson prepared for another presidential nomination.

Presidency

In the presidential election of 1800, Jefferson faced Adams in another competitive campaign. Two Democratic-Republicans, Jefferson and Aaron Burr of New York, tied for victory with 73 electoral votes apiece, and Adams finished with 65 electoral votes. At that time the U.S. Constitution prevented electors from distinguishing between their choice of president and vice president. Although the voters preferred Jefferson, Burr refused to relinquish the presidency to him. The election went to the House of Representatives, which after more than 30 ballots chose Jefferson for president and Burr for vice president.

Jefferson was inaugurated on March 4, 1801. As president he reduced the authority of the U.S.

In a painting by John Trumbull entitled The Declaration of Independence, *Thomas Jefferson (standing at table) presents the Declaration to John Hancock, president of the Continental Congress.*

As secretary of state, Jefferson (left) meets Citizen Genêt, the French minister to the United States, in Philadelphia in 1793.

government by dismantling the military, lowering taxes, and decreasing the national debt. He also dispensed with much of the ceremony and formality that had attended the office of president to that time.

Tripolitan War. Jefferson faced his first foreign challenge from the North African Barbary state of Tripoli (now the capital of Libya). The Barbary states of Algiers, Tunis, Morocco, and Tripoli required tribute from U.S. ships traveling in the Mediterranean Sea in exchange for immunity from attacks. In 1801, after Jefferson refused to meet Tripoli's increased demands, Tripoli declared war on the United States. Jefferson deployed U.S. warships to the North African coast, and for the next four years the United States and Tripoli engaged in a naval war. The combination of a U.S. naval blockade and a U.S. land offensive into Tripoli ended the conflict. A peace treaty signed in 1805 abolished all tribute from the United States.

Louisiana Purchase. The Mississippi River was a valuable waterway for U.S. settlers who relied on it for commerce. When Jefferson and Secretary of State Madison learned that Spain had ceded the Louisiana Territory to France in 1800, the U.S. leaders worried about losing access to the vital trade port at New Orleans.

Jefferson instructed the U.S. ambassador to France to negotiate with French officials for the purchase of New Orleans. In a surprise move, Napoleon I offered to sell the entire Louisiana Territory, which stretched from west of the Mississippi River to the Rocky Mountains, to the United States for 15 million dollars. In 1803 U.S. delegates signed a treaty with Napoleon I for the

Louisiana Purchase, which doubled the land area of the country. The purchase was Jefferson's most celebrated achievement as president.

Soon afterward Jefferson sent Meriwether Lewis and William Clark to explore the Louisiana Territory and find a passage to the Pacific Ocean. Lewis and Clark's expedition departed St. Louis, Mo., in May 1804 and reached the Pacific in November 1805. Lewis and Clark returned to St. Louis in September 1806 with detailed journals and maps and various plant and animal specimens for research. Their trail to the Pacific paved the way for future explorers and traders who sought to colonize the West.

Domestic and foreign challenges. Jefferson coasted to an easy victory in the presidential election of 1804 against the Federalist candidate, Charles Cotesworth Pinckney of South Carolina. George Clinton, a former governor of New York, replaced Aaron Burr as Jefferson's vice president.

When the Napoleonic Wars resumed between Great Britain and France in 1803, Jefferson insisted that the United States uphold the Proclamation of Neutrality issued by President Washington in 1793. However, both European countries distrusted the United States. British and French naval ships, protecting their own interests, seized U.S. merchant vessels that were suspected of carrying war supplies. In response to the harassment, Jefferson signed the Embargo Act in 1807, which closed all U.S. ports to import and export shipping. Jefferson theorized that restricting trade with the United States would convince Great Britain and France to honor U.S. neutrality. Instead, the Embargo Act backfired and wrecked the U.S. economy. By the time he left office in March 1809, Jefferson was a tired and beaten man.

Retirement

In the years following his presidency, Jefferson entertained many visitors at Monticello. He and his daughter Patsy hosted dinner parties and rented rooms to their guests. To provide a private home away from the activity at Monticello, Jefferson built a new mansion, named Poplar Forest, on his Bedford estate 90 miles (140 kilometers) from Monticello.

Another of Jefferson's architectural efforts was the University of Virginia in Charlottesville, which opened in 1825, Jefferson planned the layout of the campus and designed the buildings. The university's policies reflected the principles that Jefferson had advocated during his political career. The school had no religious affiliation, was regulated by an honor system for students rather than a code of conduct, and had no president or administration.

Jefferson and John Adams made amends and renewed their friendship in 1812. Over the next 14 years, the former presidents exchanged 158 letters on topics such as politics, philosophy, and religion. Their letters became the most famous correspondence between two U.S. statesmen. The two died within hours of each other on July 4, 1826—the 50th anniversary of the adoption of the Declaration of Independence.

JAMES MADISON

The Granger Collection, New York

**4th President of the United States
(1751–1836; president 1809–17)**

**Vice Presidents: George Clinton (1739–1812; vice president 1809–12)
Elbridge Gerry (1744–1814; vice president 1813–14)**

Called the Father of the Constitution, James Madison did more than any of the other Founding Fathers to shape the U.S. Constitution in 1787. He went on to serve in the new U.S. House of Representatives from 1789 to 1797 and then as secretary of state under President Thomas Jefferson. In 1809 Madison succeeded Jefferson to become the fourth president of the United States. The War of 1812 was fought during his presidency.

Early Life

James Madison, Jr., was born on March 16, 1751, in Port Conway, Va. His parents were James Madison, Sr., and Eleanor (Nelly) Conway. A prominent landowner, James Madison, Sr., raised his family on the Montpelier plantation near the Blue Ridge Mountains in Virginia. Young James attended a boarding school and also was tutored at Montpelier. A dedicated student, he entered the College of New Jersey (now Princeton University) in 1769. While in college he joined the American Whig Society, a student club that opposed British rule.

After earning his bachelor's degree in 1771, Madison returned to Montpelier and studied politics, history, and law independently. He became interested in law but never pursued admission to the bar. He remained undecided about his career until his father offered him an opportunity in politics. Madison was elected to his first public office in 1774 with the Orange County Committee of Safety, an organization his father chaired.

First Years in Government

In 1776 Madison was elected as a delegate to the Virginia state convention. There he worked alongside Thomas Jefferson in writing the state constitution, which became the model for the U.S. Constitution. Through this work Madison and Jefferson formed a lifelong friendship and political alliance.

After serving two years in the Virginia governor's cabinet, Madison was elected in 1780 to the Continental Congress. He quickly became a leader in the Congress. He sat in the assembly during the stormy closing years of the American Revolution, hammering out laws, treaties, and plans to keep the young country alive. He opposed the issue of paper money by individual states, he fought for the right of Congress to tax imports, and he battled to keep the country's right to sail through the Spanish-held delta of the Mississippi River. He worked hard to strengthen the feeble powers of the central government.

After retiring from the Congress, Madison reentered the Virginia legislature in 1784. His work there led to the Annapolis Convention of 1786, a meeting of delegates from five states to address concerns over interstate commerce. The delegates determined that they could not

---

First Lady Dolley Madison (1768–1849)

A very popular first lady, Dolley Madison was renowned for her charm, warmth, and social graces. Born Dolley Payne, she married John Todd in 1790 but was widowed three years later. In 1794 she married James Madison, then a U.S. senator. After the election of President Thomas Jefferson in 1800, Dolley assisted the widowed president as hostess at official events. After James became president in 1809, Dolley established the tradition that the White House would reflect the first lady's tastes and ideas about entertaining. At weekly receptions she opened the doors to virtually anyone who wanted to come and then moved among the guests, greeting all with charming ease. Even after James's death in 1836, Dolley remained the country's most prestigious hostess and was a frequent White House guest.

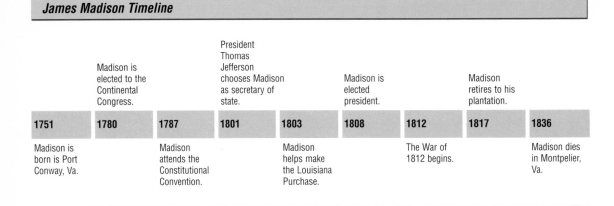

James Madison Timeline

1751	1780	1787	1801	1803	1808	1812	1817	1836

Madison is elected to the Continental Congress. (1780)

President Thomas Jefferson chooses Madison as secretary of state. (1801)

Madison is elected president. (1808)

Madison retires to his plantation. (1817)

Madison is born is Port Conway, Va. (1751)

Madison attends the Constitutional Convention. (1787)

Madison helps make the Louisiana Purchase. (1803)

The War of 1812 begins. (1812)

Madison dies in Montpelier, Va. (1836)

handle such matters under the Articles of Confederation, which had served as the constitution of the United States since 1781. They planned to hold a convention in Philadelphia the following year to revise the Articles.

Father of the Constitution

At the Constitutional Convention of 1787 Madison presented the Virginia Plan, a set of resolutions that outlined a federal government composed of three branches—executive, legislative, and judicial—with power balanced among them. The Virginia Plan provided the basic framework for the U.S. Constitution, earning Madison the title Father of the Constitution. To promote the Constitution, Madison collaborated with Alexander Hamilton and John Jay to write the Federalist papers, a collection of essays explaining the document and the federal system of government. The essays helped to ensure ratification of the Constitution.

Elected to the U.S. House of Representatives in 1789, Madison sponsored the Bill of Rights, the first 10 amendments to the Constitution that guaranteed the freedoms of religion, speech, and the press. Madison served in the House throughout President George Washington's administration.

Madison's lifelong home was Montpelier, a plantation in Virginia.

Lee Snider—Photo Images/Corbis

National Politics

During Madison's tenure in the House, political parties emerged within the government. The leaders divided over policies concerning the power of the federal government. The Federalist party, led by Vice President John Adams and Treasury Secretary Alexander Hamilton, advocated a strong central government. Jefferson and Madison created the Republican party (from 1798, the Democratic-Republican party), which favored more power for the states.

In 1794 Madison married a young widow named Dolley Payne Todd. Dolley had one child, John Payne Todd, from her previous marriage. The couple raised John Todd but never had children together.

Madison left Congress in 1797, but in the next year the passage of the Alien and Sedition Acts inspired him to action. These laws restricted immigration and incriminated anyone who printed criticism of the federal government. In response, Madison and Thomas Jefferson drafted the Virginia and Kentucky Resolutions. The resolutions held that the Alien and Sedition Acts were unconstitutional because they violated the freedom of speech clause of the Constitution.

In 1801 Madison was appointed secretary of state by Jefferson, the newly elected president. He held this office for the eight years of Jefferson's presidency, and they worked closely together. Their great joint achievement was the Louisiana Purchase, in which the United States acquired the Louisiana Territory from France. The purchase doubled the country's size. However, Madison and Jefferson stumbled in their efforts to maintain neutrality in a war between Great Britain and France. The Embargo Act of 1807, which closed U.S. ports to foreign trade, was meant to stop Great Britain and France from harassing U.S. ships. Instead, the act caused an economic downturn in the United States.

Presidency

Despite the failed Embargo Act, Madison was elected president in 1808 to succeed Jefferson. His vice president was George Clinton of New York. When Madison took office in 1809, the country faced naval threats from both

Major World Events During Madison's Administration

Russia. *Napoleon invades and retreats, 1812*

Great Britain *fights United States in War of 1812, 1812–14*

Holland *annexed to France, 1810*

France. *Napoleon tries to reconquer during Hundred Days, 1815*

Austria. *Congress of Vienna, 1814–15*

Austria *loses territory to France by Treaty of Schönbrunn, 1809*

Bettmann/Corbis

Madison (right) confers with his friend and political ally Thomas Jefferson.

Great Britain and France. In place of the Embargo Act, Madison offered to resume trade with either of the two countries that agreed to respect U.S. shipping. Napoleon I of France accepted these terms as a ploy, while the British continued to seize U.S. ships and force U.S. sailors into military service. Great Britain also contributed weapons and supplies to Native Americans who were fighting settlers along the northwestern boundaries of the United States.

Madison sought peace with Great Britain but accepted war as inevitable. Encouraged by the so-called War Hawks in Congress, Madison signed a declaration of war in 1812. As commander in chief in the ensuing War of 1812, Madison was unable to convince Congress to increase funds for the military, hampering the U.S. effort. The small U.S. Navy won some impressive victories, but U.S. land forces were routed.

Amid the defeats on the battlefield came the presidential election of 1812. During the campaign New England Federalists who opposed the war labeled Madison as an incompetent leader. Nevertheless, the president had little difficulty in defeating his Federalist opponent, DeWitt

Clinton of New York, to gain a second term. Elbridge Gerry of Massachusetts was elected vice president.

The war continued through 1814. In August of that year British troops marched into Washington, D.C., and burned the White House, the Capitol, and several other government buildings. Madison and his Cabinet fled to Virginia during the attack. The war ended without a conclusive victor when the Treaty of Ghent was signed on Dec. 24, 1814. Nevertheless, many Americans proclaimed the result a U.S. triumph.

As the war was ending, a group of New England Federalists met secretly in Hartford, Conn. They were accused of plotting New England's secession from the Union. The charge of disloyalty caused the death of the Federalist party and a resurgence of Madison's popularity.

Madison's Democratic-Republican party favored states' rights and a strict interpretation of the Constitution. Despite its stand, however, a new nationalism began to develop. This was shown in the new protective tariff law and in the charter of the second Bank of the United States, both passed in 1816. Louisiana was admitted as a state in 1812, and Indiana in 1816. Improved roads, new canals, and a better land allotment method helped develop the West. A series of Supreme Court decisions on constitutional law broadened national powers and limited those of the states. The Era of Good Feeling was starting.

Retirement

Madison was succeeded by James Monroe in 1817. He spent the next 19 years managing his 5,000-acre (2,000-hectare) farm at Montpelier. The cultivation techniques he used are regarded today as modern innovations. Madison also contributed funds to help Thomas Jefferson build the University of Virginia campus in Charlottesville, which was chartered in 1819. Later he followed Jefferson as rector of the university.

Although a slave owner, Madison worked to abolish slavery by supporting the American Colonization Society. It called for the government to purchase slaves and resettle them in the colony of Liberia on the west coast of Africa. Madison's final political activity came in 1829, when he took part in Virginia's constitutional convention. Madison died in his home on June 28, 1836.

JAMES MONROE

The Granger Collection, New York

**5th President of the United States
(1758–1831; president 1817–25)**

Vice President: Daniel D. Tompkins (1774–1825)

James Monroe

The fifth president of the United States was James Monroe. His most celebrated achievement was the Monroe Doctrine, a groundbreaking policy for the defense of North and South America against foreign intrusion. Monroe's two terms as president, from 1817 to 1825, brought growing national wealth and unity. His generally calm and prosperous administration has been called the Era of Good Feeling.

Early Life

James Monroe was born on April 28, 1758, in Westmoreland County, Va. His family lived on a modest 600-acre (240-hectare) estate. When his father died in 1774, James became proprietor of the estate. In the same year he enrolled at the College of William and Mary in Williamsburg but he left in 1776 to fight in the American Revolution.

Monroe served in the Army for two years. As a lieutenant, he crossed the Delaware River with Gen. George Washington in 1776 to take part in the battle of Trenton. Monroe suffered a near fatal shoulder wound

and had to be carried from the field. For his heroism in combat, Washington promoted him to captain. Upon recovering, Monroe fought in the battles of Brandywine and Germantown. Advanced to major, Monroe served during the harsh winter of 1777–78 at Valley Forge. At the battle of Monmouth, N.J., in 1778, Monroe led a scouting party for General Washington. Later that year Monroe resigned his commission in the army and returned to Williamsburg.

State and National Politics

In Williamsburg Monroe studied law under Thomas Jefferson, then governor of Virginia. His first public office was in the Virginia state assembly. In 1783 he was elected to the Continental Congress, where he served for three years. He worked for granting frontier settlements to veterans of the American Revolution, for acquiring new territories and admitting new states in the West, and for the free navigation of the Mississippi River.

While serving in the Congress, Monroe met the socially prominent Elizabeth Kortright. James and Elizabeth were married in 1786 in New York City. The couple had two daughters, Eliza and Maria, and a son who died in infancy.

That same year Monroe retired from the Congress and moved to Fredericksburg, Va., where he practiced law. Soon he was in politics again, first in the state assembly and then in the state convention called to ratify the new U.S. Constitution. He voted against the Constitution because it lacked a bill of rights, but after the document was ratified he supported it.

First Lady Elizabeth Monroe (1768–1830)

Although noted for her beauty and elegance, Elizabeth Monroe was an unpopular first lady because she largely ignored the role of hostess. Born Elizabeth Kortright in New York City, she married James Monroe in 1786. While her husband served as a diplomat, Elizabeth lived in Paris and then London. Her experiences abroad influenced her greatly but also harmed her image among the American public, which came to regard her as too European and elitist. As first lady, Elizabeth refused to follow the practice of her predecessor, Dolley Madison, in making or receiving social calls. Washingtonians reacted by boycotting the few parties that she hosted. Elizabeth is best remembered for her role in redecorating the presidential mansion in elegant French style.

The Granger Collection, New York

James Monroe Timeline

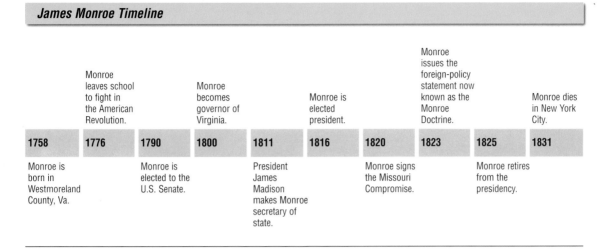

1758	1776	1790	1800	1811	1816	1820	1823	1825	1831

Monroe leaves school to fight in the American Revolution. *(1776)*

Monroe becomes governor of Virginia. *(1800)*

Monroe is elected president. *(1816)*

Monroe issues the foreign-policy statement now known as the Monroe Doctrine. *(1823)*

Monroe dies in New York City. *(1831)*

Monroe is born in Westmoreland County, Va. *(1758)*

Monroe is elected to the U.S. Senate. *(1790)*

President James Madison makes Monroe secretary of state. *(1811)*

Monroe signs the Missouri Compromise. *(1820)*

Monroe retires from the presidency. *(1825)*

In 1790 Monroe was elected to the U.S. Senate, where he vigorously opposed the Federalist-controlled government of President George Washington. Nevertheless, in 1794 Washington appointed Monroe as U.S. minister to France. Monroe received a warm welcome in France and showed great enthusiasm for the French Revolution, which he regarded as a successor to the American Revolution. Monroe's French sympathies displeased the Federalists. Believing that Monroe could not represent his government properly, Washington recalled him late in 1796. Monroe returned to the United States and published a lengthy defense of his support for France and criticism of Washington's administration.

Monroe still held the confidence of the Virginia voters, who elected him governor in 1799. Serving until 1802, he worked to clear Virginia's rivers, enlarge the state school system, and erect state capital buildings. He also rallied support for Thomas Jefferson's successful presidential run in 1800.

Foreign Minister and Secretary of State

In 1803 President Jefferson and Secretary of State James Madison convinced Monroe to resume his diplomatic career. Monroe was sent to France to assist with negotiations for the purchase of New Orleans, an essential port for U.S. trade along the Mississippi River. The Americans were astonished when Napoleon I offered to sell the entire Louisiana Territory to the United States for 15 million dollars. The Louisiana Purchase doubled the land area of the United States.

Upon completing his duties in France, Monroe was named U.S. minister to Great Britain. His primary goal was to convince the British to cease their attacks on U.S. ships and stop forcing U.S. sailors into service in the British Navy. An agreement he made with the British in 1806 was rejected by Jefferson as inadequate.

Monroe returned to the United States in 1807. He was elected to the Virginia legislature in 1810 and became governor again in 1811. In November of that year he resigned to become secretary of state under President James Madison. In this office he had to confront the

ongoing crisis with Great Britain, as the British Navy persisted in harassing U.S. ships. Madison and Monroe accepted that war was the only solution, and in 1812 Congress declared war on Great Britain. The conflict, called the War of 1812, continued through 1814. In the latter part of the war Monroe served as secretary of war in addition to secretary of state.

Presidency

In 1816 Monroe was elected president as the Democratic-Republican candidate, defeating the Federalist candidate Rufus King. Monroe took office on March 4, 1817, with Daniel D. Tompkins, former governor of New York, as vice president. He was reelected in 1820.

First Seminole War. At the beginning of Monroe's presidency U.S. authorities were attempting to recapture runaway slaves who had fled to Spanish-held Florida to

Monroe (right) signs the Louisiana Purchase in Paris in 1803. The other signers are French statesman François, marquis de Barbé-Marbois, and U.S. minister Robert R. Livingston.

The Granger Collection, New York

Major World Events During Monroe's Administration

Great Britain. George III dies; George IV becomes king, 1820

France. Napoleon I dies, 1821

German States form Zollverein (customs union), 1818

Mexico. Independence proclaimed, 1821

Brazil. Independence proclaimed, 1822

Chile. Independence proclaimed, 1818

live among the Seminole people. The escaped slaves had joined the Seminole in raiding U.S. settlements in Georgia. When Spain refused to intervene, Monroe dispatched Gen. Andrew Jackson to suppress the raids. In 1817 Jackson led a U.S. invasion of Florida—attacking Seminole villages, seizing the towns of St. Marks and Pensacola, and overthrowing the Spanish governor—in what became known as the First Seminole War. As a result of the war, Spain ceded Florida to the United States in 1819.

Missouri Compromise. Monroe faced the country's first conflict over slavery after the territory of Missouri applied for statehood in 1817. Missouri wanted no restrictions on slavery, but Northern congressmen tried to limit the practice. Representatives from the Southern states were outraged. Amid a fierce debate over slavery and the government's right to restrict it, Congress adjourned without resolving the Missouri question.

Although a slave owner, Monroe was a member of the American Colonization Society, which tried unsuccessfully to free the slaves and resettle them in

Africa. Nevertheless, Monroe refused to support banning slavery in Missouri because the U.S. Constitution included a slavery provision for new states entering the Union.

After Maine applied for statehood in 1819 as a free state, the North and the South compromised under the direction of Speaker of the House Henry Clay. Maine would enter the United States as a free state and Missouri as a slave state, but slavery was banned from then on in territories north of Missouri's southern border. Maine was admitted as the 23rd state in 1820, and Missouri was admitted as the 24th state in 1821. Though the Missouri Compromise ended the crisis peacefully, it marked the beginning of the prolonged conflict over slavery that led to the American Civil War.

Monroe Doctrine. Monroe made a lasting contribution to U.S. foreign policy with a statement to Congress in 1823. The statement came in response to the threat that European powers would help Spain reclaim its recently lost colonies in North and South America. The United States also worried that Russia would try to establish a colony in the Northwest.

Monroe made four basic points: The United States would not interfere in the political affairs of Europe; the United States recognized and would not interfere with existing colonies in Latin America; the Western Hemisphere was closed to future colonization; and any attempt by a European country to oppress or control any country in the Americas would be considered a hostile act against the United States. As the United States grew into a world power, future presidents, such as James K. Polk and Theodore Roosevelt, upheld and expanded on Monroe's principles. In the 1850s his statement became known as the Monroe Doctrine.

Retirement

After his second term ended in 1825, Monroe retired to his plantation at Oak Hill, Va. In 1826 he was named to the governing board of the University of Virginia. Three years later Monroe was a member of the convention called to amend Virginia's constitution. When his wife died in 1830, Monroe was stricken with grief. He moved to New York City to live with his daughter Maria. He died there on July 4, 1831.

President Monroe presides over a Cabinet meeting in 1823 that led to the foreign-policy statement known as the Monroe Doctrine.

The Granger Collection, New York

JOHN QUINCY ADAMS

The Granger Collection, New York

**6th President of the United States
(1767–1848; president 1825–29)**

Vice President: John C. Calhoun (1782–1850)

J Q. Adams

Son of President John Adams, John Quincy Adams became the sixth president of the United States in 1825. Although he was knowledgeable and dedicated to his country, Adams was an unsuccessful president, largely because of relentless opposition from supporters of his political adversary, Andrew Jackson. Adams' accomplishments as a diplomat and congressman overshadowed his uneventful presidency.

Early Life

John Quincy Adams was born on July 11, 1767, in Braintree (now Quincy), Mass. The son of John and Abigail Adams, he grew up amid the colonial uprisings leading up to the American Revolution. He heard his father's accounts of the Boston Massacre in 1770 and the Boston Tea Party in 1773. During the American Revolution he witnessed the battle of Bunker Hill from atop Penn's Hill.

As the eldest son in the family, Adams assumed the responsibilities of the household when his father was away attending to colonial affairs in Boston. Because

schools in Braintree were closed during the war, Adams received his early education from his parents and from tutoring by his father's law clerks. Accompanying his father to France in 1778, Adams attended the Passy Academy in Paris while his father administered to U.S. foreign affairs with the French government. Adams and his father returned to Braintree briefly in 1779 before embarking on another diplomatic mission to the Netherlands, where Adams enrolled at the University of Leiden in 1780.

At age 14 Adams was chosen to accompany Francis Dana, U.S. envoy to Russia, to the St. Petersburg court. French was the official language of diplomacy in Russia, and Adams served as Dana's private secretary and French interpreter. After a 14-month stay in St. Petersburg, Adams toured the Netherlands, Scandinavia, and Germany before joining his father in Paris.

When his father was appointed U.S. minister to Great Britain in 1785, Adams returned to Massachusetts and entered Harvard College. He graduated from Harvard in 1787 and began studying law under Theophilus Parsons (later chief justice of Massachusetts). Adams was admitted to the Massachusetts bar in 1790 and opened a law office in Boston. His law practice attracted few clients, however, and he occupied much of his time writing political articles. President George Washington read the articles and appointed Adams U.S. minister to the Netherlands in 1794.

Diplomat and Senator

In the Netherlands Adams stayed abreast of all European affairs and reported back to the U.S.

First Lady Louisa Adams (1775–1852)

Born Louisa Catherine Johnson in London, England, Louisa Adams was the daughter of an American businessman and an Englishwoman. She was the only first lady born abroad. Raised in England and France, she studied briefly in an English boarding school and was also tutored at home. She married John Quincy Adams in 1797. As her husband sought the presidency, Louisa helped his cause by staging lavish parties and making many social calls despite her fragile health. As first lady she took no part in political affairs and complained about the intense public scrutiny she faced. She was much happier during John Quincy's later years in Congress, working alongside him as he fought for the end of slavery.

Hulton Archive/Getty Images

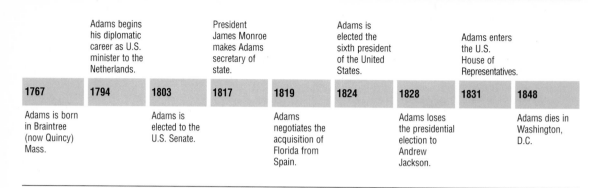

John Quincy Adams Timeline

1767	1794	1803	1817	1819	1824	1828	1831	1848

Adams begins his diplomatic career as U.S. minister to the Netherlands. (1794)

President James Monroe makes Adams secretary of state. (1817)

Adams is elected the sixth president of the United States. (1824)

Adams enters the U.S. House of Representatives. (1831)

Adams is born in Braintree (now Quincy) Mass. (1767)

Adams is elected to the U.S. Senate. (1803)

Adams negotiates the acquisition of Florida from Spain. (1819)

Adams loses the presidential election to Andrew Jackson. (1828)

Adams dies in Washington, D.C. (1848)

government. He also wrote personal letters to his father, the vice president at the time, describing the political state of Europe. President Washington recognized the versatility of Adams as a diplomat and named him U.S. minister to Portugal in 1796. When Adams' father succeeded Washington as president in 1797, Adams was reassigned as U.S. minister to Prussia.

Back in London before his departure to Berlin, Adams married Louisa Catherine Johnson on July 26, 1797. He had met her in France during one of his father's diplomatic assignments. Born in London, Louisa was the daughter of Joshua Johnson, a U.S. consul in Great Britain. The couple had three sons.

In Berlin, Adams' only significant accomplishment was negotiating a treaty of commerce with Prussia. His father recalled him from this post after Thomas Jefferson was elected president of the United States in 1800. Adams returned to Boston and served in the Massachusetts Senate for one year before his election to the U.S. Senate in 1803.

Although Adams did not embrace the concept of political parties, he was considered a Federalist. Nevertheless, he advocated many of President Jefferson's Democratic-Republican policies, including the Louisiana Purchase in 1803 and the Embargo Act in 1807. The embargo closed U.S. ports in an effort to force Great Britain and France into recognizing U.S. neutrality rights at sea. The Federalists were bitterly opposed to the embargo and were enraged over Adams' support for Jefferson's administration. The Federalist legislators in Massachusetts forced Adams to resign his seat in the Senate in 1808. He immediately allied himself with the Democratic-Republicans and endorsed James Madison in the presidential election of 1808.

In 1809 President Madison sent Adams to St. Petersburg as U.S. minister to Russia. Adams witnessed the disaster that befell Napoleon I's French army as it invaded Russia in 1812. He was still in St. Petersburg when the War of 1812 broke out between the United States and Great Britain. In 1814 Adams led a delegation to Belgium to negotiate the Treaty of Ghent, which ended the war. For the next two years Adams worked in London as U.S. minister to Great Britain.

Secretary of State

In 1817 Adams returned to the United States to become secretary of state in President James Monroe's Cabinet. In 1818 he met with British officials to establish the U.S.-Canadian border at the 49th parallel (49° N. latitude), which extended from what is now Minnesota to the Rocky Mountains. The United States and Great Britain also agreed to joint claims on the Oregon Territory, where the fur trade was thriving.

Adams also played the leading part in the acquisition of Florida from Spain. In 1819, after long negotiations, he succeeded in getting the Spanish minister to agree to a treaty in which Spain would abandon all claims to territory east of the Mississippi River. In exchange, the United States granted Spain sovereignty over what is now Texas.

Adams worked closely with President Monroe to formulate the U.S. foreign policy guidelines called the Monroe Doctrine. The doctrine, proclaimed in 1823,

Adams speaks in the House of Representatives.

Major World Events During John Quincy Adams' Administration

Russia. *Alexander I dies; Nicholas I becomes ruler, 1825*

Great Britain. *Corn Law passed, 1828*

Turkey. *War with Russia, 1828–29*

Persia. *War with Russia, 1825–28*

Uruguay. *Independence proclaimed, 1828*

Argentina. *War with Brazil over Uruguay, 1825–28*

stated that any attempt by a European power to colonize in the Western Hemisphere would be considered an act of aggression against the United States. The Monroe Doctrine remained a cornerstone of foreign policy in future presidential administrations.

Presidency

As President Monroe's second term came to a close in 1824, four candidates vied to replace him: Adams, Treasury Secretary William H. Crawford, Speaker of the House Henry Clay, and Gen. Andrew Jackson. Jackson won the popular vote, but none of the candidates received a necessary majority of electoral votes. Jackson finished with 99, Adams with 84, Crawford with 41, and Clay with 37. The decision was then turned over to the House of Representatives. Clay was dropped from consideration because the House could select from only the top three candidates. Clay endorsed Adams, giving Adams the votes he needed for victory. Upon his election, Adams appointed Clay as secretary of state.

After a stroke, Adams collapses on the floor of the House on Feb. 21, 1848.

Jackson and his followers were outraged over what they called a "corrupt bargain." Jackson felt deprived of the presidency after winning the popular vote, and he believed that Clay had thrown his support behind Adams in exchange for a Cabinet appointment. Jackson's supporters (called Jacksonians) were determined to undermine the Adams Administration at every turn.

Adams was inaugurated on March 4, 1825, aware of the sentiment against him. He acknowledged to the people of the United States in his inaugural address that he was "less possessed of your confidence…than any of my predecessors." John C. Calhoun was his vice president.

Adams outlined a forward-thinking agenda for his presidency. He supported the conservation and gradual development of Western territories. He petitioned Congress for federal aid to build more roads and canals. To strengthen higher education and stimulate science, he proposed creating a national university, a naval academy, and national astronomical observatories. However, the Jacksonians in Congress rejected his plans.

Adams faced further hostility in 1828 when he proposed a high tariff on imported industrial goods. The tariff was intended to protect New England factories from European competitors. Southerners opposed the tariff, believing that it would harm their economy. The Jacksonians in Congress tried to defeat the tariff, but it was approved nevertheless. Southerners called it the Tariff of Abominations.

In 1828 Adams ran for reelection on the National Republican ticket. His opponent was Jackson, representing the Democrats. The unpopularity of the tariff helped to propel Jackson to victory. Adams refused to attend the inauguration of his rival.

Later Years

Adams returned to his home in Quincy in 1829, but his retirement was brief. In 1830 Massachusetts elected him to the U.S. House of Representatives, where he served for the remainder of his life. In Congress Adams argued against the expansion of slavery. He also oversaw the establishment of the Smithsonian Institute in Washington, D.C. On Feb. 21, 1848, while speaking on the floor of the House, Adams suffered a stroke and collapsed. He died in the Capitol two days later.

ANDREW JACKSON

South Carolina, and the weight of evidence supports his assertion. Andrew's father died a few weeks before the boy's birth, leaving his mother to raise their three sons on her own. The area offered little opportunity for formal education, and what little schooling Andrew received was interrupted by the American Revolution.

Andrew joined the colonial militia and fought in several backwoods skirmishes against the British. In 1781 he was captured by British soldiers. When a British officer commanded Andrew to clean his boots, the boy refused and was struck across the face with a saber. His mother and two brothers died during the closing years of the war, direct or indirect casualties of the war. These tragic experiences fixed in Jackson's mind a lifelong hostility toward Great Britain.

After the end of the Revolution, Jackson moved to Salisbury, N.C., where he studied law for two years before beginning a law practice in 1787. Not keen on city life, Jackson soon traveled west to Nashville, which was still a frontier village. Jackson became a successful prosecuting attorney, quickly earning a favorable reputation among landowners, creditors, and bankers. These prominent citizens became his strongest allies during his turbulent political career.

Jackson lived in the home of Mrs. John Donelson, widow of Col. John Donelson, one of the founders of Nashville. There he met and married their daughter, Rachel Donelson Robards. The couple had no children of their own, but in 1809 they adopted a nephew of Rachel's. Their home outside of Nashville, called the Hermitage, became one of the most famous plantations in the country.

Library of Congress, Washington, D.C.

7th President of the United States
(1767–1845; president 1829–37)

Vice Presidents: John C. Calhoun (1782–1850; vice president 1829–32)
Martin Van Buren (1782–1862; vice president 1833–37)

Andrew Jackson

A military hero with a humble political background, Andrew Jackson became the seventh president of the United States in 1829. His election is commonly regarded as a turning point in U.S. history. Jackson was the first president from west of the Appalachian Mountains and the first to be elected through a direct appeal to the people rather than through the backing of an established political organization. The Democratic party, developed in the 1830s, is a legacy of his presidency.

Early Life

Andrew Jackson was born on March 15, 1767, in Waxhaw, a settlement on the western frontier of the Carolinas. The area was disputed between North and South Carolina, and both states have claimed him as a native son. Jackson maintained that he was born in

---

First Lady Rachel Jackson (1767–1828)

Rachel Jackson came from a prominent Virginia family. Born Rachel Donelson, she enjoyed an excellent education for a woman living on the frontier. As a teenager she married Lewis Robards, who proved to be an abusive husband. The couple separated and, hearing mistakenly that Robards had divorced her, Rachel married Andrew Jackson in 1791. When they discovered their mistake they remarried. Nevertheless, as Andrew pursued the presidency in 1828, his political opponents spread malicious rumors about the couple's alleged adultery. A deeply religious woman, Rachel was devastated by the attacks. As she reluctantly prepared to move to Washington, D.C., following Andrew's victory, she died of a heart attack. A young niece, Emily Donelson, took her place as White House hostess.

Andrew Jackson Timeline

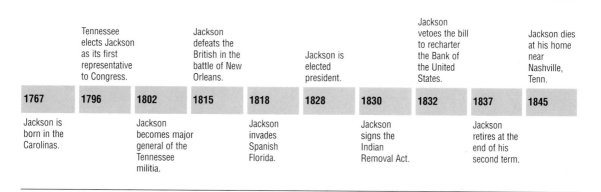

1767	1796	1802	1815	1818	1828	1830	1832	1837	1845

1796 — Tennessee elects Jackson as its first representative to Congress.

1815 — Jackson defeats the British in the battle of New Orleans.

1828 — Jackson is elected president.

1832 — Jackson vetoes the bill to recharter the Bank of the United States.

1845 — Jackson dies at his home near Nashville, Tenn.

1767 — Jackson is born in the Carolinas.

1802 — Jackson becomes major general of the Tennessee militia.

1818 — Jackson invades Spanish Florida.

1830 — Jackson signs the Indian Removal Act.

1837 — Jackson retires at the end of his second term.

In 1796 Jackson took part in the convention that wrote a constitution for the new state of Tennessee. That same year he was elected as the first Tennessee member of the U.S. House of Representatives, and in 1797 he was elected to the U.S. Senate. He resigned from the Senate in 1798 and was soon elected judge of the superior court of Tennessee, a post he held until 1804.

Military Career

In 1802 Jackson was made a major general in the Tennessee militia. When war broke out between the United States and Great Britain in 1812, Jackson offered the services of his militia to the United States. Sent to the Alabama-Georgia region to fight the Creek Indians, who were allied with the British, Jackson and his militia crushed the Creek at the battle of Horseshoe Bend in 1814. The Creek campaign was typical of Jackson as a general. He was not a great military strategist, but he had a strong determination. His troops considered him "tough as hickory," thus they nicknamed him Old Hickory. The victory over the Creek made Jackson the hero of the West, and he was commissioned as a major general in the U.S. Army.

In November 1814 Jackson marched into Spanish-held Florida and captured Pensacola, preparing for the U.S. occupation of Florida. Prior to Jackson's arrival, the British army had evacuated the city and advanced by sea to Louisiana. Jackson marched his army overland to New Orleans. A series of small skirmishes culminated in the battle of New Orleans on Jan. 8, 1815. Jackson's forces decisively defeated the British army and forced it to withdraw. The victory did not affect the outcome of the war as, unknown to Jackson, a peace treaty had already been signed. Nevertheless, it raised the country's morale and made Jackson a national hero.

In 1817 Jackson was again sent to the Alabama-Georgia region, this time to defend U.S. settlers against attacks by Seminole Indians from Florida. Without awaiting orders, Jackson marched into Spanish-held Florida, burned Seminole villages, and captured Pensacola and St. Marks in what became known as the First Seminole War. These bold actions brought sharp protest from Spain as well as harsh criticism in Congress, but Secretary of State John Quincy Adams defended Jackson and defused the crisis.

When Spain ceded Florida to the United States in 1821, President James Monroe appointed Jackson the governor of the territory. Tiring of politics, Jackson resigned this post in late 1821 and retired to private life. However, in 1823 he was again elected to the U.S. Senate.

Road to the Presidency

The United States was entering a new age as the presidential election of 1824 drew near. Foreign affairs were now of less concern than the internal development of the country. With the expansion of the West and the increase of small businesses and industries in the East, the changes in the country called for a new voice to

Refusing to clean the British officer's boots, 14-year-old Andrew Jackson tries to ward off a saber blow. His older brother, Robert (right), watches in horror but also refuses.

The Granger Collection, New York

Major World Events During Jackson's Administration

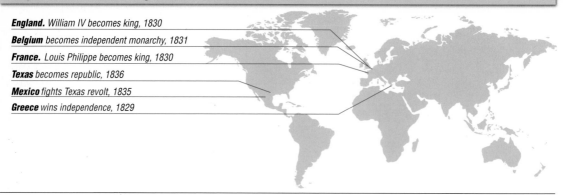

England. William IV becomes king, 1830

Belgium becomes independent monarchy, 1831

France. Louis Philippe becomes king, 1830

Texas becomes republic, 1836

Mexico fights Texas revolt, 1835

Greece wins independence, 1829

express the will of the "common people." The Western farmers and the Eastern workers wanted a leader unbound by tradition.

Against this backdrop, the Tennessee legislature nominated Jackson for the presidency in 1824. Jackson received the most electoral votes, but none of the four candidates received a majority. The election then passed to the House of Representatives. One of the candidates, Henry Clay, gave his votes to John Quincy Adams, who thus became president. When Adams named Clay his secretary of state, Jackson and his followers alleged that Clay supported Adams in exchange for a Cabinet appointment.

Jackson resigned from the Senate in 1825, but his allies in Congress, called the Jacksonians, worked to undermine all of Adams' policies. The Jacksonians created the Democratic party and used Adams' term to promote Jackson for president in the election of 1828.

Presidency

Jackson, the Democratic party candidate, swept the presidential election of 1828, defeating Adams by an electoral count of 178 to 83. John C. Calhoun was reelected vice president. Jackson took office on March 4, 1829. The celebration of his inauguration riotously heralded a new era in U.S. politics. Hordes of people swarmed through the White House to cheer their hero. Many people in the East actually feared Jackson, however, believing him dangerously unfit for office.

Spoils system. In making decisions and policy Jackson relied on an informal group of newspaper editors and politicians who had helped elect him; they came to be known as his "kitchen cabinet." Jackson's loyalty to his supporters led him to expand what is known as the spoils system—the practice of replacing

Astride his white horse, General Jackson and an aide study the British attack in the battle of New Orleans. The mix of uniforms in Jackson's army shows frontiersmen, regulars, and militia.

Mansell—Time Life Pictures/Getty Images

officeholders from the defeated party with members of the winning party. In defense of Jackson's political appointments, Senator William L. Marcy of New York replied, "To the victor belong the spoils." Although Jackson was charged with abusing the spoils system, he in fact replaced less than 20 percent of federal officeholders.

Conflict over nullification. Because of Jackson's poor health, the question of his successor became an issue soon after he assumed the presidency. Vice President Calhoun was a leading candidate, as was Secretary of State Martin Van Buren. When news leaked in 1830 that Calhoun, as secretary of war in 1818, had condemned Jackson's conduct in the First Seminole War, the president alienated Calhoun.

An intense rivalry developed between Jackson and Calhoun over a protective tariff. In 1828 President Adams had approved a tariff on imported industrial goods to protect New England factories from foreign competitors. Calhoun argued that the tariff favored the North at the expense of the South. South Carolina, Calhoun's home state, was especially hostile toward the tariff and fought for nullification—the right of states to declare federal laws null and void within their borders.

Although not an avid supporter of the tariff, Jackson opposed nullification because he felt that it exceeded the limitations of states' rights and threatened the Union. To ease the tension with South Carolina, Jackson issued a revised tariff in 1832 that was less burdensome than the original. Not satisfied, the South Carolina legislature passed a resolution that declared the tariff null and void. South Carolina also threatened to secede from the Union if the federal government tried to enforce the tariff in the state. At the end of 1832, disgruntled with Jackson's policies, Calhoun resigned as vice president. Van Buren replaced him.

The situation grew dire as Jackson threatened to send troops to South Carolina to collect the tariff. The crisis was averted in 1833 when Congress passed two compromise bills. The first bill reduced the tariff; the second, named the Force Bill, authorized the president to use the military to enforce federal laws. South Carolina repealed its nullification bill.

Native American policy. Jackson's stern stance against South Carolina contrasts with his inaction when Georgia defied federal law. Beginning in 1829 Georgia extended its territory into land that had been guaranteed to the Cherokee Indians in a treaty with the U.S. government. Even though the U.S. Supreme Court twice ruled in favor of the Cherokee, Georgia continued its illegal land seizure. Refusing to interfere, Jackson instead signed the Indian Removal Act of 1830, which required all Native American tribes east of the Mississippi River to move to reservations in the West. In the fall and winter of 1838–39 the Cherokee were forced to march west in a journey that became known as the Trail of Tears. Along the way nearly a quarter of them died of starvation, illness, and exposure. In addition, Jackson sent U.S. troops to fight the Seminole who refused to abandon their lands in Florida.

President-Elect Jackson greets supporters in a small town on his way to his inauguration.

Bank War. As the presidential election of 1832 approached, Jackson's opponents hoped to embarrass him by posing a new dilemma. The charter of the Bank of the United States was due to expire in 1836. Jackson was unhappy with the monopoly held by the bank, but he had not clearly defined his position. Jackson's opponents pushed through Congress a bill to renew the charter, forcing Jackson to take a stand. Jackson vetoed the bill in July 1832, declaring that the bank's control of the country's money was a menace both to private businesses and to democratic government. The election centered on the issue of the bank, and the voters sided with Jackson. He easily defeated Henry Clay of the National Republican party, winning 219 electoral votes to Clay's 49.

The veto of the bank charter bill ignited a conflict over financial policy that persisted throughout Jackson's second term. The prolonged struggle has been called the Bank War. Although the bank's old charter still had three years to run, Jackson removed government funds from it and deposited them in state banks. The state banks granted credit freely and printed large quantities of paper money, leading to wild land speculation in the West. As inflation soared and banks failed, a panic was in the making. It did not strike, however, until after Jackson's successor, Martin Van Buren, took office in 1837.

Retirement

Jackson retired to his Tennessee home, the Hermitage. He received visitors and continued to have a lively interest in public affairs, advising leaders of the Democratic party. For decades in poor health, Jackson was virtually an invalid during the last eight years of his life. He died in his home on June 8, 1845.

MARTIN VAN BUREN

8th President of the United States
(1782–1862; president 1837–41)

Vice President: Richard M. Johnson (1780–1850)

Elected in 1836, Martin Van Buren was the eighth president of the United States. Before the presidency he served in the U.S. Senate and then as secretary of state and vice president under President Andrew Jackson. Along with Jackson, he was a founder of the Democratic party.

Early Life

Martin Van Buren was born on Dec. 5, 1782, in Kinderhook, N.Y., a village south of Albany on the Hudson River. Of Dutch descent, he was the son of Abraham and Maria Hoes Van Buren. Abraham was a farmer and tavern keeper. Called Little Mat as a child, Martin began his education at the village school and later attended Kinderhook Academy.

After graduating from the academy at age 14, Martin was apprenticed to the lawyer Francis Silvester. He quickly became skilled in legal argument. At age 15 he participated in his first court case. The jury in the Kinderhook courthouse was amazed at his knowledge of legal affairs. With only one year's experience as a law clerk, he helped to win the case. In 1801 Van Buren entered a New York City law office and completed his law studies under the renowned attorney William P. Van Ness.

Upon admission to the New York bar in 1803, Van Buren returned to Kinderhook and became a partner in the law office of his half brother, James Van Alen. In 1807 Van Buren married his distant cousin Hannah Hoes. Together they had four sons—Abraham, John, Martin Jr., and Smith.

State and National Politics

Van Buren earned a reputation as a distinguished lawyer, but politics was his chief interest. From his first public office as surrogate of Columbia County in 1808, he moved up rapidly through state politics. Elected to the New York state senate in 1812, Van Buren created the Albany Regency, an informal political organization composed of local committees, state public officials, and journalists. The organization dominated New York politics for many years. A cunning politician, Van Buren was known as Little Magician to his friends—and the Red Fox of Kinderhook to his enemies.

Van Buren regarded himself as a disciple of Thomas Jefferson. Elected to the U.S. Senate in 1821, he supported the Jeffersonian ideas of states' rights and a limited federal government. From 1825 to 1829 Van Buren led the opposition to President John Quincy Adams. He brought together a diverse coalition of Jeffersonian Republicans, including followers of Andrew Jackson, William H. Crawford, and John C. Calhoun, to found a new political party, which was soon named the Democratic party.

Van Buren resigned from the U.S. Senate in 1828 and successfully ran for governor of New York. His primary

---

First Lady Hannah Van Buren (1783–1819)

Like her husband, Hannah Van Buren was a native of Kinderhook, N.Y. Born Hannah Hoes, she was a distant cousin and childhood sweetheart of Martin Van Buren. They married in 1807, after he had set up his law practice in Kinderhook. Little is known about Hannah, who died of tuberculosis 18 years before her husband became president in 1837. At the time their four sons were all bachelors. Former first lady Dolley Madison, believing that the White House needed a woman's touch, invited her young cousin Angelica Singleton up from South Carolina to meet the Van Burens. In 1838 Abraham Van Buren married Angelica, who served as White House hostess until Martin's term ended in 1841.

Martin Van Buren Timeline

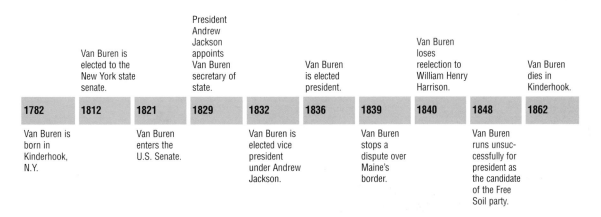

1782	1812	1821	1829	1832	1836	1839	1840	1848	1862

Van Buren is elected to the New York state senate. *(1812)*

President Andrew Jackson appoints Van Buren secretary of state. *(1829)*

Van Buren is elected president. *(1836)*

Van Buren loses reelection to William Henry Harrison. *(1840)*

Van Buren dies in Kinderhook. *(1862)*

Van Buren is born in Kinderhook, N.Y. *(1782)*

Van Buren enters the U.S. Senate. *(1821)*

Van Buren is elected vice president under Andrew Jackson. *(1832)*

Van Buren stops a dispute over Maine's border. *(1839)*

Van Buren runs unsuccessfully for president as the candidate of the Free Soil party. *(1848)*

Library of Congress, Washington, D.C. (neg. no. LC-USZC4-2859)

In 1840 Van Buren was overwhelmingly defeated by William Henry Harrison of the Whig party. A political cartoon from the campaign shows Van Buren driving a carriage called "Uncle Sam's Cab," which wrecks on a pile of "Clay," representing powerful Whig senator Henry Clay. Harrison, depicted as a locomotive, bears down on Van Buren. The locomotive is in the form of a hard cider barrel, one of Harrison's campaign symbols.

purpose in running was to garner support in the state for Jackson, the Democratic candidate, in the presidential election. Van Buren served as governor for only three months, resigning in March 1829 to become U.S. secretary of state in President Jackson's Cabinet.

From his experiences in the often corrupt politics of New York, Van Buren was familiar with the power of the spoils system—in which supporters of the victorious party were appointed to replace public officeholders from the defeated party. He helped Jackson extend the spoils system to the federal government. Van Buren was a central figure in the group of Jackson's close personal advisers who were referred to as his "kitchen cabinet." In the spring of 1831 Van Buren resigned as secretary of state to allow Jackson to reorganize his Cabinet. Assigned as minister to Great Britain, he served briefly in London.

During the first national convention of the Democratic

party, held in 1832, Van Buren was nominated as Jackson's running mate for the upcoming presidential election. The Democrats were victorious. As vice president, Van Buren faithfully supported Jackson's policies, including the relocation of Native American tribes and the removal of federal funds from the national bank to state banks.

Presidency

With Jackson's endorsement, Van Buren was unanimously nominated for president in May 1835. In the election the following year, Van Buren faced three candidates fielded by the newly formed Whig party. The Whigs comprised former Democrats and National Republicans who were disgruntled with Jackson's administration. The Whig strategy was to have three candidates representing different parts of the country as a means of preventing Van Buren from winning a majority of the votes. Benefiting from Jackson's fame and influence, Van Buren defeated the Whigs William Henry Harrison, Daniel Webster, and Hugh Lawson White. He was inaugurated on March 4, 1837, with Richard M. Johnson of Kentucky as vice president.

As Van Buren took office, a financial panic was spreading throughout the country. The crisis came about partly because of the transfer of federal funds from the Bank of the United States to state banks during Jackson's second term. Easy credit granted by the state banks had led to rampant land speculation in the West. As the panic struck and banks collapsed, Van Buren moved to guard the federal government's money by signing the Independent Treasury Act in 1840. It provided for the transfer of national funds from the state banks to federally supervised treasuries. Conservative Democrats who favored the state banks bitterly opposed the treasuries, and they abandoned the party to join the Whigs.

Van Buren faced further criticism for continuing Jackson's policy of relocating Native American tribes east of the Mississippi River to reservations in the West. In addition, Van Buren inherited the Second Seminole War (1835–42), in which the Seminole defended their

Major World Events During Van Buren's Administration

Canada. Papineau-Mackenzie revolts, 1837–38

Canada. Act of Union, 1840

England. Victoria becomes queen, 1837

Brazil. Pedro II begins reign, 1840

South Africa. Great Trek, 1837

Library of Congress, Washington, D.C. (neg. no. LC-USZC2-2465)

Martin Van Buren ran for president in 1848 as the candidate of the antislavery Free Soil party. His running mate was Charles F. Adams. The party's historic slogan was "Free Soil, Free Speech, Free Labor, and Free Men."

Florida homeland against U.S. troops. Thousands of lives were lost on both sides, and the war cost the U.S. government between 40 and 60 million dollars.

Meanwhile, Van Buren had to manage the undeclared and bloodless Aroostook War, a dispute between Maine and the British-controlled Canadian province of New Brunswick over Maine's northeast border on the Aroostook River. In 1839 both sides dispatched troops to the area. Van Buren sent Gen. Winfield Scott, who negotiated a truce with British officials in March 1839. The Webster-Ashburton Treaty of 1842 established a permanent boundary line between Maine and New Brunswick.

As the presidential election of 1840 approached, Van Buren lost support in the South with his handling of the question of the annexation of Texas. Texas had won its independence from Mexico in 1836 and applied for U.S. statehood in the summer of 1837. Northerners opposed the acquisition of Texas because it would add another slave state to the Union. Although Van Buren felt that slavery should remain an internal concern for individual states, he rejected the annexation of Texas to avoid any sectional conflicts that would divide the country even further over the issue. This decision disappointed Southern Democrats.

To regain favor with the South before the election, Van Buren sided against the African slaves who stood trial in the United States for their mutiny in 1839 aboard the Spanish slave ship *Amistad*. Nevertheless, Van Buren still lost many Southern voters to the Whigs. In addition, the enduring economic crisis haunted Van Buren in the election of 1840. A more united Whig faction nominated William Henry Harrison as their candidate, and he soundly defeated Van Buren.

Later Years

Van Buren returned to New York, where he remained active in defending his political principles. He fought the expansion of slavery and remained opposed to the annexation of Texas. In 1844 the Missouri legislature nominated Van Buren for president, but his stance on the Texas issue prevented him from securing the Democratic nomination. He lost to James K. Polk, who became the 11th president of the United States in 1845.

Over the next four years Van Buren gathered support from antislavery Democrats, known as Barnburners, to form the Free Soil party in 1848. Van Buren ran as the party's candidate in the presidential election of 1848. The Free Soil ticket won only 10 percent of the popular vote, but it drew votes away from the Democratic candidate, thus securing victory for the Whig candidate, Zachary Taylor.

Exhausted from public life, Van Buren finally retired to his Lindenwald estate in Kinderhook. He tended to his farms and kept abreast of national politics. Van Buren's health slowly deteriorated in his last year, and he died at Lindenwald on July 24, 1862.

WILLIAM HENRY HARRISON

The Granger Collection, New York

**9th President of the United States
(1773–1841; president March 4–April 4, 1841)**

Vice President: John Tyler (1790–1862)

W. H. Harrison

On March 4, 1841, Gen. William Henry Harrison was inaugurated ninth president of the United States. The former Army officer was 68 years old—the oldest man to become president in the 19th century. Just one month later, on April 4, he died in the White House, becoming the first president to die in office.

Early Life

William Henry Harrison was born on Feb. 9, 1773, at Berkeley, the family plantation on the James River in Charles City County, about 20 miles (32 kilometers) southeast of Richmond, Va. He was the third son of Benjamin Harrison and Elizabeth Bassett Harrison. Benjamin Harrison, a landed aristocrat and governor of Virginia, was usually called "the Signer" because he signed the Declaration of Independence. William was educated at home until he attended Hampden-Sydney College in Virginia (1787–90). He then studied medicine in Richmond, Virginia, and in Philadelphia with Benjamin Rush.

The death of his father in 1791 changed his plans. Under the old Virginia law, most of the Berkeley estate went to his older brothers. Young Harrison decided on an army career. President George Washington appointed him an ensign in the Army, which at that time numbered only one infantry regiment and one artillery battalion.

In Philadelphia the 18-year-old ensign recruited a force of 80 soldiers. He marched them afoot through the mountains to the Ohio River, then by flatboats to Fort Washington at Cincinnati—a little settlement of some 30 log cabins. This was Harrison's first post in the vast Northwest Territory—the pioneer land he was to serve for the rest of his life.

Service on the Frontier

Thrust into the brawling, drinking life of a frontier post, Harrison had to win the respect of his unit. He was determined to succeed in the Army, making himself three promises—to be temperate, to never be provoked into a duel, and to learn all he could about military science. He was so successful that in just two years he became aide to Gen. "Mad Anthony" Wayne. In Wayne's campaign against the Native Americans, Harrison served with distinction at the battle of Fallen Timbers (1794), which ended 20 years of border warfare. As a lieutenant, Harrison then commanded Fort Washington.

Marriage and New Career

While at Fort Washington, Harrison eloped in 1795 with Anna Symmes, 20-year-old daughter of Judge John Cleves Symmes, a wealthy landowner at North Bend, near Cincinnati. The marriage was long and happy despite many periods of debts and scrimping. The

---

First Lady Anna Harrison (1775–1864)

Born in New Jersey as Anna Tuthill Symmes, Anna Harrison came from a prominent family and attended prestigious girls' schools on the East Coast. In 1795 she married William Henry Harrison despite the opposition of her father, who objected to the young man's lack of any profession "but that of arms." When William won the presidency in 1840, she did not accompany him to the White House because of illness. The couple asked their daughter-in-law, Jane Irwin Harrison, to serve as first lady until Anna could come to Washington. As Anna began packing in April 1841, she learned of William's death. She lived more than two decades after her husband's death. Her grandson Benjamin Harrison was the country's 23rd president.

William Henry Harrison Timeline

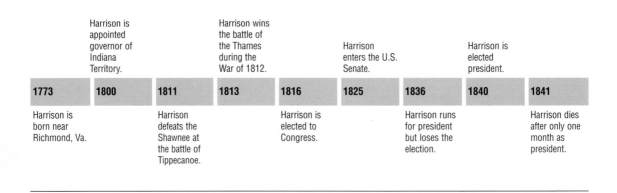

	Harrison is appointed governor of Indiana Territory.		Harrison wins the battle of the Thames during the War of 1812.		Harrison enters the U.S. Senate.		Harrison is elected president.	
1773	**1800**	**1811**	**1813**	**1816**	**1825**	**1836**	**1840**	**1841**
Harrison is born near Richmond, Va.		Harrison defeats the Shawnee at the battle of Tippecanoe.		Harrison is elected to Congress.		Harrison runs for president but loses the election.		Harrison dies after only one month as president.

Harrisons had 10 children—six sons and four daughters. Harrison was promoted to captain in 1797 but resigned the next year and settled on a farm at North Bend.

The growing family lived in a four-room log cabin, which Harrison gradually enlarged to 16 rooms. Through the years the large family was visited almost daily by friends, travelers, territorial officials, and politicians. Harrison's hospitality was so extensive that most of his farm produce went toward feeding his guests. The expense often drained his income, but he managed to give his sons a college education.

Government Work

In June 1798 President John Adams appointed Harrison secretary of the Northwest Territory. In 1799 he was its first delegate to Congress. To aid the people, Harrison pushed through a bill changing the government's land policy. Formerly the land was sold in huge tracts, which only the wealthy could buy. Harrison's bill put smaller tracts, on easier terms, within reach of settlers with less money.

A campaign badge from the election of 1840 emphasizes Harrison's frontier identity and highlights his military triumph in the battle of Tippecanoe.
The Granger Collection, New York

In 1800, when the Territory was divided into Ohio and Indiana territories, Harrison became governor of Indiana Territory. He also served as superintendent of Indian affairs, with headquarters in Vincennes.

At scores of council fires Harrison made treaties with Native American tribes. He gained millions of acres for settlement in Indiana and Illinois. He sympathized with the Native Americans, but his duty was to the government. Tecumseh, a chief of the Shawnee people, claimed that the land cessions were not valid until all the tribes agreed. This led to a war in which Harrison defeated the Native Americans at Tippecanoe River, near Lafayette, Ind., in 1811. This victory brought national acclaim to Harrison and the admiring nickname Old Tippecanoe.

In the War of 1812 Harrison, appointed a brigadier general, commanded all forces in the Northwest. After Oliver Hazard Perry's naval victory on Lake Erie, Harrison took the offensive. Relieving British-held Detroit, he led his army into Canada. On Oct. 5, 1813, he defeated the British in the battle of the Thames, ending the war in Upper Canada.

Congress and the Presidency

In 1814 Harrison resigned his commission as general. He farmed in North Bend but also undertook several disastrous business ventures. He was, however, enormously popular in Ohio and was elected successively to Congress, the state Senate, and the United States Senate. In 1828–29 he was minister to Colombia.

In 1836 the Whigs nominated him for the presidency, but he lost to Martin Van Buren. The Whigs again nominated him in 1840; John Tyler of Virginia was named the vice presidential candidate.

The campaign, based on the slogan "Tippecanoe and Tyler too," was like a giant carnival. The Whigs promised "better days for everyone" in the wake of the severe recession of 1837, and Harrison won 234 electoral votes to Van Buren's 60. The strain of the campaign, however, and the pressure of office seekers were too great for the aging Harrison. He died of pneumonia on April 4, 1841.

JOHN TYLER

The Granger Collection

**10th President of the United States
(1790–1862; president 1841–45)**

Vice President: none

John Tyler [signature]

Soft-spoken John Tyler was never expected to be president of the United States. When he was elected vice president in 1840, with William Henry Harrison as president, he was just a political pawn. Harrison, however, died after only a month in office, and Tyler became president—the first vice president to succeed to the presidency by the death of a president.

Early Life

John Tyler was born on March 29, 1790, at Greenway, the family plantation on the James River about 30 miles (48 kilometers) southeast of Richmond, Va. His parents were John and Mary Armistead Tyler. John Tyler, Sr., was a governor of Virginia and had been a roommate of Thomas Jefferson at the College of William and Mary.

John attended a local school until the age of 12, when he entered the grammar school division of the College of William and Mary in Williamsburg, Va. Later he took the college classical course. He was especially interested in Latin, Greek, ancient history, Shakespeare, and poetry

and liked playing the violin. He graduated at age 17 and studied law. At 19 he was admitted to the bar.

In 1813 Tyler married Letitia Christian. They made Greenway their home. Of their eight children, seven lived to see Tyler as president.

Political Career

Tyler easily won election to the Virginia House of Delegates in 1811, when he was only 21 years old. His flair for public speaking, in the somewhat florid style of the day, won him immediate attention. He was reelected four times; then, in 1816, he was elected to the U.S. Congress. In 1821 ill health kept him from seeking reelection.

Tyler returned to political life in 1823. He won every office he sought—state representative, governor, and U.S. senator. His service in Washington was marked by his support of states' rights and his strict constructionist interpretation of the Constitution. Though a slaveholder, he sought to prohibit the slave trade in the District of Columbia, provided Maryland and Virginia agreed. He voted against the protective tariffs of 1828 and 1832 but also condemned South Carolina's attempted nullification of these measures.

Presidency

In the election year of 1840, Tyler was a political hybrid. He had been a Democrat; but, when Andrew Jackson became president, he opposed some of Jackson's policies

---

First Ladies Letitia Tyler (1790–1842) and Julia Tyler (1820–89)

John Tyler and Letitia Christian met in about 1808 and married in 1813. Letitia devoted most of her time to her family and took little interest in her husband's political career. A stroke suffered in 1839 left her unable to perform her duties as first lady when her husband became president in 1841. Her daughter-in-law, Priscilla Cooper Tyler, served as White House hostess. In 1842 Letitia died, and two years later John married Julia Gardiner. In her eight months as first lady, Julia entertained in high style and became very popular. She hosted many formal balls and began the custom of having the president greeted with the anthem "Hail to the Chief."

The Granger Collection, New York

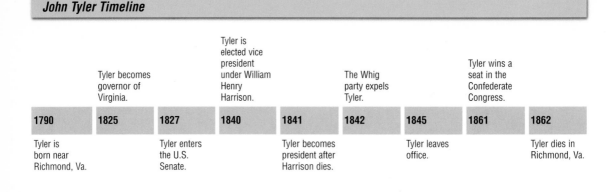

John Tyler Timeline

1790	1825	1827	1840	1841	1842	1845	1861	1862

Tyler becomes governor of Virginia. *(1825)*

Tyler is elected vice president under William Henry Harrison. *(1840)*

The Whig party expels Tyler. *(1842)*

Tyler wins a seat in the Confederate Congress. *(1861)*

Tyler is born near Richmond, Va. *(1790)*

Tyler enters the U.S. Senate. *(1827)*

Tyler becomes president after Harrison dies. *(1841)*

Tyler leaves office. *(1845)*

Tyler dies in Richmond, Va. *(1862)*

and became a Whig. Many Southern Democrats joined him. To capture those votes, the Whigs in 1840 nominated Tyler as vice president, with William Henry Harrison for president. They did not care what Tyler thought politically because he was not the presidential candidate. In the noisy Whig campaign for "Tippecanoe and Tyler too," Tyler was just part of a slogan.

Harrison's sudden death created a constitutional crisis. A shocked Congress did not even know what Tyler's title should be. There was no precedent, and the Constitution was silent on the matter. The Cabinet suggested that he call himself "Vice President of the United States, acting President." Tyler calmly ignored this suggestion. Defying his opponents, who called him "His Accidency," Tyler decided that he was president and moved into the White House. By assuming all the powers and responsibilities of the presidency, Tyler established the precedent for future vice presidents called to the office.

After Tyler vetoed a national bank bill supported by the Whigs, all but one member of the Cabinet resigned. The Whigs then expelled Tyler from the party, disclaiming any responsibility for his acts. Tyler became a president without a party. Henry Clay, a Whig leader, expressed their feelings: "If a God-directed thunderbolt were to strike and annihilate the traitor, all would say that 'Heaven is just.' "

Tyler's administration was stormy. Personally he was mild and gracious. Politically he had nothing but enemies. Time and again angry crowds burned him in effigy, even within sight of the White House. Nevertheless, he managed to accomplish a great deal. He led Congress to reorganize the Navy, to establish the nucleus of the present Naval Observatory, and to promote a national telegraph system, which became the heart of the Weather Bureau. His leadership helped to end the costly Seminole Indian wars. His mediation led to the Webster-Ashburton Treaty, which established the boundary of Maine and Canada. His calm judgment ended Dorr's Rebellion against the state government of Rhode Island. He helped negotiate the treaty with China to open its ports for the first time. Finally, in his last days as president he obtained a resolution from Congress to annex Texas.

Letitia Tyler died in the White House in 1842. In 1844 Tyler married Julia Gardiner, a wealthy young New York woman, becoming the first president to marry while in office. Julia and John Tyler had seven children.

Having been rejected by the Whigs and finding only lukewarm support among the Democrats, Tyler entered the presidential election of 1844 as the candidate of his own party, which he created from a core of loyal appointees. His candidacy attracted little support, however. In August 1844 he withdrew in favor of the Democratic nominee, James K. Polk.

Retirement

At the end of his term Tyler retired to Sherwood Forest, a plantation on the James River in Virginia. He continued to take an active interest in public affairs and remained a strong champion of Southern interests. However, on the eve of the Civil War he stood firmly against secession, and in 1861 he served as chairman of a peace conference in Washington. When the conference failed, he urged Virginia to secede. He was elected to the Confederate House of Representatives, but he died before taking office, on Jan. 18, 1862.

In 1840 the Whigs tried to bolster presidential candidate William Henry Harrison's backwoods image with raucous campaign events featuring miniature log cabins and jugs of hard cider. John Tyler's status as an afterthought in the campaign was evident in the slogan "Tippecanoe and Tyler too."

Bettmann/Corbis

JAMES K. POLK

**11th President of the United States
(1795–1849; president 1845–49)**

Vice President: George Mifflin Dallas (1792–1864)

James K Polk

When the Democrats nominated James K. Polk for the presidency in 1844, he was well known in political circles for his years in the House of Representatives. To most of the public, however, Polk was unfamiliar—the first "dark horse" nominee in the history of the presidency. Extremely conscientious, serious, and methodical, he lacked the dramatic personality that caught public attention. Nevertheless, his administration's accomplishments had a lasting impact on the United States. Under his leadership the country acquired vast territories along the Pacific coast and in the Southwest.

Early Life

James Knox Polk was born on Nov. 2, 1795, in Mecklenburg County, N.C. He was the eldest child of Samuel and Jane Knox Polk. His ancestors were Scots-Irish. The first to come to America settled in Maryland early in the 18th century. As the frontier moved westward, the Polks pioneered into North Carolina. In 1806 Samuel Polk, a prosperous farmer, moved his

family to new land in the Duck River valley in west-central Tennessee.

As a boy, James's chief interest was learning. Even though ill health made formal schooling impossible during his childhood, he qualified to enter the University of North Carolina as a sophomore in 1815. He studied so hard that he further weakened his health, but he took first honors in mathematics and the classics and graduated in 1818.

Polk then returned to Tennessee and studied law for two years. In 1820 he was admitted to the bar and started to practice law in Columbia, Tenn. In less than a year he was a leading lawyer and earning a substantial income.

On New Year's Day in 1824 Polk married Sarah Childress, the daughter of a wealthy farmer. The social prominence of her family, coupled with her personal charm and bearing, furthered Polk's rise to political power. The couple had no children.

Political Career

Polk's ability as an orator led him naturally into politics. He was elected in 1823 to the Tennessee legislature. With the backing of his close friend Andrew Jackson, he ran for Congress in 1825, and his tireless campaign won over veteran politicians. He served 14 years in the House of Representatives. For four years Polk was speaker of the House, a trying position in those turbulent times. He fought the policies of President John Quincy Adams, Jackson's rival. When Jackson became president, Polk skillfully piloted Old Hickory's controversial measures through the House. Nevertheless, politicians from both parties respected his fairness and integrity.

First Lady Sarah Polk (1803–91)

Born Sarah Childress in Murfreesboro, Tenn., Sarah Polk was the daughter of a prominent businessman and planter. She received an excellent education for a woman of her time, attending the Moravian Female Academy in Salem, N.C., one of the best schools in the South. After marrying James K. Polk in 1824, she quickly came to share her husband's political ambitions, becoming a valuable political ally. As first lady she proved to be the most politically dominant president's wife since Abigail Adams. Her influence was so great that she was often referred to as "the Presidentress." Dignified and gracious, even to political foes, she opened the White House for receptions twice a week, but, in keeping with her religious views, she forbade dancing and music on Sundays.

James K. Polk Timeline

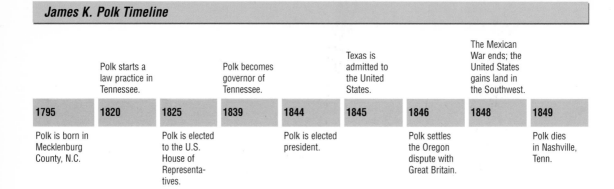

1795	1820	1825	1839	1844	1845	1846	1848	1849

1820 — Polk starts a law practice in Tennessee.

1839 — Polk becomes governor of Tennessee.

1845 — Texas is admitted to the United States.

1848 — The Mexican War ends; the United States gains land in the Southwest.

1795 — Polk is born in Mecklenburg County, N.C.

1825 — Polk is elected to the U.S. House of Representatives.

1844 — Polk is elected president.

1846 — Polk settles the Oregon dispute with Great Britain.

1849 — Polk dies in Nashville, Tenn.

After every session of Congress, Polk returned to Columbia to practice law. In the autumn he and his wife returned to Washington by stage or in their own carriage. At that time few representatives had their own homes in Washington. Usually two or more families would "mess" together—taking rooms in the same house and using a common dining room and parlor. Among the Polks' messmates and neighbors were two future presidents, Martin Van Buren and Franklin Pierce.

In 1839 Polk ran for governor of Tennessee. He was elected, much to the delight of Andrew Jackson, but he was defeated in his reelection bids of 1841 and 1843.

To reward Polk for his devoted service to the party, the Democrats planned to nominate him for the vice presidency in 1844. The party had more-prominent presidential contenders in Martin Van Buren, Lewis Cass, and James Buchanan. A bitter dispute arose, however, over who should be the presidential candidate. Unable to reconcile their differences, the Democrats selected Polk as a compromise candidate for the presidency. The news came as a surprise to many. During the campaign the Whigs tried to exploit the candidate's relative obscurity with the taunt "Who is James K. Polk?"

During his campaign Polk surprised the country by taking a positive stand on two burning issues of the day. Whereas other candidates hedged on the question of whether to annex Texas, which had been independent of Mexico since 1836, he demanded annexation. Whereas other candidates evaded the problem of the joint occupation of Oregon with Great Britain, he openly laid claim to the whole territory. The campaign slogan "Fifty-four Forty or Fight" meant that the United States should receive the territory up to latitude 54° 40′, its northern border. In the election Polk benefited from the presence of a third party; the Liberty party took enough votes from the Whig candidate, Henry Clay, to let Polk win.

Presidency

When Polk was inaugurated in 1845 he was only 49 years old—the youngest president up to that time. His vice president was George Mifflin Dallas of Pennsylvania. As president, Polk showed remarkable skill in the selection and control of his advisers and,

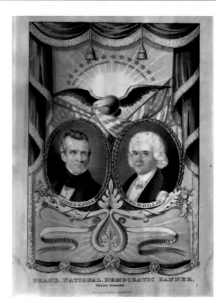

Currier & Ives/Library of Congress, Washington, D.C.

A campaign banner produced by Nathaniel Currier for the 1844 election features James K. Polk and his vice-presidential running mate, George Mifflin Dallas. The campaign slogan "Polk, The Young Hickory. Dallas and Victory" appears in a rising sun.

drawing on his legislative experience, handled Congress deftly. When his party was firmly united behind a policy he himself opposed, he yielded to the wishes of Congress. When he disagreed strongly with Congress and decided to make an issue of it, he called on executive precedent to strengthen his position.

Unlike most presidents before him, Polk knew exactly what he wanted his administration to accomplish. He declared: "There are four great measures—one, reduction of the tariff; another, an independent treasury; third, settlement of the Oregon boundary question; and lastly, the acquisition of California." The program was ambitious, but Polk succeeded in carrying it through. Unlike many presidents he could afford to be

Major World Events During Polk's Administration

Ireland. *Great potato famine, 1846*

Britain–United States. *Oregon boundary fixed, 1846*

Mexico. *War with United States ends, 1848*

Hawaiian Islands. *King abolishes feudal land holdings, 1848*

Portugal. *Civil war, 1846*

Europe. *France, Italy, Germany, Denmark, Austria–Hungary torn by revolts, 1848*

independent, because he announced at the start that he would not run for a second term.

In 1846, against strong opposition from manufacturers, he obtained his lower tariff bill, the country's first real approach to free trade. In the same year he managed to establish the national treasury, setting up the government financial system that has endured through the years almost without change.

In the dispute with Great Britain over the Oregon boundary, Polk showed his firmness. Despite his rousing campaign slogan, he knew that neither the United States nor Great Britain had a valid claim to the whole territory. He instructed his secretary of state, James Buchanan (later president of the United States), to propose a boundary at the 49th parallel. The British minister refused. Polk then told Buchanan to claim the whole territory. When Buchanan and others protested that this might lead to war with Great Britain, Polk stood firm. Britain then accepted Polk's first offer.

In a political cartoon from 1846, President Polk (right) looks on as Gen. Winfield Scott (center) pours soup on Gen. Zachary Taylor. Polk, who had recently sent Scott to replace Taylor as U.S. commander in the Mexican War, urges on Scott: "We must smother him!" The cartoon suggests that Polk had made this move to squelch the great popularity of Taylor, who had won impressive victories in early battles.

DISTINGUISHED MILITARY OPERATIONS WITH A HASTY BOWL OF SOUP.

Library of Congress, Washington, D.C. (neg. no. LC-USZ62-62676)

Polk's determination to acquire California helped lead to war with Mexico. After the United States annexed Texas in 1845, the United States and Mexico disagreed over the southern border of Texas. Polk sent a diplomat to negotiate the dispute and to purchase New Mexico and California, but Mexico refused to receive him. In response to the snub, Polk sent troops to occupy the disputed land. The Mexican War was unpopular, but the peace treaty in 1848 gave the United States 522,000 square miles (1,350,000 square kilometers) in the Southwest. The acquisition reopened the bitter debate between the North and South over the extension of slavery.

The expansion of the country westward led to the creation of a new agency, the Department of the Interior, during Polk's presidency. His administration also established the U.S. Naval Academy at Annapolis, Md., and the Smithsonian Institution, a national foundation for all areas of science.

The Presidential Burden

No president was more aware of his position and responsibility than Polk. In his private diary he referred frequently to himself as "the President." Up at six o'clock in the morning, he worked well into the night. He seemed to feel that the entire government—and country—rested on him.

In Polk's time people did not accord to the presidency the dignity it holds today. Office seekers crowded into Polk's office every morning until noon. In his diary he wrote bitterly, "The importunity for office, it would seem, will never cease." On Christmas Day in 1846 he wrote to his mother: "My official term has nearly half expired. My responsibilities and cares are very great, and I shall rejoice . . . when I can bid adieu to public life forever." The only time he spent away from work was for an occasional White House reception, a few horseback rides, visits to sick associates, and Sunday attendance at church.

When Polk left the presidency in 1849, he was worn out. He looked forward to a life of retirement in the home, Polk Place, he had just recently bought in Nashville, Tenn. He died only three months later on June 15, 1849.

ZACHARY TAYLOR

**12th President of the United States
(1784–1850; president 1849–50)**

Vice President: Millard Fillmore (1800–74)

Zachary Taylor

The first U.S. president elected after the Mexican War was a popular hero of that war, Gen. Zachary Taylor. After 40 years in the Army, he became the first man to occupy the country's highest office without previous political experience. The biggest problem he faced was how to organize the large Southwest territory acquired from Mexico. Amid a national crisis between the North and the South over the territory, Taylor died suddenly on July 9, 1850, only 16 months after his inauguration.

Early Life

Zachary Taylor was born in Montebello, Va., on Nov. 24, 1784. Both of his parents, Richard and Sarah Strother Taylor, came from leading Virginia families. A few months after Zachary's birth, the family moved across the Appalachian Mountains into what is now northern Kentucky. The boy grew up on his father's pioneer plantation in Jefferson County. There were no schools nearby, so Zachary received his only formal education from a private tutor.

In the evenings Zachary and his four brothers heard many soldier stories from their father, who had been an Army officer in the American Revolution. When the boys were grown, all but one of them joined the Army. Zachary, however, always kept his interest in farming, and later he operated plantations in Louisiana and Mississippi.

Military Career

In 1808 Taylor received a commission as first lieutenant in the infantry. During the next 40 years he served at several frontier posts and fought in the War of 1812, in wars against Native Americans in the Northwest Territory and Florida, and in the Mexican War. Among those who served under him were Abraham Lincoln, in the Black Hawk War, and Ulysses S. Grant and Jefferson Davis, in the Mexican War. An able and respected military commander, Taylor earned the nickname Old Rough and Ready for his endurance in combat.

In 1810 Taylor married Margaret (Peggy) Smith of Maryland. They had six children, two of whom died in childhood. The only son, Richard, later served as a lieutenant general in the Confederate Army. His daughter Sarah Knox married Jefferson Davis, future president of the Confederacy.

In 1837 Taylor defeated the Seminole Indians in a bitter battle at Lake Okeechobee, Fla. He was then promoted to brigadier general. Three years later he became commander at Fort Smith, Ark., and then Fort Jesup, La. During this time he established his home in Baton Rouge, La.

Mexican War

Early in 1846 General Taylor was ordered to occupy disputed territory between the Rio Grande and the

---

First Lady Margaret Taylor (1788–1852)

Born in Maryland, Margaret Smith was the daughter of wealthy plantation owners. She was educated at home. While visiting her sister in Kentucky she met Zachary Taylor, whom she married in 1810. Her husband's military career took the family to a variety of outposts and forts in unsettled areas of the Midwest, and Margaret patiently managed homes that lacked the comforts she had known in her youth. Margaret disapproved of her husband's acceptance of the Whig party's presidential nomination in 1848. Following his election, she moved with him to Washington, D.C., but delegated White House hostess duties and social appearances to her daughter Betty Bliss. One of the most elusive of all first ladies, no portrait of her made during her lifetime has survived.

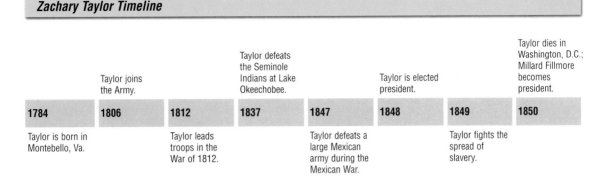

Zachary Taylor Timeline

1784	1806	1812	1837	1847	1848	1849	1850

Taylor joins the Army. *(1806)*

Taylor defeats the Seminole Indians at Lake Okeechobee. *(1837)*

Taylor is elected president. *(1848)*

Taylor dies in Washington, D.C.; Millard Fillmore becomes president. *(1850)*

Taylor is born in Montebello, Va. *(1784)*

Taylor leads troops in the War of 1812. *(1812)*

Taylor defeats a large Mexican army during the Mexican War. *(1847)*

Taylor fights the spread of slavery. *(1849)*

Nueces River in what is now Texas. Both Mexico and the United States claimed this strip of land. The government of Mexico had previously been provoked by the annexation of Texas by the United States in 1845. On April 24, 1846, Taylor's troops clashed with Mexican soldiers. Two weeks later Taylor's forces won the battles of Palo Alto and Resaca de la Palma. Congress declared war on Mexico on May 13, 1846.

In September 1846 Taylor captured the city of Monterrey, Mexico, and granted the Mexican army an eight-week armistice. Displeased, President James K. Polk sent Gen. Winfield Scott to Mexico as chief U.S. commander. Most of Taylor's troops were reassigned to Scott's command. Learning of Taylor's weakened position, Santa Anna, the Mexican commander, launched a powerful attack at Buena Vista. Despite a four-to-one superiority in numbers, the Mexicans were defeated in February 1847. This victory ended the war in northern Mexico and made Taylor a national hero.

In December 1847 Taylor returned to his Baton Rouge home to supervise his plantation. When he was first mentioned as a possible candidate for president, he was cool toward the idea. Later he asserted that he would not seek the office but would accept the nomination if it were offered to him.

Presidential Election of 1848

The Whig national convention of 1848 met in Philadelphia. The party was seeking its second victory in a presidential election. Eight years earlier the Whigs had won with a military hero, Gen. William H. Harrison. Now they again turned to a soldier, Gen. Zachary Taylor, as their nominee. Millard Fillmore of New York was chosen for vice president. The Democratic party nominated Lewis Cass, a former Army officer and U.S. senator from Michigan.

Taylor campaigned on his military record and on his promise of a nonpolitical administration. The Democrats also adopted a vague platform. Both parties avoided the vital issue of the time—the expansion of slavery in the territories. As a result, most antislavery factions formed a Free Soil party headed by a former president, Martin Van Buren.

In the election Taylor polled 163 electoral votes to Cass's 127. The Free Soilers failed to win an electoral

Currier & Ives/Library of Congress (neg. no. LC-USZ62-7555)

General Taylor commands his troops during the battle of Buena Vista.

vote, but the strength they drew away from the Democratic party ensured Taylor's victory.

Presidency

The greatest achievement of President Taylor's administration was in foreign affairs. In 1850 his secretary of state, John M. Clayton, arranged the Clayton-Bulwer Treaty with Great Britain. This agreement paved the way for the building of the Panama Canal half a century later.

At home the breach between the free and the slave states gradually widened. Although a slaveholder himself, Taylor opposed the unrestricted expansion of slavery. When California asked to be admitted as a free state, he recommended that Congress grant the request. Taylor also took a firm stand against Southern threats of secession from the Union.

In an effort to settle the differences between the North and the South, Senator Henry Clay of Kentucky introduced eight compromise resolutions in early 1850. These measures produced the greatest debate in Senate history. President Taylor did not live to see Clay's proposals adopted as the Compromise of 1850, which temporarily settled the slavery crisis. On July 9, 1850, Taylor died of cholera in Washington, D.C. He was succeeded by Vice President Fillmore.

MILLARD FILLMORE

**13th President of the United States
(1800–74; president 1850–53)**

Vice President: none

Millard Fillmore (signature)

In 1850 the United States was close to civil war over the thorny issue of slavery. A proposed compromise had touched off the greatest political storm in the country's history. Amid this bitter struggle President Zachary Taylor suddenly died on July 9, 1850. Succeeding to the presidency was Vice President Millard Fillmore, a Whig from New York. Fillmore worked hard to secure the passage of five separate measures dealing with the slavery problem. This set of laws, called the Compromise of 1850, postponed war for another 10 years. It also ended Fillmore's political career. The Whig party refused to nominate him for a second term in 1852, and Fillmore thus became the country's last Whig president.

Early Life

Millard Fillmore was born on Jan. 7, 1800, in a log cabin on a frontier farm in Cayuga County, N.Y. He was the oldest son of Nathaniel and Phoebe Millard Fillmore. Work on the farm took up most of young Millard's time, and he was unable to attend school more than three months each year.

When Millard was 14 years old his father hired him out as a woolworker. After five years in the apprenticeship he went to Buffalo, where he worked in a law office for room and board. To earn extra money he taught school.

Fillmore studied law and was admitted to the bar in 1823. For seven years he practiced law in East Aurora, N.Y., and then he moved to Buffalo. In a few years his law firm was one of the best known in the state.

In 1826 Fillmore married Abigail Powers of Stillwater, N.Y. They had two children, Mary Abigail and Millard Powers. Abigail Fillmore died in 1853. Five years later Fillmore married Caroline Carmichael McIntosh, from Albany.

Political Career

In 1828 Fillmore was elected to the New York legislature. His chief legislative contribution was outlawing imprisonment for debt in New York. In 1832 he was elected to the U.S. Congress, where he joined the Whig party in opposition to Andrew Jackson.

Except for one term (1835–37) Fillmore served in Congress continuously until 1843. He took a leading part in framing the tariff law of 1842, which set high duties on imports. The following year he helped provide Samuel F.B. Morse with 30,000 dollars to aid in perfecting the telegraph.

Defeated in a campaign for governor in 1844, Fillmore won election as state comptroller three years later. Meanwhile, supported by Senator Henry Clay of Kentucky, he had become one of the most prominent members of the Whig party. On the burning question of slavery he followed a moderate course. This made him acceptable to both Northern and Southern Whigs and led to his nomination and election as Zachary Taylor's vice president in 1848.

First Lady Abigail Fillmore (1798–1853)

Abigail Fillmore was born Abigail Powers in Upstate New York. Her parents placed great importance on education, and she developed an early interest in books. By age 16 she was teaching at a school in New Hope, N.Y., where Millard Fillmore was one of her students. The two married in 1826. As a newlywed Abigail supplemented the couple's income by continuing to teach, making her the first president's wife to work outside the home following marriage. In 1830 they moved to Buffalo. Sickly when her husband took office in 1850, Abigail delegated many social duties to her teenage daughter Mary. Disappointed to find that the White House had no library, she persuaded Congress to appropriate money to start one.

Millard Fillmore Timeline

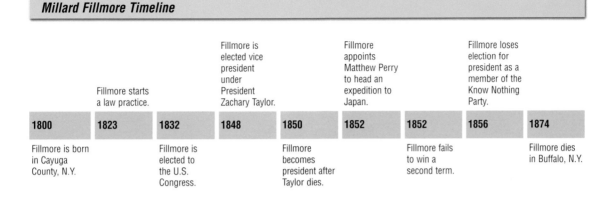

			Fillmore is elected vice president under President Zachary Taylor.		Fillmore appoints Matthew Perry to head an expedition to Japan.		Fillmore loses election for president as a member of the Know Nothing Party.	
1800	**1823**	**1832**	**1848**	**1850**	**1852**	**1852**	**1856**	**1874**
Fillmore is born in Cayuga County, N.Y.	Fillmore starts a law practice.	Fillmore is elected to the U.S. Congress.		Fillmore becomes president after Taylor dies.		Fillmore fails to win a second term.		Fillmore dies in Buffalo, N.Y.

A campaign ribbon promotes Fillmore's unsuccessful bid for the presidency in 1856, when he was the candidate of the Know Nothing party. His vice-presidential running mate was Andrew Jackson Donelson.

David J. and Janice L. Frent/Corbis

As vice president, Fillmore had to preside over the Senate during a time of bitter political quarrels. For 20 years no vice president had tried to maintain discipline when the senators became too heated in debate. Fillmore, however, insisted on dignity and brought order to the Senate chamber.

Presidency

When President Taylor died, Fillmore became president. He immediately formed a new Cabinet with the famous orator Daniel Webster as secretary of state. Though he personally opposed slavery, he gave his full support to the Compromise of 1850 because he felt that this was the only way to preserve the Union. These pieces of legislation, devised by Henry Clay, were designed to settle the slavery issue to the South's satisfaction in the new territories that had been won in the Mexican War (1846–48). Without the compromise, civil war was becoming a genuine threat.

Except for this series of measures there was no important legislation passed during Fillmore's term. In foreign affairs, the president made an important contribution to world trade by sending an expedition under Commodore Matthew Perry to Japan. This led to a treaty in 1854 that opened Japanese ports to U.S. ships and helped set Japan on its way to modern industrialization.

Like the other presidents between Jackson and Lincoln, Fillmore could not win a second term. He lost the backing of Whigs in the North with his support of the Compromise of 1850—especially the provision called the Fugitive Slave Act, which required the federal government to help capture and return runaway slaves to their owners. In retrospect it has been realized that his goal in accepting the compromise was much the same as Lincoln's a decade later. He wanted to preserve the Union at all costs, regardless of the outcome of the slavery issue. The Whig convention of 1852 ignored the president and nominated Gen. Winfield Scott, a national hero of the Mexican War. Scott, however, was defeated by the Democratic candidate, Franklin Pierce. This proved to be the last campaign in which the Whigs took an effective part.

Later Years

At the next presidential election, in 1856, the dying Whig party formed an alliance with the Know Nothing, or American, party. They made Fillmore their candidate for president. He carried only one state (Maryland), running far behind Democrat James Buchanan and John C. Frémont, the first presidential nominee of the new Republican party.

The presidential campaign of 1856 was Fillmore's last political service, but he continued to have an active interest in public affairs. He opposed Lincoln's conduct of the Civil War and supported Gen. George B. McClellan for president in the 1864 election. After the war he sided with the Reconstruction policies of President Andrew Johnson. Fillmore was also a leader in Buffalo's civic and cultural life, becoming the first chancellor of the University of Buffalo. He died in the city on March 8, 1874.

FRANKLIN PIERCE

Bettmann/Corbis

**14th President of the United States
(1804–69; president 1853–57)**

Vice President: William R. King (1786–1853)

Franklin Pierce

In 1852 the Democrats could not agree on one of their party leaders for a presidential nomination. They finally turned to a little-known New Hampshire lawyer, Franklin Pierce, as their candidate. At the time of Pierce's election the slavery issue had been temporarily quieted by the Compromise of 1850. When the problem suddenly recurred during his administration, Pierce had little success in dealing with it. His shifting views made him unpopular, especially in the North, and he failed to win a second term.

Early Life

Franklin Pierce was born on a frontier farm in Hillsboro, N.H., on Nov. 23, 1804. His father, Benjamin Pierce, served 13 years in the New Hampshire state legislature and two terms as governor of that state. During his youth Franklin attended private schools, and in 1824 he graduated from Bowdoin College in Maine. After studying law for three years he was admitted to the bar in Hillsboro County, N.H. In 1834 Pierce married Jane

Appleton, daughter of Jesse Appleton, a former president of Bowdoin College.

Political Career

In 1829 Pierce was elected to the New Hampshire state legislature. He served four years in this office, and in 1831–32 he was speaker of the lower house. At the age of 29 Pierce was elected a representative in the U.S. Congress. A supporter of President Andrew Jackson's policies, he was sent to the Senate in 1837. He was the youngest senator at that time. Handsome, affable, and charming, Pierce made many friends in Congress, but his career there was otherwise undistinguished. Overshadowed by such orators as Daniel Webster, Henry Clay, and John C. Calhoun, he seldom took part in debate.

Pierce resigned from the Senate in 1842 to practice law in Concord, N.H. When the Mexican War broke out he enlisted in the Army as a private. Soon commissioned as a brigadier general, he served under Gen. Winfield Scott in the campaign against Mexico City. Pierce resigned from the Army after the war.

Although he had refused all offers of public office after his resignation from the Senate, Pierce had maintained an active interest in politics. When the Democratic national convention met in 1852, there were so many strong candidates for the presidential nomination that none could win the required two-thirds vote. To break the deadlock a coalition of New England and Southern delegates proposed Pierce, whom they called "Young Hickory"—a reference to Andrew Jackson, who had been known as "Old Hickory." The

---

First Lady Jane Pierce (1806–63)

Born Jane Appleton in Hampton, N.H., Jane Pierce attended boarding school in New Hampshire and studied piano in Boston. She married Franklin Pierce in 1834. While Franklin served in the state legislature and then in the U.S. Congress, Jane performed the social duties of a political wife, though she found them agonizing and tried to avoid them. Jane fainted when she learned that the Democrats had nominated her husband for the presidency, and she prayed for his defeat. Eventually she accepted Franklin's victory, but the tragic death of their son weeks before the inauguration caused her to sink into a deep depression. During Franklin's presidency she rarely left the White House, and female relatives presided at most of the social events.

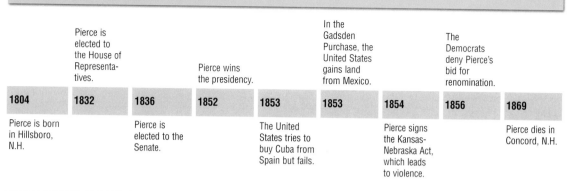

Franklin Pierce Timeline

1804	1832	1836	1852	1853	1853	1854	1856	1869
	Pierce is elected to the House of Representatives.		Pierce wins the presidency.		In the Gadsden Purchase, the United States gains land from Mexico.		The Democrats deny Pierce's bid for renomination.	
Pierce is born in Hillsboro, N.H.		Pierce is elected to the Senate.		The United States tries to buy Cuba from Spain but fails.		Pierce signs the Kansas-Nebraska Act, which leads to violence.		Pierce dies in Concord, N.H.

convention finally nominated Pierce on the 49th ballot. William R. King of Alabama was the candidate for vice president.

Opposing Pierce was the Whig nominee, General Scott. Though largely unknown nationally, Pierce unexpectedly carried all but four of the 31 states, receiving an electoral vote of 254 to Scott's 42. His triumph was quickly marred by tragedy, however. A few weeks before his inauguration, he and his wife witnessed the death of their only surviving child, 11-year-old Bennie, in a railroad accident. Jane Pierce, who had always opposed her husband's candidacy, never fully recovered from the shock.

Presidency

At the time of his election, Pierce, age 47, was the youngest man to have been elected to the presidency. For the sake of harmony and business prosperity, he tried to satisfy both sides of the slavery debate. He appointed both Northerners and Southerners to his Cabinet.

Pierce also tried to draw attention away from the hostilities between North and South by promoting U.S. territorial expansion abroad. His effort to buy Cuba from Spain led to the Ostend Manifesto of 1854. This document, declaring that if Spain would not sell Cuba, the United States should take the island by force, caused great controversy. The administration was forced to disavow the document, and Pierce recalled his minister to Spain.

In 1855 an American adventurer, William Walker, led an expedition into Central America with the hope of establishing a proslavery government under the control of the United States. In Nicaragua he established himself as military dictator and then as president. Pierce's administration recognized Walker's dubious regime.

A more lasting diplomatic achievement came from the expedition that President Millard Fillmore had sent to Japan in 1853 under Commodore Matthew C. Perry. In 1854 Perry concluded a treaty with Japan that gave U.S. ships limited access to Japanese ports.

Among Pierce's domestic policies were preparations for a transcontinental railroad and the opening of the

Northwest for settlement. In 1853, in order to create a southerly route to California, the U.S. minister to Mexico, James Gadsden, negotiated the purchase of a strip of Mexican territory now in southern Arizona. The Gadsden Purchase fixed the southern boundary of the United States.

To encourage migration to the Northwest and to ease construction of a central route to the Pacific, Pierce signed the Kansas-Nebraska Act in 1854. This measure opened two new territories for settlement and provided that the status of the territories as "free" or "slave" would be decided by popular sovereignty. The Kansas-Nebraska Act repealed the Missouri Compromise of 1820, which had prohibited slavery in the territories north of Missouri's southern border, and led to violent clashes in Kansas. The Act angered many Democrats and spurred formation of the antislavery Republican party.

Pierce sought his party's renomination for president in 1856, but the Democrats denied him, nominating James Buchanan instead. When his term ended, Pierce returned to New Hampshire to practice law. He died on Oct. 8, 1869, in Concord.

Pierce takes the oath of office at the U.S. Capitol on March 4, 1853.

JAMES BUCHANAN

15th President of the United States
(1791–1868; president 1857–61)

Vice President: John C. Breckinridge (1821–75)

James Buchanan

When James Buchanan became president in 1857 he had a record of 42 years of almost continuous public service. Even with this experience, he was not a successful leader in a time of great crisis for the United States. The problems of slavery had gradually divided the country into two hostile parts—the North and the South. As his term was ending, seven slave states of the Deep South used the event of Abraham Lincoln's election to secede from the Union. They set up an independent government, the Confederate States of America. Buchanan was unable to prevent this action. The result was the American Civil War, which began during the administration of his successor, Abraham Lincoln.

Early Life

James Buchanan was born near Mercersburg, Pa., on April 23, 1791. His parents were James Buchanan, a successful storekeeper and landowner, and Elizabeth Speer Buchanan. He attended Dickinson College in Carlisle, Pa., graduating in 1809, and then studied law in Lancaster. He was admitted to the bar three years later and established a successful law practice, aided by his great ability as a public speaker.

Political Career

After working as a lawyer for two years, Buchanan entered politics. In 1814 he was elected to the Pennsylvania House of Representatives for the first of two terms. During his service in the state capital Buchanan became engaged to Ann Coleman. The engagement was broken by a quarrel, however, and the young lady died soon after. Buchanan was heartbroken. He never married, and later he became the country's only bachelor president.

In 1820 Buchanan was elected to the U.S. House of Representatives. There he served 10 years, first as a moderate Federalist and then as a Jacksonian Democrat. He became minister to Russia in 1832 and negotiated the first commercial treaty with that country for the United States. Two years later he was elected to the U.S. Senate. Twice reelected, he served until 1845, when he resigned to become secretary of state under President James K. Polk. In this position he presided over the annexation of Texas and helped settle the Oregon boundary dispute. He also tried unsuccessfully to buy Cuba from Spain.

At the end of Polk's administration, Buchanan retired to his newly purchased estate, Wheatland, near Lancaster, Pa. He was a strong candidate for the Democratic nomination for president in 1852 but lost to Franklin Pierce. He supported Pierce in the campaign and was named minister to Great Britain.

First Lady Harriet Lane (1830–1903)

Harriet Lane served as first lady during the term of her uncle James Buchanan, the only unmarried U.S. president. Born in Mercersburg, Pa., she was orphaned at age 11 and requested that Buchanan be appointed her legal guardian. She attended boarding schools in Virginia and then the Academy of the Visitation Convent in Washington, D.C. During Buchanan's presidency Harriet was a popular hostess who was hailed by the press as the Democratic Queen. Women copied her hair and clothing styles, and parents named their daughters for her. She used her position to promote social causes, such as improving the living conditions of Native Americans on reservations. For both her popularity and her advocacy work, she has been described as the first of the modern first ladies.

James Buchanan Timeline

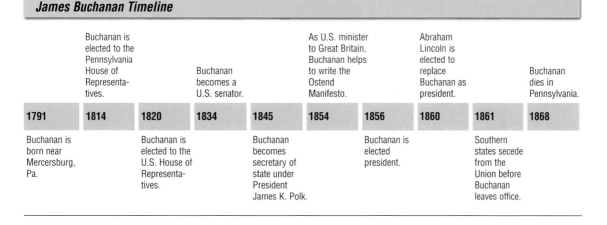

	Buchanan is elected to the Pennsylvania House of Representatives.		Buchanan becomes a U.S. senator.		As U.S. minister to Great Britain, Buchanan helps to write the Ostend Manifesto.		Abraham Lincoln is elected to replace Buchanan as president.		Buchanan dies in Pennsylvania.
1791	**1814**	**1820**	**1834**	**1845**	**1854**	**1856**	**1860**	**1861**	**1868**
Buchanan is born near Mercersburg, Pa.		Buchanan is elected to the U.S. House of Representatives.		Buchanan becomes secretary of state under President James K. Polk.		Buchanan is elected president.		Southern states secede from the Union before Buchanan leaves office.	

In 1854 Buchanan played a large part in framing the Ostend Manifesto. The recommendation—to take Cuba by force if necessary—increased Buchanan's popularity at home because the country was eager to pursue its "manifest destiny" by acquiring more territory.

At the Democratic convention of 1856 Buchanan was unanimously nominated for president. John C. Breckinridge of Kentucky was nominated for vice president. Opposing Buchanan was the Republican party's first presidential candidate, John Charles Frémont. Former President Millard Fillmore was the nominee of the American (Know Nothing) party. Although they received fewer than half of the popular votes cast, "Buck and Breck" were elected with a total of 174 electoral votes; Frémont received 114 and Fillmore, 8.

Presidency

Socially, Buchanan's administration was an outstanding success. He had been chosen as the guardian of his orphaned niece, Harriet Lane, and she acted as his hostess and entertained brilliantly. In foreign affairs the administration was popularly received. In domestic affairs, however, the president could find no way to deal effectively with the critical question of slavery. The split between the slave and the free states steadily widened, and the danger of secession became ever greater.

President Buchanan (standing center) poses with his Cabinet.

Library of Congress, Washington, D.C.

Civil war was already raging in Kansas, where slaveholders and Free-Soilers tried to gain control of the state government. Influenced by threats of secession from radical Southerners, Buchanan urged Congress to admit Kansas as a state under the 1858 Lecompton Constitution. This would have permitted slavery in the state. Congress refused to accept the constitution, and Kansas was kept out of the Union for another three years.

In 1860 the Democratic party split into two groups. Neither of the groups would accept Buchanan as its nominee because it was obvious he could not win. The Northern Democrats named Stephen A. Douglas for president; the Southern Democrats chose Vice President Breckinridge. This split secured the election of Republican candidate Abraham Lincoln.

Buchanan's administration reached a crisis during the winter of 1860–61, between the election and the inauguration of Lincoln. The victory of a Republican president opposed to the extension of slavery led to secession by Southern states. On Dec. 20, 1860, South Carolina withdrew from the Union. By Feb. 1, 1861, Mississippi, Florida, Alabama, Georgia, and Louisiana had seceded, and on March 2 Texas joined the Confederacy. Although he opposed secession, Buchanan believed that there was no way for him to prevent it. This wavering attitude angered leaders on both sides. Six Cabinet members resigned within six weeks.

Buchanan refused to surrender any of the federal forts that he could hold, however. In January 1861 he sent a steamship to resupply besieged Fort Sumter at Charleston, S.C. When the ship was turned back by the Confederates, Buchanan abandoned all attempts to assist federal outposts in the South.

Retirement

When Buchanan retired in March 1861, he was under attack from critics in both the North and the South for his compromise tactics. Although he upheld President Lincoln's policies during the American Civil War, he claimed that as president he could not have acted other than as he did. In 1866 he published a book defending his actions. Buchanan died on June 1, 1868, near Lancaster, Pa.

ABRAHAM LINCOLN

**16th President of the United States
(1809–65; president 1861–65)**

*Vice Presidents: Hannibal Hamlin (1809–91; vice president 1861–65)
Andrew Johnson (1808–75; vice president 1865)*

The 16th president of the United States, Abraham Lincoln ranks among the greatest of all American statesmen. When he took office in 1861, the country was at the brink of civil war. During this difficult time Lincoln was firm in his determination to hold the Union together. Along the way he helped bring about the end of slavery in the United States, earning the title of the Great Emancipator. His relevance has endured especially because of the passion with which he championed democracy.

Early Life

Abraham Lincoln was born on Feb. 12, 1809, in a one-room log cabin near Hodgenville, Ky. His parents, Thomas and Nancy Hanks Lincoln, were pioneer farmers. When Abe was two years old the family moved to a nearby farm on Knob Creek. Like all farm boys in those days, he learned to plant, hoe, husk corn, build fires, and chop wood. In 1816 the Lincolns moved to southwestern Indiana, settling on Little Pigeon Creek in Spencer County. Abe helped his father build a log cabin and take care of the family's crops.

After Abe's mother died in 1818, Thomas married a widow, Sarah Bush Johnston. She encouraged Abraham's desire to learn. She also made Thomas send the 11-year-old to school. In all, the boy attended school for less than a year, but he made up for it by reading. When he was 15 years old Abe often worked as a hired hand on other farms. Usually, while he plowed or split fence rails, he carried a borrowed book to read while he lunched or rested.

Life in Illinois

In 1830 the Lincoln family moved to Illinois. At the age of 21, Lincoln was about to begin life on his own. Having no desire to be a farmer, he tried his hand at a variety of occupations. As a rail-splitter, he helped to clear and fence his father's new farm. As a flatboatman, he made a voyage down the Mississippi River to New Orleans, La.

Upon his return to Illinois he settled in New Salem, a village of about 25 families on the Sangamon River, about 20 miles (32 kilometers) northwest of Springfield. There he worked from time to time as storekeeper, postmaster, and surveyor. When the Black Hawk War broke out in 1832, Lincoln enlisted as a volunteer and served three months.

Meanwhile, aspiring to be a legislator, Lincoln was defeated in his first bid for the Illinois General Assembly. He won a seat in 1834, however, and was reelected in 1836, 1838, and 1840. Lincoln soon became popular in the legislature. By the time he started his second term he

---

First Lady Mary Todd Lincoln (1818–82)

Born Mary Ann Todd in Lexington, Ky., Mary Todd Lincoln came from a wealthy family. She received an excellent education for a young woman of her time. In 1839 Mary moved to Springfield, Ill., where she met Abraham Lincoln, then a struggling country lawyer. The couple married in 1842. Mary became first lady on the eve of the Civil War. Her position was a difficult one given her Southern birth and the fact that some of her relatives were fighting for the Confederacy. Her gracious performance as hostess drew initial praise, but she was later criticized for her extravagant spending. She began to behave erratically, a condition that worsened after the assassination of her husband. She spent her last years in declining health.

Abraham Lincoln Timeline

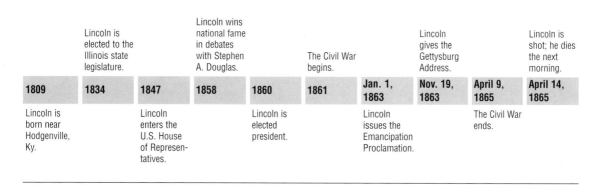

1809	1834	1847	1858	1860	1861	Jan. 1, 1863	Nov. 19, 1863	April 9, 1865	April 14, 1865
	Lincoln is elected to the Illinois state legislature.		Lincoln wins national fame in debates with Stephen A. Douglas.		The Civil War begins.		Lincoln gives the Gettysburg Address.		Lincoln is shot; he dies the next morning.
Lincoln is born near Hodgenville, Ky.		Lincoln enters the U.S. House of Representatives.		Lincoln is elected president.		Lincoln issues the Emancipation Proclamation.		The Civil War ends.	

was a skilled politician and a leader of the Whig party in Illinois. Encouraged by friends in the legislature, Lincoln decided to become a lawyer. Between terms he borrowed law books to study. In 1836 he received his law license.

Lincoln in Springfield

The next year Lincoln led the drive to have the Illinois capital transferred from Vandalia to Springfield. The legislature did not meet there until 1839, but in April 1837 Lincoln left New Salem to make his home in Springfield.

Lincoln established a reputation for himself as a lawyer in Springfield and took part in the busy social life of the city. One of the society belles was a young woman named Mary Todd, who shared Lincoln's love of literature. Her wealthy, aristocratic family was opposed to Lincoln, who was considered to be "uncouth, full of rough edges." Nevertheless, Mary married Lincoln on Nov. 4, 1842. They had four sons. As he prospered in his law practice, he and Mary gave large dinner parties and became noted as generous and gracious hosts.

By the time he began to be prominent in national politics, Lincoln had made himself one of the most distinguished and successful lawyers in Illinois. He was noted for his shrewdness, common sense, fairness, and honesty, earning the nickname Honest Abe.

National Politics

In 1847 Lincoln went to Washington, D.C., to serve in the U.S. House of Representatives. The Mexican War was on, and Lincoln opposed it. His antiwar speeches displeased his political supporters. He knew they would not reelect him. At the end of his term in 1849 he returned to Springfield and resumed his law practice.

The threat of slavery being expanded brought Lincoln back into politics in 1854. He did not suggest interfering with slavery in states where it was already lawful. The Kansas-Nebraska Act of 1854, however, enabled the people of each new territory to vote on whether the territory would be slave or free, thus threatening to extend slavery. Lincoln gave a series of speeches protesting the act.

An American flag banner promotes Abraham Lincoln for president in 1860.
The Granger Collection, New York

Major World Events During Lincoln's Administration

Denmark. *Defeated by Austria and Prussia, 1864*

Ireland. *Great emigration after famine, 1863*

Italy. *Victor Emmanuel unites nation, 1861*

Mexico. *France invades, 1862; Maximilian emperor, 1864*

West Indies. *Dutch abolish slavery, 1863*

Central America. *Honduras and El Salvador war on Guatemala and Nicaragua, 1863*

In 1856 he helped to organize the Illinois branch of the new Republican party, a political party formed by people who wanted to stop the spread of slavery. Lincoln became the leading Republican in Illinois. When the Republicans nominated John C. Frémont for the presidency of the United States, Lincoln received 110 votes for nomination as vice president. This brought Lincoln to the attention of the country.

The Republicans lost the presidential election, but in 1858 Lincoln won the Republican nomination for senator from Illinois. Lincoln's opponent in the senatorial election was Stephen A. Douglas, a Democrat and Lincoln's political rival. Douglas was running for reelection and had supported the Kansas-Nebraska Act. Lincoln challenged him to a series of debates on the slavery issue. Although he overwhelmed Douglas in the debates, Lincoln lost the election. The debates, however, began earning him a national reputation.

Realizing his countrywide fame, Lincoln's friends sought the Republican presidential nomination for him in 1860. He himself worked tirelessly to win support. He now knew what he wanted—to be president of the United States in its time of crisis. He was determined to preserve the Union. At the Republican national convention in Chicago, he was nominated on the third ballot.

Campaign and Election

The Democratic party was split, with the North nominating Stephen A. Douglas and the South choosing John C. Breckinridge. Throughout the campaign Lincoln stayed quietly in Springfield, directing party leaders from a makeshift office in the Capitol. To avoid stirring up controversy and perhaps splitting the Republicans, he did not make a single political speech.

The strategy worked. Lincoln was elected 16th president of the United States. Although he received only two fifths of the popular vote, he won by a large margin in the electoral college. He was the first Republican to become president. His vice president was Hannibal Hamlin of Maine.

Alarm spread through the Southern states. They thought a Republican president would not respect their

Library of Congress, Washington, D.C. (neg. no. LC-B8171-7929)

Two weeks after the Union victory at Antietam, Lincoln visits the battlefield in Maryland. With him are detective Allan Pinkerton (left), who led espionage efforts in the South, and Maj. Gen. John A. McClernand (right).

rights or property. They felt that secession was their only hope. Before Lincoln's inauguration seven Southern states seceded from the Union. In his inaugural address Lincoln assured the South that he would respect its rights. Nevertheless, less than six weeks later, on April 12, 1861, the Civil War began.

Presidency

The Civil War completely consumed Lincoln's administration. He excelled as a wartime leader. When he had trouble finding capable generals early in the war, he read all he could on military science and directed

A painting shows the Lincoln family in the White House in 1862, after the death of Lincoln's son Willie. Tad sits at Lincoln's knee. Robert, the eldest son, stands between his father and mother.

Library of Congress, Washington, D.C. (neg. no. LC-USZ62-5459)

much of the strategy for the Union Army and the Navy himself. He made mistakes but, on the whole, he was a successful commander in chief. When he found a capable general, such as Ulysses S. Grant, he supported him steadfastly despite great criticism. For the greater part of the war most of the newspapers and people bitterly criticized Lincoln's policies.

Considering the dangers of the time, Lincoln was quite liberal in his treatment of political opponents and the press. He was by no means the dictator critics often accused him of being. Nevertheless, his suspension of some civil liberties disturbed Democrats, Republicans, and even members of his own Cabinet. For example, he let his generals shut down several newspapers, though only for short periods of time.

Emancipation Proclamation. Lincoln believed that his primary task in the war was to save the Union. Nevertheless, he knew that the slavery question must be settled if the United States, founded on the principles of liberty and equal rights for all, were to survive as a country. During 1862 Lincoln worked out a plan to free the slaves. His Cabinet approved issuing the proclamation after the next Union victory. The summer passed with no victory. Then on Sept. 17, 1862, the Union's forces stopped the advancing Confederate armies at Antietam.

On Sept. 22, 1862, Lincoln put forth his preliminary proclamation, promising freedom for slaves in any Confederate state that did not return to the Union that year. When the South ignored him, he issued the final Emancipation Proclamation on Jan. 1, 1863. It was a landmark moment that transformed the war from a struggle to preserve the Union into a crusade for human freedom.

Gettysburg Address. In July 1863 the Union armies turned back the Confederate forces at Gettysburg, Pa. On Nov. 19, 1863, the battlefield was dedicated as a national cemetery. The chief speaker was Edward Everett, a noted orator. As an afterthought, President Lincoln was invited to speak. He worked and reworked his speech, seeking to make it as perfect as possible.

The crowd listened for two hours to Everett's extravagant oratory. Lincoln finished his speech, now called the Gettysburg Address, in a little less than three minutes. He thought it a failure, as did most of the newspapers. Only a few recognized it as one of the noblest speeches ever made. Everett wrote to him: "I should be glad if I could flatter myself that I came as near the central idea of the occasion in two hours as you did in two minutes."

Reelection. By November 1864 Lincoln was nearly exhausted by the burden of the war and grief at the death of his son Willie in the White House. Wherever he turned he read or heard criticism of himself and his generals. He prepared a memorandum for his Cabinet, forecasting his defeat in the coming election. The people, however, at last rallied to him and reelected him, with Andrew Johnson as vice president. His platform had included passage of the 13th Amendment outlawing slavery; the amendment was ratified in 1865.

When Lincoln gave his inaugural address on March 4, 1865, the end of the war was in sight. He looked forward to welcoming the Southern states back into the Union and to making their readjustment as easy as possible. He expressed that thought in these words: "With malice toward none, with charity for all, with firmness in the right as God gives us to see the right, let us strive on to finish the work we are in, to bind up the nation's wounds, to care for him who shall have borne the battle and for his widow and orphan, to do all which may achieve and cherish a just and lasting peace among ourselves and with all nations."

Victory and Death

Little more than a month later, on April 9, 1865, Confederate Gen. Robert E. Lee surrendered. To celebrate the end of the war, Lincoln took Mary and two guests to Ford's Theatre on the night of April 14. During the play John Wilkes Booth, a young actor who was proslavery and a Confederate sympathizer, crept into the presidential box and shot Lincoln in the head. Early the next morning, on April 15, 1865, Lincoln died. Vice President Johnson assumed the presidency.

ANDREW JOHNSON

Library of Congress, Washington, D.C.

**17th President of the United States
(1808–75; president 1865–69)**

Vice President: none

Andrew Johnson became a public figure during the country's greatest crisis—the American Civil War. Although as a senator he represented the slave state of Tennessee, Johnson worked to preserve the Union even after the state seceded. For his efforts he won the vice presidency, and he was elevated to the presidency when Abraham Lincoln was assassinated in 1865. In his time Johnson's administration was widely condemned. His Reconstruction policies were bitterly opposed in Congress by the Radicals, the majority faction of the Republican party. The resulting political struggles led to an unsuccessful attempt to remove him from office.

Early Life

Andrew Johnson was born in Raleigh, N.C., on Dec. 29, 1808. He was the younger son of Jacob Johnson and Mary (Polly) McDonough Johnson. His father died three years after Andrew was born. The family was very poor even after Andrew's mother married again. Unable to attend school, young Andrew was hired out to a tailor at an early age. He learned the trade but was so unhappy at his job that he refused to serve out his apprenticeship.

In 1826 the Johnsons moved to Tennessee, settling in Greeneville. Johnson opened his own tailor shop and hired a man to read to him while he worked with needle and thread. From a book containing some of the world's great speeches he began to learn history. Another subject he studied was the Constitution of the United States, which he was soon able to recite from memory in large part. In 1827 Johnson married Eliza McCardle, daughter of a Scottish shoemaker, who also read to him while he worked and helped him improve his reading, writing, and general education. The couple had five children.

Meanwhile, Johnson became an important figure in Greeneville. His lack of formal schooling and his homespun quality helped him to build a political base of poor people seeking a fuller voice in government. His tailor shop became a center for political discussion with Johnson as the leader. Before he was 21, he organized a workingman's party that elected him first an alderman and then mayor of Greeneville.

In 1835 Johnson was elected to the state legislature, where he served two terms in the House of Representatives and one term in the Senate. Politically, he found a natural home in the Democratic party of Andrew Jackson. He championed the cause of the working people against the interests of the wealthy classes.

Congressman, Governor, and Vice President

In 1843 Johnson began his first of five consecutive terms in the U.S. Congress. His most notable achievement

---

First Lady Eliza Johnson (1810–76)

Eliza Johnson was born Eliza McCardle in Greeneville, Tenn. She was educated at home and at the Rhea Academy in Greeneville. In 1827 she married Andrew Johnson, an aspiring tailor. The young couple started a tailor shop and worked together while she helped him to continue his education and perfect his speaking skills. Although she encouraged his political ambitions, she did not enjoy the limelight that his success focused on her. Instead she preferred to concentrate on raising their children and maintaining the house. In middle age she contracted tuberculosis, and during her husband's presidency she rarely appeared in public. She left the role of hostess mostly to her daughter Martha Patterson, who won praise for her simple ways and hard work.

Library of Congress, Washington, D.C. (neg. no. LC-USZ62-25821)

Andrew Johnson Timeline

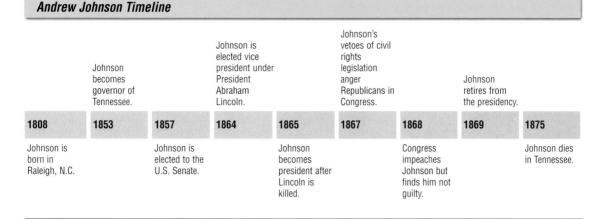

1808	1853	1857	1864	1865	1867	1868	1869	1875

Johnson becomes governor of Tennessee. (1853)

Johnson is elected vice president under President Abraham Lincoln. (1864)

Johnson's vetoes of civil rights legislation anger Republicans in Congress. (1867)

Johnson retires from the presidency. (1869)

Johnson is born in Raleigh, N.C. (1808)

Johnson is elected to the U.S. Senate. (1857)

Johnson becomes president after Lincoln is killed. (1865)

Congress impeaches Johnson but finds him not guilty. (1868)

Johnson dies in Tennessee. (1875)

Bettmann/Corbis

Johnson hosted many informal political debates at his tailor shop in Greeneville, Tenn. The building is now part of the Andrew Johnson National Historic Site.

there was the introduction of the first homestead bill. This would have cut up Western public lands into many small holdings for poor farmers. Johnson's bill was defeated by Southern representatives.

Johnson was elected governor of Tennessee in 1853 and reelected in 1855. In this position he secured the passage of the first tax in Tennessee to be levied in support of popular education. He also directed the creation of a state board of agriculture.

In 1857 Johnson became a U.S. senator from Tennessee. He again tried to enact a homestead law but the measure was vetoed by President James Buchanan. (Such a bill was not passed until 1862, after the secession of the slave states.)

When secession came in 1860–61, Johnson attracted the attention of the North by his arguments for the Union. People in the North took note of him because he

was the only Southern senator who did not resign and side with his state when it seceded.

In March 1862 President Lincoln appointed Johnson military governor of Tennessee. Although Tennessee had seceded in 1861, eastern Tennessee remained loyal to the Union. Johnson set out to restore civil government in Tennessee after the defeat in 1863 of the last remaining Confederate forces holding out there.

In the Republican convention of 1864 Lincoln's renomination for president was assured. In choosing a vice-presidential candidate the convention wanted to name a man who would appeal to Democrats and Republicans alike. Johnson was selected because of his work for the Union and his political label as a "war Democrat." Under the name Union party, this ticket won an easy victory.

Presidency

Upon the assassination of Lincoln on April 14, 1865, Johnson was elevated to the presidency. He now had to face a series of difficult problems. The Civil War was over, but its damages were still to be repaired and the Union restored. The bitterness of the people in the North was increased by the death of Lincoln. Many held the South responsible for this tragedy, and majorities in both houses of Congress were demanding harsh measures against the defeated states.

At first many Congressional leaders liked the idea of Johnson as president. They felt that Lincoln would have been too merciful to the South and that Johnson would be more unforgiving. During his early weeks in office the new president seemed to justify this belief. He denounced Confederates as traitors, saying they must be punished and "impoverished."

Quarrels with Congress. Soon Johnson changed his attitude. Before Congress met in December 1865 he had recognized state governments in nearly all the seceding states that had not been reconstructed under Lincoln. But the Republican majority refused to seat Congressmen from these states, claiming the right to judge the qualifications of prospective Southern members. The remainder of Johnson's administration was dominated by a long and bitter struggle with

Major World Events During Andrew Johnson's Administration

Alaska. *Purchased by United States, 1867*

Canada. *Dominion of Canada created, 1867*

Germany. *North German Confederation formed, 1867*

Austria. *Austria-Hungary monarchy formed, 1867*

Midway Island. *United States occupies, 1867*

Mexico. *Maximilian executed, 1867*

Library of Congress, Washington, D.C. (neg. no. LC-USZ61-269)

The Senate chamber was filled to capacity for the impeachment trial of President Johnson in 1868. The vote fell one short of the total needed to remove him from office.

Congress about the supremacy of legislative over executive rule.

Johnson believed firmly in states' rights. Consequently, he vetoed a bill that would have increased the powers of the Freedmen's Bureau, established as a guardian of the freed slaves. He also vetoed a civil rights bill that placed all cases involving the rights of blacks in the federal rather than state courts. Congress passed both of these bills over his vetoes and then passed the 14th Amendment to the Constitution. This gave citizenship to all people born or naturalized in the United States and guaranteed them equal protection under the law. It also excluded from office all who had taken part in the rebellion until they were pardoned by a two-thirds vote of each house. Against Johnson's objections, the amendment was ratified

Politics and impeachment. Before the Congressional elections of 1866, the president appealed to the people to support his policies. He made a tour through the country—called a "swing around the circle"—in which he spoke bitterly of Congress. The effort proved to be a complete failure. His personal abuse of his opponents lost Johnson what little support he had.

In 1867 and 1868 Congress passed a series of four Reconstruction acts establishing military rule and conditions of readmission for 10 Southern states. Johnson vetoed every one of these measures, but each time Congress overrode the president's disapproval.

In 1868 the quarrel between Johnson and the Radical Republicans in Congress came to a head. The president sought to remove Edwin M. Stanton as his secretary of war. This action violated the Tenure of Office Act, which had been passed by Congress in 1867 to limit the powers of the presidency. Stanton refused to give up the office, and the Senate supported him.

Charges of impeachment were then brought against Johnson by the House of Representatives. The grounds of the charges were clearly political. Acting as a court of trial the Senate voted 35 for removal from office and 19 against it. As 36 votes—two thirds of the membership—were necessary for conviction, Johnson's impeachment was not upheld.

The struggle over Reconstruction overshadowed two important international developments. During the Civil War the French emperor, Napoleon III, had installed Archduke Maximilian of Austria on the Mexican throne. In 1867 Johnson forced the French troops to withdraw. Maximilian was then overthrown by Mexican patriots.

In 1867 Alaska was purchased from Russia for 7.2 million dollars on the advice of Secretary of State William H. Seward. Gold had not yet been found there, and many people thought it a bad bargain. They called it "Seward's folly."

Later Years

Johnson left office in 1869 under a storm of abuse. In 1872 he ran for congressman-at-large from Tennessee but was defeated. Two years later he campaigned for senator and this time he won. In 1875 he took his seat in the Senate, which he had left 13 years before. Johnson thus became the only ex-president ever elected to the Senate. He suffered a paralytic attack several months later and died near Carter Station, Tenn., on July 31, 1875.

ULYSSES S. GRANT

Library of Congress, Washington, D.C. (neg. no. LC-USZ62-13018)

**18th President of the United States
(1822–85; president 1869–77)**

**Vice Presidents: Schuyler Colfax (1823–85; vice president 1869–73)
Henry Wilson (1812–75; vice president 1873–75)**

From humble beginnings, Ulysses S. Grant rose to command all the Union armies in the Civil War and lead them to victory. So great was his popularity that the people twice elected him to the presidency. He was less successful as a president, however, than he had been as a general.

Early Life

Hiram Ulysses Grant was born on April 27, 1822, in Point Pleasant, Ohio, near Cincinnati. His parents were Jesse Root Grant, a tanner, and Hannah Simpson Grant. When Ulysses was a year old, the family moved a few miles east to Georgetown. There his father bought a farm, built a house, and set up a tannery of his own. Lyss, as he was called, did chores on the farm and learned to manage horses skillfully. Three months each winter he went to a one-room schoolhouse.

When Lyss was 17, his father obtained for him an appointment to the United States Military Academy at West Point, N.Y. The academy mistakenly recorded his name as Ulysses S. Grant, and he eventually accepted

the name. The initials U.S. suggested Uncle Sam to Ulysses' classmates, who called him Sam. He was the finest horseman at the academy, and he was so good in mathematics that he hoped to teach the subject.

Upon graduation Grant was assigned to Jefferson Barracks, near St. Louis, Mo. From 1846 to 1848 he fought in almost every battle of the Mexican War. Grant came back from Mexico a brevet captain. He then married Julia Boggs Dent, with whom he had four children. In 1852 Grant's regiment was ordered to the Pacific coast. Homesick, he resigned from the Army in 1854.

Julia's father gave Grant 80 acres (30 hectares) to farm near St. Louis. After failing at farming, Grant turned to selling real estate in St. Louis. He failed again and walked the streets looking for something to do. Finally he joined his brothers in their leather business in Galena, Ill.

Civil War

When the Civil War broke out in April 1861, President Abraham Lincoln issued a call to arms. Within two weeks Grant was recruiting and drilling volunteers in Galena. He took his troops to the Illinois capital, Springfield, where the governor made him a clerk. In June 1861 Grant was made colonel of an unruly volunteer regiment, which he trained within a month. Then, before even engaging the enemy, he was appointed brigadier general.

Grant reached his headquarters at Cairo, Ill., on Sept. 4, 1861. In February 1862 he and his forces won the first major Union victory of the war, capturing Fort Donelson on the Cumberland River in Tennessee. While he was

---

First Lady Julia Grant (1826–1902)

A popular first lady, Julia Grant was noted for her informal manner and extravagant entertaining. Born Julia Boggs Dent near St. Louis, Mo., she was the daughter of a successful merchant and plantation owner. She attended local schools and then spent seven years at a St. Louis boarding school. After marrying Ulysses S. Grant in 1848, her fame rose along with her husband's military rank. During Grant's years in the White House, Julia became the first president's wife to receive national attention. Her attractive children became favorites of the press, and her daughter's wedding was celebrated with national fanfare. Julia spent lavishly on entertaining, White House furnishings, and her own wardrobe. Strong-willed and forthright, she also supported women's rights and considered Susan B. Anthony to be a friend.

Brady-Handy Collection/Library of Congress, Washington, D.C. (neg. no. LC-USZ62-25791)

Ulysses S. Grant Timeline

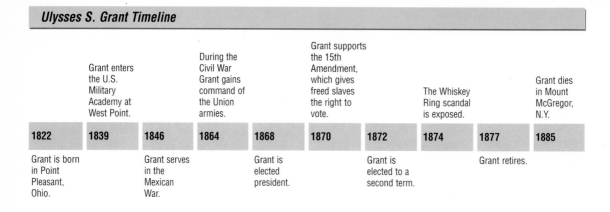

1822	1839	1846	1864	1868	1870	1872	1874	1877	1885

Above the timeline:

- **1839** — Grant enters the U.S. Military Academy at West Point.
- **1864** — During the Civil War Grant gains command of the Union armies.
- **1870** — Grant supports the 15th Amendment, which gives freed slaves the right to vote.
- **1874** — The Whiskey Ring scandal is exposed.
- **1885** — Grant dies in Mount McGregor, N.Y.

Below the timeline:

- **1822** — Grant is born in Point Pleasant, Ohio.
- **1846** — Grant serves in the Mexican War.
- **1868** — Grant is elected president.
- **1872** — Grant is elected to a second term.
- **1877** — Grant retires.

The Granger Collection, New York

General Grant and his Union troops engage the Confederate forces of Gen. Robert E. Lee during the battle of Spotsylvania Court House in Virginia in May 1864.

besieging this fort, the Confederate general asked for an armistice. Grant replied, "No terms except an unconditional and immediate surrender can be accepted. I propose to move immediately upon your works." The Confederates surrendered the fort with some 15,000 prisoners. Newspapers in the North were filled with praise of "Unconditional Surrender" Grant, and Lincoln named him a major general.

The objective of the campaign in the West was to cut the Confederacy in two by winning the Mississippi Valley. The first major success came the next year in the battle of Shiloh in southern Tennessee. In two days of fighting—April 6 and 7, 1862—Grant pushed the Confederate forces back to Corinth in Mississippi.

Losses on both sides were heavy. Grant was severely criticized for his conduct in this battle because he had failed to anticipate an attack by the enemy. Grant made no excuses but spent the rest of 1862 making plans to take Vicksburg, the great Confederate stronghold on the Mississippi River that served as a transportation point for the Confederacy. Vicksburg was a brilliant operation and showed Grant at his best. The fort surrendered unconditionally on July 4, 1863. Five days later Port Hudson, the last Confederate post on the Mississippi, fell.

When Grant returned to Tennessee, he set out to relieve a Union army penned up in Chattanooga. The Confederates occupied the heights of Lookout Mountain and Missionary Ridge, which controlled the approaches to the city. On November 24 and 25 Union troops stormed the heights, and the Confederates fled into Georgia. All Tennessee was now captured, and the power of the Confederacy west of the Alleghenies was effectively broken.

Meanwhile, the war in the East had been dragging. In March 1864 Lincoln, still looking for a general to match against Robert E. Lee, appointed Grant lieutenant general and gave him command of all the Union armies. While Gen. William T. Sherman rampaged across Georgia, Grant attacked Lee's forces in Virginia. On April 9, 1865, Lee surrendered, bringing the war to an end. In 1866 Congress revived for Grant the rank of full general, a title not used since George Washington had held it.

Presidency

Grant had never been interested in politics and belonged to no political party. President Andrew Johnson hoped to put through Lincoln's lenient plan for Reconstruction— that is, for bringing the Southern states back into the Union. The Radical Republicans in Congress demanded a harsh policy. Johnson hoped to have Grant's support, but Grant quarreled with him and was won over by the Radicals.

In 1868 the Republican convention in Chicago unanimously nominated Grant for president, with Schuyler Colfax of Indiana for vice president. His Democratic opponent was Horatio Seymour, a former governor of New York. The campaign was fought over problems of Reconstruction. Although Grant's popular majority was small, he received 214 electoral votes against 80 for Seymour. At 46, Grant was the youngest man yet elected president.

Grave problems confronted the country as Grant took office. The war had brought poverty and desolation to the South. To the North it had brought prosperity. Speculation was rife, and there was widespread corruption in both political and business life.

In 1869 two speculators, Jay Gould and James Fisk, attempted to corner the market on gold and pressured

Major World Events During Grant's Administration

London. *Queen Victoria crowned empress of India, 1876*

Canada. *Buys vast territories from Hudson's Bay Company, 1869; Red River Rebellion, 1870*

Franco–Prussian War. *1870–71. Defeated French depose Napoleon III and proclaim Third Republic, 1870*

German Empire. *Proclaimed at Versailles, 1871*

Rome. *Taken from Pope and made capital of Italy, 1870*

Suez Canal. *Opened, 1869*

Library of Congress, Washington, D.C. (neg. no. LC-USZ62-3983)

A Republican campaign banner from 1872 invokes the working-class roots of Grant and his running mate, Henry Wilson. Grant is depicted as a tanner and Wilson as a shoemaker.

Grant to keep the U.S. treasury from selling it. Foreign trade was almost stopped. On Black Friday, Sept. 24, 1869, the U.S. treasury, with Grant's approval, suddenly put up for sale 4 million dollars in gold. The price plunged, causing the ruin of many speculators.

The Radical Republicans hoped to gain the votes of blacks in the South with the 15th Amendment to the Constitution (1870), which provides that "the right of citizens of the United States to vote shall not be denied or abridged . . . on account of race, color, or previous condition of servitude." The immediate result of the amendment was an increase of terrorist acts against blacks to prevent their voting.

In foreign policy Grant usually supported his capable secretary of state, Hamilton Fish. The United States had claims against Great Britain for damage done by the British-built Confederate cruiser *Alabama*. In 1871 a treaty was signed in Washington agreeing to submit the *Alabama* claims to an arbitration tribunal in Geneva, Switzerland. This was the first important case of arbitration in U.S. history.

In 1872 reformers in the Republican party set out to defeat Grant for reelection. They organized the Liberal Republican party, which joined with the Democrats in supporting Horace Greeley, founder of the *New York Tribune*, for the presidency. The regular Republicans, called Stalwarts, renominated Grant. Grant won easily.

Grant's popularity declined as evidence of serious political corruption came to light. The government had given money and land grants to the new railways in the West. In 1873 it was found that certain members of Congress had been bribed to vote in the interests of the Union Pacific Railroad. The bribes were in the form of stock in a railway construction company, the Crédit Mobilier. In 1874 the Whiskey Ring scandal was uncovered. The ring was a combination of distillers and tax officers who defrauded the treasury of the revenue tax on whiskey. Grant was not personally implicated in the scandals, but he gave appointments to unfit people and stood by them after they had been shown to be dishonest.

Later Years

Grant reluctantly announced that he would not be a candidate for a third term because he knew that the scandals of his administration had turned the voters against him. After leaving office in 1877, he toured Europe and Asia and then moved to New York City.

Grant unwisely invested all his money in a brokerage firm co-owned by his son. When his son's partner defrauded the firm, it crashed and left Grant in poverty. To earn money, he turned to writing. His friend Mark Twain offered to publish his memoirs. Grant finished his book about a week before he died on July 23, 1885.

RUTHERFORD B. HAYES

Library of Congress, Washington, D.C. (neg. no. LC-USZ62-13019)

**19th President of the United States
(1822–93; president 1877–81)**

Vice President: William A. Wheeler (1819–87)

R.B.Hayes

The presidential election of 1876 between Rutherford B. Hayes and Samuel Tilden was among the most bitterly contested in U.S. history. Both the Democrats and the Republicans accused each other of fraud. Not until March 2, two days before President Ulysses S. Grant's term expired, was the issue at last settled. The electoral commission decided in favor of the Republican candidate, Hayes. After eight years of corruption in Washington, Hayes tried to establish new standards of integrity in the White House.

Early Life

Rutherford Birchard Hayes was born in Delaware, Ohio, on Oct. 4, 1822. He was the son of Rutherford Hayes, a farmer, and Sophia Birchard Hayes. His father died 10 weeks before Rutherford was born. His mother taught him reading and spelling at home.

At age 14 Rutherford was sent to school in Norwalk, Ohio. The next year he attended an academy in

Middletown, Conn. At 16 he entered Kenyon College in Gambier, Ohio. A serious student who excelled in debating. he graduated at the head of his class in 1842. Hayes then attended Harvard Law School in Cambridge, Mass., receiving a bachelor of laws degree in 1845.

Returning to Ohio, Hayes established a successful legal practice in Cincinnati. He joined the Literary Club, where he made influential friends, and the Sons of Temperance, for whom he made his first public speech. He also entered local politics in the new Republican party. Within a few years he had made a name for himself as a criminal lawyer. In 1852 he married Lucy Ware Webb, a cultured and unusually well-educated woman for her time. They had eight children.

Congressman and Governor

While serving in the Union Army during the Civil War, Hayes was nominated and elected to the U.S. Congress. Refusing to leave his command until the war was over, he took his seat in the House of Representatives in December 1865 and was reelected in 1866. He made few speeches and took no part in the rancorous debates over Reconstruction but voted consistently with his party.

In 1867 and again in 1869 Hayes was elected governor of Ohio. He proved a capable and economical administrator. He took great interest in prison reform and in hospitals for the mentally ill. He attracted national attention with his strong advocacy of a sound currency backed by gold.

In 1873 Hayes declared he was finished with politics, but his retirement was brief. After one year he was

---

First Lady Lucy Hayes (1831–89)

The first presidential wife to graduate from college was Lucy Hayes. Born Lucy Ware Webb in Ohio, she earned a liberal arts degree from Wesleyan Female College in Cincinnati in 1850. She married Rutherford B. Hayes in 1852. During Rutherford's governorship of Ohio, Lucy performed many of the charitable and social-service activities that would later become routine for first ladies, such as visiting schools and hospitals and lobbying for funding for orphanages and veterans' families. Although family inheritances had made her wealthy, she kept her humble style and frugal habits as first lady. This endeared her to people who had tired of the extravagant lifestyle of her predecessor, Julia Grant. Partly as a result of Lucy's popularity, the title first lady became more common during her tenure.

Library of Congress, Washington, D.C. (neg. no. LC-USZ62-25792)

Rutherford B. Hayes Timeline

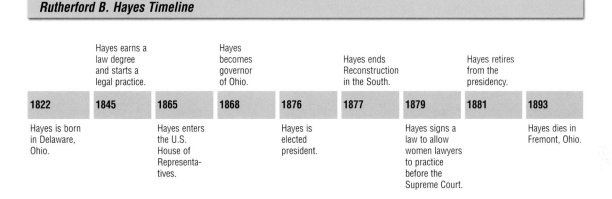

	Hayes earns a law degree and starts a legal practice.		Hayes becomes governor of Ohio.		Hayes ends Reconstruction in the South.		Hayes retires from the presidency.	
1822	**1845**	**1865**	**1868**	**1876**	**1877**	**1879**	**1881**	**1893**
Hayes is born in Delaware, Ohio.		Hayes enters the U.S. House of Representatives.		Hayes is elected president.		Hayes signs a law to allow women lawyers to practice before the Supreme Court.		Hayes dies in Fremont, Ohio.

persuaded to run for Congress, but the Democrats swept the country in 1874 and he was defeated. Ohio itself had elected a Democratic governor in 1873. The Republicans, knowing Hayes to be a good vote getter, nominated him for governor again in 1875. Hayes's success in a hard-fought campaign made him a presidential possibility in 1876.

The Disputed Presidential Election

The Republican nominating convention met in Cincinnati. President Grant's decision not to seek a third term left the field open. The leading candidate, Senator James G. Blaine of Maine, had been accused of graft, and reformers controlled the convention. Hayes suited the reformers as well as the practical politicians; moreover, he would bring in the needed Ohio vote. Gradually the drift to Hayes gathered strength, and Ohio's "favorite son" won out over the brilliant senator. Congressman William A. Wheeler of New York was nominated for vice president.

The Democratic party also nominated a reform candidate—Samuel J. Tilden, who had helped to overthrow the circle of corrupt New York City politicians known as the Tweed Ring. The campaign was bitterly fought, though the platforms of the two major parties differed little. Both were for "hard money," civil service reform, and an end to corruption in government. The Republicans had many handicaps—the scandals of Grant's administrations, the abuses of Reconstruction in the South, and a lingering economic depression.

On election night Hayes went to bed convinced that he had lost the election. The next day, however, the Republican campaign manager, Zachary Chandler, boldly proclaimed Hayes the victor. Three Southern states—South Carolina, Florida, and Louisiana—had sent in double returns. In these states the election boards were dominated by Republicans, some of them from the North. They refused to accept the apparent Democratic majorities and certified that the states had gone Republican. The Democrats, however, sent in their own returns. On both sides there was undoubtedly fraud.

Week after week Congress debated the election. The Senate, which was Republican, declared for Hayes. The House, which was Democratic, said Tilden had won.

The Granger Collection, New York

A Republican campaign poster for the 1876 election features presidential candidate Rutherford B. Hayes and his vice-presidential running mate William A. Wheeler.

The year ended with no decision reached. Finally Congress appointed an electoral commission to re-count the entire vote. The commission consisted of eight Republicans and seven Democrats. The vote on every count was eight to seven.

When it became clear that the commission would decide for Hayes, the Southern Democrats agreed to accept him if the Republicans would enter into a "bargain." More than the election of Tilden, they wanted federal troops withdrawn from the South and the return of self-government to the states. The Republicans agreed,

Major World Events During Hayes's Administration

Russo–Turkish War, *1877–78*

Congress of Berlin, *1878, reduces Russia's gains*

Africa. *Stanley reaches mouth of Congo, 1877, after crossing Africa*

Chile, Peru, Bolivia. *War of the Pacific begins, 1879*

MPI/Getty Images

The electoral commission established to resolve the disputed presidential election of 1876 holds a secret session by candlelight. In March 1877 the commission awarded the election to Rutherford B. Hayes.

and on March 2 the commission announced that Hayes had 185 electoral votes and Tilden 184.

Hayes had to set off for Washington before he knew with certainty what the commission's decision would be. Although he felt some doubt, he sincerely believed he was entitled to the election. Some Northern Democrats sharply disagreed; they referred to Hayes as His Fraudulency.

Presidency

The presidency was weak and Congress strong when Hayes moved into the White House. Powerful senators had impeached President Johnson and subdued Grant. They expected to control Hayes also and were by no means pleased with the tone of his inaugural address. The people of the country, however, applauded his much-quoted statement, "He serves his party best who serves his country best."

Hayes incurred the enmity of many Republican leaders by carrying out the "bargain." The Southern Republican governments to which Hayes owed his election collapsed, and the South thereafter became

solidly Democratic. In April 1877 the last federal troops were withdrawn from the South, and the long, bitter period of Reconstruction was at last ended.

Hayes's policies toward the South angered conservative Republicans known as the Stalwarts. The president further offended this group with his efforts to end the corrupt "spoils system"—the giving of government jobs to party workers as a reward for securing votes. Congress refused to pass civil service legislation or to appropriate money to administer civil service examinations. Hayes did awaken public interest on the issue, however, and civil service reform clubs sprang up in many states.

The worst abuses of the spoils system were in the customhouse of New York City. Hayes ignited a bitter dispute with Senator Roscoe Conkling of New York by dismissing Conkling's political friends from the top posts. One of the officials he dismissed was Chester A. Arthur, collector of the port of New York, who was later to become the 21st president of the United States. The other official he dismissed, Alonzo B. Cornell, became governor of New York in 1879.

Another achievement of Hayes's term was the return to a stable paper currency backed by gold. This meant that every paper dollar the federal government printed was matched by a gold dollar that the government kept in reserve. This increased the public's confidence in the money supply. Hayes's "hard money" policy helped pull the country out of its economic depression. When Hayes left the White House the country was again prosperous.

Retirement

Hayes had said before his election that he would not be a candidate for a second term. No one pressed him to change his mind. He stayed away from the nominating convention of 1880 and took no part in the campaign, though he approved of the candidate chosen—James A. Garfield. After leaving office Hayes was a man without a party, but he had won the affection and admiration of many people.

Back in Fremont, Ohio, Hayes devoted himself to humanitarian causes, working for prison reform and for improved education and training for blacks in the South. He died in Fremont on Jan. 17, 1893.

JAMES A. GARFIELD

Brady-Handy Collection/Library of Congress, Washington, D.C. (neg. no. lc-usz62-13020)

20th President of the United States
(1831–81; president March 4–Sept. 19, 1881)

Vice President: Chester A. Arthur (1829–86)

JAGarfield

Born in a log cabin, James A. Garfield rose by his own efforts to become a college president, a major general in the Civil War, a leader in Congress, and finally president of the United States. Four months after his inauguration, he was shot by an assassin. After weeks of suffering he died.

Early Life

James Abram Garfield was born near Orange, Ohio, on Nov. 19, 1831. He was the son of Abram Garfield and Eliza Ballou. After his father's death in 1833, his mother continued to run the family's impoverished farm. James early showed a love for books and his mother determined that he should have an education. When he was 4 years old, a log schoolhouse was built on the Garfields' lot.

When he was 15, James was hired out to the neighbors for chopping wood, washing sheep, planting, plowing, and sowing. When he was 16, he decided to become a sailor and see the world. Unable to get a job on a lake steamer, the boy worked for three months on a boat on the Ohio Canal between Cleveland, Ohio, and Pittsburgh, Pa.

Always a serious student, Garfield attended the Western Reserve Eclectic Institute (now Hiram College) at Hiram, Ohio. In 1852 he began to teach there. He saved his money so that he could spend his last two years of school at an Eastern college. In 1856 he graduated with high honors from Williams College in Williamstown, Mass.

Garfield returned to Hiram to teach again at the Eclectic Institute and after one year he was made president. The next year, in 1858, he married Lucretia Rudolph, a former classmate of his. The couple had seven children, though two died in infancy.

Military and Political Career

Garfield studied law and was ordained as a minister in the Disciples of Christ church, but he soon turned to politics. He joined the new Republican party and was elected to the Ohio senate in 1859.

When the Civil War broke out in 1861, Garfield was appointed lieutenant colonel of an Ohio regiment. Skilled as a public speaker, he recruited his own volunteers, many of them his students. At Middle Creek, Ky., on Jan. 10, 1862, Garfield won a victory that gained for him the rank of brigadier general. In April he fought at the battle of Shiloh in Tennessee. In 1863 he was transferred to the Army of the Cumberland as chief of staff. For his distinguished service in the battle of Chickamauga, he was rewarded with the rank of major general.

In 1862, while still in the Army, Garfield was elected to the U.S. House of Representatives. He took his seat in the House in December 1863. Serving until 1880,

---

First Lady Lucretia Garfield (1832–1918)

Born Lucretia Rudolph in Hiram, Ohio, Lucretia Garfield met her future husband, James A. Garfield, while they both attended Western Reserve Eclectic Institute. The couple married in 1858. Trained as an educator, Lucretia taught until the birth of their first child in 1860. Although Lucretia held strong views on women's rights and her own independence, she tempered her positions as her husband's political career advanced. In May 1881, after only a few months as first lady, she became ill with malaria and went to New Jersey to recuperate. When she received word that her husband had been shot, she returned to Washington to nurse him through the final weeks of his life. After James's death Lucretia dedicated herself to her children and to preserving his memory.

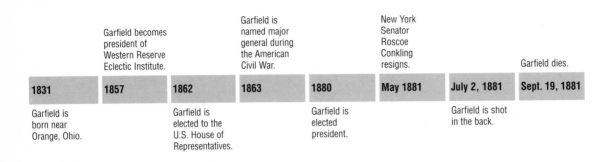

James A. Garfield Timeline

	Garfield becomes president of Western Reserve Eclectic Institute.		Garfield is named major general during the American Civil War.		New York Senator Roscoe Conkling resigns.		Garfield dies.
1831	**1857**	**1862**	**1863**	**1880**	**May 1881**	**July 2, 1881**	**Sept. 19, 1881**
Garfield is born near Orange, Ohio.		Garfield is elected to the U.S. House of Representatives.		Garfield is elected president.		Garfield is shot in the back.	

The Granger Collection, New York

President Garfield reels after being shot in the back at a Washington railroad station. Secretary of State James G. Blaine supports the president as his assailant, Charles J. Guiteau, is captured at left.

Garfield became an expert on the financial problems facing the country—currency, taxation, and the public debt. He also supported strict policies of Reconstruction for the South. When the great orator James G. Blaine left the House for the Senate, Garfield became the House Republican leader.

Garfield lost respect for President Ulysses S. Grant because of the political corruption of his administration. When Rutherford B. Hayes became president, Garfield supported him strongly, fighting for civil-service reform and a sound currency.

Nomination and Election

The Ohio legislature elected Garfield to the U.S. Senate in 1880. Before he could take his seat, however, he was unexpectedly nominated for the presidency.

The Stalwarts, a faction of the Republican party that opposed Hayes's civil-service reform policies, pressed for a third term for Grant. The leader of the Stalwarts was Roscoe Conkling, a senator from New York who was boss of the Republican organization in his state. The next leading candidate was Blaine, who was labeled a "Half-Breed" (moderate) Republican. Garfield went to the convention in Chicago as head of the Ohio delegation to put forward the name of Ohio's favorite son, John Sherman. Garfield's speech nominating Sherman was so well received that he, not the candidate, became the focus of attention.

Grant led all other candidates for 35 ballots, but he failed to command a majority. On the 36th ballot the nomination went to a dark horse, Garfield. He was still trying to remove his name from nomination as the bandwagon gathered speed. Chester A. Arthur of New York was chosen as the vice-presidential candidate.

The Democrats nominated Gen. Winfield Scott Hancock of Pennsylvania. Garfield's victory in the popular vote was small—about 10,000 votes—but the electoral vote was 214 to 155.

Presidency

True to his civil-service principles, President Garfield followed Hayes's example in attacking the spoils system. Senator Conkling had built up his political machine by giving out public offices to reward party workers. Garfield accepted nobody's domination in making appointments. When he named Conkling's bitterest political foe to be collector of the New York Custom House, Conkling resigned from the Senate in protest. The incident strengthened the independence and power of the presidency.

Garfield complained of the steady stream of office seekers. One was Charles J. Guiteau, a disreputable politician. When the president refused his request, Guiteau resolved to kill him. On the morning of July 2, 1881, Garfield entered the Pennsylvania Railroad Station in Washington, D.C. When he reached the waiting room, Guiteau stepped forward, fired two pistol shots, and shouted, "I am a Stalwart! Arthur is president now." One bullet grazed Garfield's arm, the other struck him in the back.

Day after day bulletins of the president's condition were telegraphed to every part of the country. In September, to escape the heat of Washington, Garfield was moved to Elberon, near Long Branch, N.J. He died there on September 19. Vice President Arthur took the oath of office the next day. Guiteau was tried and sentenced to death; on June 30, 1882, he was hanged.

CHESTER A. ARTHUR

Library of Congress, Washington, D.C.
**21st President of the United States
(1829–86; president 1881–85)**

Vice President: none

When President James A. Garfield was assassinated in 1881, Chester A. Arthur, the vice president, rose to the highest office of the United States. Arthur took the presidential oath on Sept. 19, 1881, amid widespread belief that he was unworthy of the office. Said to be hurt by the public's low regard for him, Arthur was determined to prove that he could rise above expectations.

Early Life

Chester Alan Arthur was born in Fairfield, Vt., on Oct. 5, 1829. His parents were William Arthur, a Baptist minister, and Malvina Stone Arthur. His father was restless, and the family moved frequently. In 1839 they settled in Union Village (now Greenwich) in eastern New York.

Five years later Chester was admitted to Union College in Schenectady, N.Y., when he was only 15. To support himself financially, he began to teach during the long winter vacations. After graduating at 18, he continued to teach while studying law.

Defender of Civil Rights

William Arthur was an abolitionist, and his son shared his views on slavery. In the minister's congregation was a congressman, Erastus D. Culver, who also had strong antislavery principles. Culver moved his law office to Brooklyn and agreed to take young Arthur into his firm to train him. Arthur entered Culver's office in 1853. The next year he was admitted to the bar and taken into partnership.

Arthur arrived in time to assist Culver in the famous Lemmon slave case. In 1852 Jonathan Lemmon and his wife had brought eight slaves from Virginia to New York by boat. They intended to stop over only until the next boat left for Texas. The court decided that slaves passing through New York became free.

Meanwhile Arthur was fighting another civil rights case. An African American woman, Lizzie Jennings, had been forced off a Brooklyn streetcar by the conductor and some of the passengers. Arthur won damages of 500 dollars for her and, more importantly, obtained a court decision forbidding discrimination in public transportation.

Political Career

In 1856 Arthur went into partnership with another young lawyer in the Wall Street district. To build up a practice, he needed to enlarge his circle of acquaintances, so he joined clubs and entered politics. He soon numbered among his friends prominent literary figures as well as politicians. In 1859 he married Ellen Lewis Herndon, with whom he had three children.

First Lady Ellen Arthur (1837–80)

Ellen Arthur was born Ellen Lewis Herndon in Culpeper, Virginia. Called Nell, she was the daughter of Capt. William Lewis Herndon of the U.S. Navy, who explored the Amazon River and was one of the founders of the Naval Observatory in Washington, D.C. Ellen was living with her mother in New York City when a cousin introduced her to Chester A. Arthur in 1856. They married three years later. The Arthurs were prosperous and liked to entertain guests in their fashionable New York City home. Shortly after Chester was elected vice president in 1880, Ellen died of pneumonia. When Arthur assumed the presidency, his sister Mary Arthur McElroy acted as White House hostess.

Chester A. Arthur Timeline

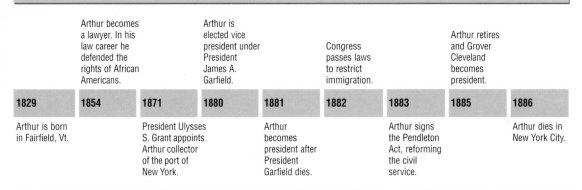

1829	1854	1871	1880	1881	1882	1883	1885	1886

Arthur becomes a lawyer. In his law career he defended the rights of African Americans. *(1854)*

Arthur is elected vice president under President James A. Garfield. *(1880)*

Congress passes laws to restrict immigration. *(1882)*

Arthur retires and Grover Cleveland becomes president. *(1885)*

Arthur is born in Fairfield, Vt. *(1829)*

President Ulysses S. Grant appoints Arthur collector of the port of New York. *(1871)*

Arthur becomes president after President Garfield dies. *(1881)*

Arthur signs the Pendleton Act, reforming the civil service. *(1883)*

Arthur dies in New York City. *(1886)*

Arthur played an important part in the organization of the new Republican party in the state of New York, but he was never interested in holding political office. His activities soon brought him to the attention of the governor, Edwin D. Morgan. On April 13, 1861, the day after the Civil War began, Morgan asked Arthur to take over the duties of quartermaster general in New York City. The post involved supplying barracks, food, uniforms, and equipment for the troops who passed through the city.

Arthur resumed his law practice in 1863. His political activities brought him into close association with Senator Roscoe Conkling, the Republican boss of New York. In 1868 Arthur worked with Conkling on Ulysses S. Grant's successful presidential campaign. In 1871 President Grant rewarded Arthur by appointing him collector of the port of New York.

The New York Custom House on Wall Street collected about two thirds of the country's tariff revenue and employed about 1,000 people. It was the usual practice for the collector to give appointments to people who had worked for the party and to accept from them "voluntary contributions" to campaign funds. Arthur was scrupulously honest but he was a practical politician, not a reformer. He did not remove good workers to make way for others, but when an appointment was to be made he looked for a qualified political friend to do the work. Like Conkling and many others in government, he believed that the spoils system ("to the victor belong the spoils") was necessary to maintain a political organization.

Civil-service reform was in full swing when Rutherford B. Hayes succeeded Grant as president in 1877. Hayes decided to organize the New York Custom House on a strictly business basis. In 1878 he suspended Arthur, who returned to his law practice.

Vice Presidency

The Republican party was seriously divided in 1880. Conkling, as leader of the Stalwart Republicans, tried to nominate Grant for a third term in 1880. The "Half-Breed" (moderate) Republicans wanted Senator James G. Blaine. The deadlock in the convention lasted until the 36th ballot, when James A. Garfield was unexpectedly

nominated as a compromise candidate. To make sure of the Stalwarts' aid in the election, the convention nominated Arthur for vice president. The Republicans won the election and Arthur took the country's second highest office.

After the election, the split in the Republican party widened. Garfield appointed Blaine, Conkling's bitter enemy, as secretary of state and refused to allow Conkling to name the secretary of the treasury, who would control the Custom House. Finally, Garfield proposed to appoint William H. Robertson, the outstanding "Half-Breed" Republican of New York State, to the Custom House.

Conkling feared Robertson would use Custom House patronage to build up his own machine, and Arthur shared his apprehension. As a protest, Conkling resigned from the Senate and took with him the junior senator from New York, Thomas C. Platt. Arthur went with them to Albany to work for their reelection.

Vice President Chester A. Arthur takes the presidential oath at his home in New York City following the death of President James A. Garfield on Sept. 19, 1881.

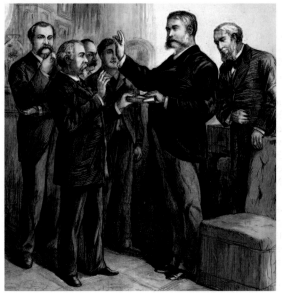

Major World Events During Arthur's Administration

Arctic. *Greely rescued, 1884*

Berlin. *Conference on partition of Africa, 1884–85*

Germany, Austria, and Italy *form Triple Alliance, 1882*

Egypt. *Occupied by British, 1882*

Chile *crushes Peru and Bolivia in war of the Pacific, 1879–83*

Presidency

On July 2, 1881, Garfield was shot by a disappointed office seeker who boasted that he was a Stalwart Republican. During the weeks when Garfield lingered between life and death, popular indignation against the Stalwarts ran high. Arthur remained in seclusion until Garfield's death in September made him president. The public considered the former customhouse collector unqualified for the office.

Arthur's simple and sincere inaugural address helped to reassure the people. In his first message to Congress he surprised everyone by coming out strongly for civil-service reform. In 1883 he signed the country's first civil-service law, the Pendleton Act. This act set up a civil-service commission to conduct competitive examinations for people seeking government jobs. It was the first important step toward replacing the spoils system with a merit-based system for filling government offices. Succeeding presidents extended the merit system.

Arthur is called the Father of the American Navy because he took a personal interest in modernizing and expanding it. The Navy had declined steadily after the Civil War. In 1882 Congress appropriated money for the country's first all-steel vessels. The so-called "white squadron," which was completed during Grover Cleveland's administration, formed the nucleus of the modern U.S. Navy.

Few governments in history had ever complained of too much money in the treasury. Each year in the 1880s, however, the U.S. government had a large surplus over ordinary expenditures. At this time government funds were stored in vaults rather than in banks. With each increase in the treasury surplus, more money was taken out of circulation, which resulted in a deflation of prices. Moreover, this was happening in a period of rapid economic expansion. The most pressing problem of the administration therefore was how to return money to circulation. The flood of money was caused largely by the high tariffs that had been imposed by the government during the Civil War. Arthur wanted to attack the surplus by lowering tariffs. He set up a commission, which recommended a reduction in duties. Manufacturers who prospered under the high tariffs,

The Granger Collection, New York

In a political cartoon from 1884, President Arthur suffers from dealing with the feuding factions of the Republican party.

however, had powerful lobbies in Washington. The so-called "Mongrel" Tariff of 1883, which Congress passed, stamped the Republicans as favoring a high protective tariff. The Democrats began to demand a lower tariff, setting off a partisan debate that would last for decades.

During Arthur's administration the first acts to restrict immigration were passed. The Chinese Exclusion Act of 1882 restricted the immigration of Chinese laborers for a 10-year period. In the same year paupers, criminals, convicts, and the insane were barred from the United States.

Arthur's popularity grew with each year of his presidency. He had struggled to hold together the bitterly divided Republican party, and he hoped to receive approval from the nominating convention of 1884. The convention, however, did not seriously consider him. Senator Blaine was nominated but lost the election to Grover Cleveland, the first Democratic president to be elected since 1856. Despondent, Arthur returned to his New York home and tried to resume his law practice, but he lacked the energy for it. He died on Nov. 18, 1886.

GROVER CLEVELAND

Library of Congress, Washington, D.C. (neg. no. LC-USZ62-48559)

**22nd and 24th President of the United States
(1837–1908; president 1885–89, 1893–97)**

**Vice Presidents: Thomas A. Hendricks (1819–85; vice president 1885)
Adlai E. Stevenson (1835–1914; vice president 1893–97)**

Democrats from all parts of the country crowded into Washington to witness the presidential inauguration of March 4, 1885. For the first time since the Civil War a Democrat had won the presidency. Grover Cleveland, an honest and principled politician, had revived the party. Elected again in 1892, he was both the 22nd and the 24th president of the United States. He was the only president ever to be reelected after a defeat.

Early Life

Stephen Grover Cleveland was born in Caldwell, N.J., on March 18, 1837. He was the son of Richard Falley Cleveland, a Presbyterian minister, and Ann Neal. Grover grew up in New Jersey and later in New York State. When his father died in 1853, Grover had to give up school to support his mother and sisters. He spent a year teaching young children at the New York Institution for the Blind. Then he decided to look for a job with more opportunity for advancement.

In Buffalo, N.Y., Grover worked as a clerk in a law office. He received no salary but was allowed to study in

the firm's library. He passed the examination to be a lawyer in 1859, when he was 22 years old.

Political Career

Before he was old enough to vote, Cleveland had become an active worker in the Democratic party because he regarded it as being more solid and conservative than the Republican. In 1863 he was appointed assistant district attorney for Erie County, and from 1870 to 1873 he served as county sheriff.

A ring of corrupt politicians was ruling Buffalo. In 1881, to oppose their choice for mayor, the Democrats wanted a reform candidate who would attract votes from dissatisfied Republicans. Cleveland, now the head of a leading law firm, had a reputation for enormous energy and stern devotion to justice. With difficulty he was persuaded to run for mayor. He won the election and became known as the "veto mayor" because he vetoed so many dishonest bills.

Cleveland had served only one year as mayor when a Democratic reform group began to look around for a principled candidate for governor to oppose New York City's Tammany Hall politicians. While Cleveland was home with his dying mother, his friends organized a movement for his nomination. He returned to Buffalo to find a statewide boom well under way. He won the election by a landslide vote and was inaugurated on Jan. 3, 1883. He broke openly with Tammany, earning himself a national reputation.

In 1884 the Republicans nominated Senator James G. Blaine for the presidency. Blaine was associated with the spoils system in government. He was also suspected of

---

First Lady Frances Cleveland (1864–1947)

Frances Cleveland was the youngest first lady in U.S. history. Born Frances Folsom in Buffalo, N.Y., she attended Wells College in Aurora, N.Y. While touring Europe after graduation, she continued her long-standing correspondence with President Grover Cleveland, who had been her father's law partner and a close family friend from before the time of Frances' birth. They married in the White House in 1886, the first time an incumbent president wed in the mansion. At 21 years old, Frances was 27 years younger than her husband. She proved to be a very popular first lady. Advertisers used her image in illustrations and sought her endorsements for their products, and many parents named their infant daughters after her.

Grover Cleveland Timeline

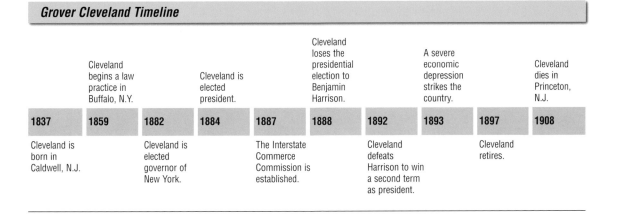

1837	1859	1882	1884	1887	1888	1892	1893	1897	1908

Above timeline:
- **1859** Cleveland begins a law practice in Buffalo, N.Y.
- **1884** Cleveland is elected president.
- **1888** Cleveland loses the presidential election to Benjamin Harrison.
- **1893** A severe economic depression strikes the country.
- **1908** Cleveland dies in Princeton, N.J.

Below timeline:
- **1837** Cleveland is born in Caldwell, N.J.
- **1882** Cleveland is elected governor of New York.
- **1887** The Interstate Commerce Commission is established.
- **1892** Cleveland defeats Harrison to win a second term as president.
- **1897** Cleveland retires.

having profited in the railroad graft of President Ulysses S. Grant's administration. Carl Schurz and other prominent reformers left the Republican party and offered to support Cleveland if the Democrats nominated him for the presidency.

When the Democrats gathered in Chicago, Tammany delegates were there to oppose Cleveland. He was far in the lead, however, on the first vote, and the second vote gave him the nomination. Thomas A. Hendricks of Indiana was nominated for vice president. The independent Republicans, called Mugwumps, became practically a Cleveland party.

The campaign was bitterly fought on personal rather than on political issues. Blaine was accused of political corruption and Cleveland of personal immorality. The story was circulated that he was the father of an illegitimate son. A week before the election, a Republican called the Democrats the party of "rum, Romanism, and rebellion." This angered the Roman Catholics and cost Blaine many votes.

The election was close. Cleveland won with a plurality of about 23,000 votes over Blaine. The electoral vote was 219 for Cleveland to Blaine's 182. The new president took office on March 4, 1885.

First Term and Defeat

Cleveland was 48 when he moved into the White House and was still a bachelor. Unlike elegant President Chester A. Arthur, whom he followed, he was a man of simple tastes. One of his sisters, Rose Cleveland, acted as hostess for him. In 1886 the president married Frances Folsom, the daughter of his former law partner. They had five children.

In the 1880s the country's greatest problem was the large surplus in the treasury. The country was so prosperous that in 1886 the unions decided to strike for an eight-hour day. This movement ended disastrously with the Haymarket Riot in Chicago when a bomb killed seven people.

Cleveland took a firm stand against corruption and extravagance. He upheld the Civil Service Commission against members of his own party who were eager for the spoils of office. He read carefully each private

pension bill for Civil War veterans and vetoed hundreds. This lost him many supporters both in and out of Congress. After the Interstate Commerce Act of 1887 was passed, he gave close attention to forming the Interstate Commerce Commission, the first regulatory agency in the United States.

Shortly after his election, Cleveland began a concentrated study of the tariff. In 1887, just before the presidential nominations, Cleveland devoted his entire annual message to Congress to attacking the high tariff and the trusts it protected. This message won him the anger of many Democrats in Congress and also of powerful business interests.

Cleveland was renominated in 1888 and made tariff reform the chief issue of the campaign. He polled about 100,000 more votes than the Republican candidate, Benjamin Harrison, but Harrison won 233 electoral votes to Cleveland's 168.

Cleveland spent the next four years working for a prominent law firm in New York City. He watched the

President Cleveland marries Frances Folsom in the White House on June 2, 1886.

Major World Events During Cleveland's Administrations

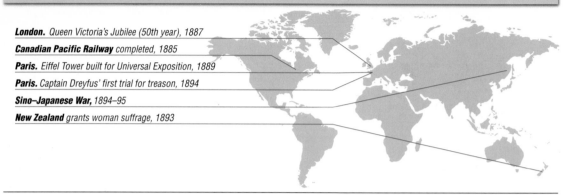

London. *Queen Victoria's Jubilee (50th year), 1887*

Canadian Pacific Railway *completed, 1885*

Paris. *Eiffel Tower built for Universal Exposition, 1889*

Paris. *Captain Dreyfus' first trial for treason, 1894*

Sino–Japanese War, *1894–95*

New Zealand *grants woman suffrage, 1893*

Harrison Administration spending money recklessly and making what he regarded as dangerous blunders. The McKinley Tariff of 1890 raised rates so high that imports almost stopped. The Sherman Silver Purchase Act of 1890 caused a steady outflow of gold from the treasury. As Harrison's term drew to a close, the country was sliding swiftly into a serious agricultural and industrial depression.

Second Term

In 1892 the Democrats nominated Cleveland on the first ballot with Adlai E. Stevenson of Illinois as vice president. This time he triumphantly defeated Harrison by a landslide popular vote of 5,556,918 to Harrison's 5,176,108 and an electoral vote of 277 to 145.

Two months after the inauguration the great Panic of 1893 swept the country. Banks closed their doors, railroads went bankrupt, and farm mortgages were foreclosed. People hoarded gold, and the treasury was fast losing its gold reserve.

Cleveland called a special session of Congress to deal with the currency situation. William Jennings Bryan, the talented orator, spoke for three hours demanding the

A political cartoon from 1894 depicts Cleveland as captain of the ship Democracy. *He tries to quell a mutiny of congressmen in his own party over his support for the gold standard and tariff reform.*

The Granger Collection, New York

free and unlimited coinage of silver. But Cleveland stood for the gold standard and succeeded in having the Sherman Silver Purchase Act repealed. Financial disaster was not staved off, however, because there was so little gold in the treasury. Cleveland turned in desperation to Wall Street bankers in New York City and asked them to sell government bonds abroad for gold. The strategy succeeded in replenishing the government's gold supply, but the crisis did not pass until 1896.

Meanwhile, there were strikes in mines, on railroads, and in textile mills. In 1894 "Coxey's Army," a group of unemployed men led by businessman Jacob S. Coxey, marched on Washington to demand relief. More serious was the great Pullman strike on the outskirts of Chicago. The American Railway Union came to the aid of the workers and refused to move any trains that included Pullman cars. Cleveland's attorney general, Richard Olney, had a federal court issue an injunction to restrain the strikers, and the president sent troops to quell the rioters. This response won Cleveland the plaudits of the business community but lost him the support of many workers.

Cleveland was unyielding in his opposition to foreign expansion. In 1893 he withdrew from the Senate a treaty calling for the annexation of Hawaii. In 1895, when the Cubans revolted against Spain, he held firmly to neutrality. He took vigorous action, however, against Great Britain in its quarrel with Venezuela and succeeded in having the boundary of British Guiana (now Guyana) settled by arbitration.

Retirement

When his second term drew to a close, Cleveland's party rejected the gold standard and nominated Bryan. The Republican candidate, William McKinley, won the election. Cleveland retired to Princeton, N.J., where he bought a mansion called Westland. He became active in the affairs of Princeton University as a lecturer in public affairs and as a trustee. Gradually public opinion changed, and Cleveland regained much of the public admiration he had earlier enjoyed. In 1904 he saw the Democratic party declare for the gold standard. He died at Westland on June 24, 1908.

BENJAMIN HARRISON

23rd President of the United States
(1833–1901; president 1889–93)

Vice President: Levi P. Morton (1824–1920)

Benjamin Harrison, a moderate Republican, won the presidency in 1888 despite losing the popular vote to Democrat Grover Cleveland. President Harrison's single term fell between Cleveland's two terms. Cleveland was popular with the people but unpopular with political leaders. Harrison, though a principled man of keen intellect, was popular with neither.

Early Life

Benjamin Harrison was born on Aug. 20, 1833, in North Bend, Ohio. He was the son of John Scott Harrison, a farmer, and Elizabeth Irwin Harrison. His grandfather, William Henry Harrison, was the ninth U.S. president. When Benjamin was 14 he went to Farmers' College, near Cincinnati, Ohio. For his junior year he moved on to Miami College in Oxford, Ohio, where he showed skill in debating. After graduating in 1852 he went to Cincinnati to study law in the office of a well-known attorney.

In 1853 Harrison married Caroline (Carrie) Lavinia, with whom he had two children. The next year they moved to Indianapolis, Ind., so Harrison could establish his own law practice. He also joined the new Republican

party and worked as reporter of the Indiana Supreme Court. During the Civil War he served as an officer in the Union army, finally reaching the rank of brevet brigadier general.

Political Career

After the war Harrison returned to his work at the Indiana Supreme Court and his law practice. In 1876 he ran for governor of Indiana. The Democrats called him "cold as an iceberg" because of his reserved manner and nicknamed him Kid-Glove Harrison for his habit of wearing gloves to guard against infection. He lost the election.

Four years later the Indiana legislature elected Harrison to the U.S. Senate. He served from 1881 to 1887 and won the goodwill of veterans by supporting the many private pension bills that came to him. Harrison also defended the interests of homesteaders and Native Americans against the railroads and fought for civil-service reform and a moderate tariff.

Great was the confusion at the Republican National Convention of 1888. Senator James G. Blaine, the leader of the party, had been defeated by Grover Cleveland in 1884 and refused to run against him again. The field was therefore open, and more than a dozen candidates vied for the presidential nomination. Harrison was finally nominated with Blaine's support. Levi P. Morton, a New York banker, was named for vice president.

Manufacturers gave money to the Republican campaign because they feared Cleveland, who demanded a lower tariff. Cleveland polled about 100,000 more votes than Harrison but lost the election because the electoral

---

First Lady Caroline Harrison (1832–92)

Born Caroline Lavinia Scott in Oxford, Ohio, Caroline Harrison was educated in the best schools of southern Ohio. An excellent student, she showed special talent in painting and music. She married Benjamin Harrison in 1853. Her husband's election to the presidency in 1888 brought Caroline enormous public attention. She oversaw an extensive renovation of the White House, including the installation of electric lighting. A history enthusiast, she was the first president general of the patriotic society called Daughters of the American Revolution. Caroline also helped to raise funds to start a medical school at Johns Hopkins University. During her husband's campaign for reelection in 1892, Caroline contracted tuberculosis, and she died in the White House.

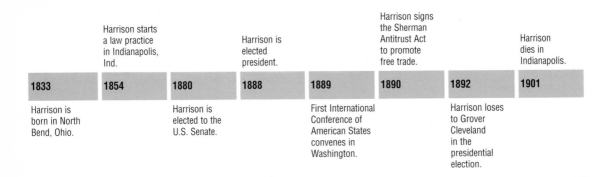

Benjamin Harrison Timeline

1833	1854	1880	1888	1889	1890	1892	1901

Harrison starts a law practice in Indianapolis, Ind.

Harrison is elected president.

Harrison signs the Sherman Antitrust Act to promote free trade.

Harrison dies in Indianapolis.

Harrison is born in North Bend, Ohio.

Harrison is elected to the U.S. Senate.

First International Conference of American States convenes in Washington.

Harrison loses to Grover Cleveland in the presidential election.

The Granger Collection, New York

President Harrison (seated center) poses with his Cabinet in 1893.

college gave him 168 votes to Harrison's 233. Harrison appointed Blaine his secretary of state.

Presidency

Harrison's administration was marked by a bold foreign policy and expanding American influence abroad. Secretary of State Blaine presided over the First International Conference of American States, held in Washington, D.C., in 1889–90. The conference established the International Union of American Republics (later called the Pan-American Union) for the exchange of cultural and scientific information. Later Harrison submitted to the Senate a treaty to annex Hawaii, but Democrats blocked its ratification.

Harrison generally kept aloof from Congress and left lawmaking to its leaders. Thomas B. Reed, speaker of the House, won the title of Czar Reed because he pushed through new parliamentary rules to speed up lawmaking. First on his list was the Dependent Pension Act. This provided money for Civil War veterans who had a disability, no matter where or when they got it. Extravagant appropriations were made also for the Navy and for rivers and harbors. The 51st Congress was the first to spend a billion dollars in peacetime. It easily disposed of the large treasury surplus that had troubled earlier administrations.

Six states were admitted to the Union during Harrison's presidency. Four were Western mining states. Congressmen from these Western states wanted more silver dollars coined to raise the price of silver. Congressmen from the East wanted higher tariffs. The two groups agreed to support each other. The McKinley Tariff Act raised duties on almost every article that competed with American products, thus making permanent the duties enacted during the Civil War. The Sherman Silver Purchase Act forced the treasury to buy 4.5 million ounces of silver each month.

The 51st Congress also passed the Sherman Antitrust Act (1890), the first legislation to prohibit business combinations that restrained trade. No serious attempt was made to enforce this law until the administration of Theodore Roosevelt.

Defeat and Retirement

As the 1892 presidential election approached, there were already warnings of the approaching Panic of 1893. Because of the Sherman Silver Purchase Act, the government was buying all the silver produced in the United States. Still, the price of silver did not rise because of the large world production. Precious gold was being drained away from the treasury, and cheap silver piled up. People and banks began to hoard gold coins. Foreign investors sent their American bonds back to be sold for gold while the precious metal was still to be had.

The Republicans renominated Harrison. The Democrats nominated Cleveland again. The new People's party, or Populists, put up James B. Weaver of Iowa. The Populists represented farmers in the West. The farmers were suffering from low prices and "tight" money. They wanted cheap money—silver or greenbacks—to raise the prices of their products.

Cleveland was elected by a large majority. Harrison's wife died on October 25, near the end of the campaign. After Cleveland's inauguration Harrison returned to his Indianapolis home to resume his law practice and to write. His excellent book on federal government, *This Country of Ours* (1897), was widely read.

In 1896 Harrison married Mary Scott Lord Dimmick, who had nursed Carrie through her last illness. With her he had a daughter. Harrison died on March 13, 1901.

WILLIAM McKINLEY

Library of Congress, Washington, D.C.

**25th President of the United States
(1843–1901; president 1897–1901)**

**Vice Presidents: Garret A. Hobart (1844–99; vice president 1897–99)
Theodore Roosevelt (1858–1919; vice president 1901)**

The 25th president of the United States was William McKinley. He was the leader of the country when, at the end of the 19th century, it suddenly became a world power by making territorial acquisitions overseas following the Spanish-American War.

Early Life

William McKinley, the son of William and Nancy Allison McKinley, was born in Niles, Ohio, on Jan. 29, 1843. When he was nine, the family moved to Poland, Ohio, so he and his siblings could attend a better school. In the Poland Seminary he organized and was elected president of a literary and debating society.

At age 17 William entered Allegheny College at Meadville, Pa. He remained only a few months, returning home because of ill health. Then feeling that he could not afford to continue in college, he taught in a country school near Poland. After school hours he worked as a clerk in the Poland post office.

When the Civil War broke out in 1861, McKinley enlisted in an Ohio regiment led by Rutherford B. Hayes, later to become president of the United States. For his bravery in the battle of Antietam, he was promoted to the rank of second lieutenant. When the war ended he had the rank of major.

After the war McKinley studied law for two years and then began a practice in Canton, Ohio. In 1871 he married Ida Saxton, the daughter of a Canton banker. The couple faced a succession of misfortunes. Within two years both of their daughters and Ida's mother died. Shattered by grief, Ida became an invalid who suffered for the rest of her life from a nervous illness. Yet McKinley remained devoted to her, and his unflagging attentiveness earned him admiration from the public.

Political Career

Drawn to politics, McKinley won his first public office in 1869, when the young Republican was elected prosecuting attorney in a Democratic county. In 1876 he was elected to the U.S. House of Representatives. He remained there for 14 years, except for one interval after the election of 1882. He rose steadily in the organization of the Republican party.

Many of the people he represented in Ohio were manufacturers. McKinley believed that a high tariff would build up American industry and bring prosperity to people of all classes. As chairman of the Ways and Means Committee, he was the author of the tariff law of 1890 known as the McKinley Act. It was the first time the tariff was systematically revised to protect all

---

First Lady Ida McKinley (1847–1907)

Born Ida Saxton in Canton, Ohio, Ida McKinley attended private schools and the Brooke Hall Seminary finishing school in Media, Pa. She met William McKinley while working as a cashier in her father's bank. The couple married in 1871. In the early years of their marriage the deaths of her mother and two young daughters left Ida an invalid. Once energetic and vibrant, she became sickly and began experiencing seizures. As first lady she was too ill to perform many of the duties assumed by her predecessors. At formal dinners she sat next to the president, close enough so William could cover her face with a handkerchief if she suffered a seizure. Although deeply grieved by her husband's death in 1901, Ida apparently suffered no more seizures for the rest of her life.

Library of Congress, Washington, D.C.

William McKinley Timeline

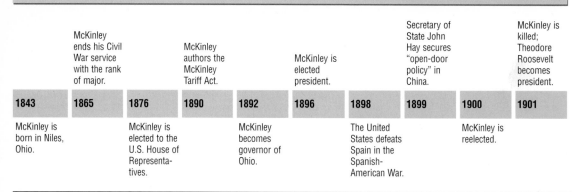

1843	1865	1876	1890	1892	1896	1898	1899	1900	1901

McKinley ends his Civil War service with the rank of major. *(1865)*

McKinley authors the McKinley Tariff Act. *(1890)*

McKinley is elected president. *(1896)*

Secretary of State John Hay secures "open-door policy" in China. *(1899)*

McKinley is killed; Theodore Roosevelt becomes president. *(1901)*

McKinley is born in Niles, Ohio. *(1843)*

McKinley is elected to the U.S. House of Representatives. *(1876)*

McKinley becomes governor of Ohio. *(1892)*

The United States defeats Spain in the Spanish-American War. *(1898)*

McKinley is reelected. *(1900)*

The Granger Collection, New York

A Republican poster from McKinley's presidential campaign of 1896 promises "prosperity at home" and "prestige abroad."

American manufacturers. The bill was very unpopular with the people, however. In the 1890 election the Republicans suffered nationwide defeat, and McKinley failed to be reelected.

From 1892 to 1896 McKinley was governor of Ohio. During this period he continued to take an active part in national party affairs. The Panic of 1893 struck the country while the Democrats were changing the tariff policy. This gave the Republican leaders an opportunity to blame the Democrats for causing the panic. In the Congressional campaign of 1894, McKinley made

hundreds of speeches throughout the country on behalf of the party's candidates. He came to be known as "the advance agent of prosperity." He was, in fact, aiming at the Republican nomination for the presidency in 1896.

McKinley was supported in this ambition by Mark Hanna, a wealthy Ohio industrialist and political leader. He managed the presidential campaign and was chiefly responsible for McKinley's election. Garret A. Hobart of New Jersey was the nominee for the vice presidency. William Jennings Bryan was the Democratic nominee.

The campaign was fought on an issue other than the tariff. The Republicans believed in a money system based on the single gold standard. The Democrats believed in bimetallism—that is, a money system based on both gold and silver. Bryan had the support of poor farmers and other people in debt, who would benefit from the unlimited coinage of silver. Behind McKinley were the bankers and manufacturers. McKinley won the election decisively by an electoral college vote of 271 to Bryan's 176 votes.

Presidency

Immediately after his inauguration McKinley called a special meeting of Congress to consider tariff revision. Within three days a bill known as the Dingley Tariff Act once more raised the tariff on many imported items. Yet domestic issues would play only a minor role in McKinley's presidency. Americans were eager for the country to play a more assertive role on the world stage. Under McKinley, the United States became an empire.

In February 1898 the U.S. battleship *Maine* exploded in the harbor of Havana, Cuba, with a loss of 260 lives. This was a climax to years of trouble between Cuba and its despotic ruler, Spain. The *Maine* had been sent to Havana to protect Americans in case war should break out between Cuba and Spain. McKinley made every effort to avoid war, and a mid-20th century investigation would later prove that the ship was destroyed by an internal explosion. Nevertheless, the "yellow" (sensational) newspapers inflamed popular opinion against Spain. Even the assistant secretary of the Navy, Theodore Roosevelt, strongly urged war. McKinley was forced to recommend to Congress that the United States free Cuba by force, and war was declared on April 25.

Major World Events During McKinley's Administration

Netherlands. *First Hague Peace Conference, 1899*

China. *Boxer uprising against foreign domination, 1900*

Australia. *Commonwealth of Australia established, 1901*

South Africa. *Boer War, 1899–1902*

The brief Spanish-American War ended with the Paris Peace Treaty of Dec. 10, 1898, which gave Puerto Rico, Guam, and the Philippines to the United States and liberated Cuba. The new responsibilities brought the United States into closer contact with the great powers of Europe and Asia.

As soon as the transfer of the Philippines was complete, Secretary of State John Hay took up the problem of European domination in East Asia. Russia, France, Germany, and Great Britain were scrambling to seize territory from China, weakened by a disastrous war with Japan. In 1899 Hay persuaded the European powers to keep China open to the trade of all countries. The "open-door policy" thus agreed upon remained a cornerstone of U.S. foreign policy for more than 40 years.

In 1900 a revolution, known as the Boxer Rebellion, broke out in China. Foreigners were besieged in the foreign quarter of Beijing. McKinley sent U.S. troops to their relief. Hay, meanwhile, persuaded the other powers not to use the revolution as an excuse for further dismemberment of China.

Insurrection in the Philippines was another problem. U.S. forces were attacked by Emilio Aguinaldo, who proclaimed his country's independence. He was

President McKinley delivers his final address at the Pan-American Exposition in Buffalo, N.Y., on Sept. 5, 1901.

captured in 1901. On July 1, 1901, a government was established with William Howard Taft as the first governor-general.

The war with Spain revealed how useful a canal across the Isthmus of Panama would be to the United States, both for reasons of commerce and to maintain a two-ocean Navy. Under the Clayton-Bulwer Treaty of 1850, Great Britain had equal rights with the United States over any interoceanic canal across Central America. After lengthy negotiations, Secretary Hay and Lord Pauncefote, British ambassador to the United States, produced the Hay-Pauncefote Treaty. It was ratified by the Senate in December 1901.

The treaty specifically set aside the Clayton-Bulwer Treaty. It gave the United States exclusive rights to build a canal across the isthmus and permitted fortification of the canal and its approaches.

Reelection and Death

Through his first four years, President McKinley continued to grow in popularity. The successful war and the country's prosperity weakened any opposition to his administration. There was no doubt of McKinley's renomination in 1900. Vice President Hobart had died in office. Theodore Roosevelt, then governor of New York, was nominated as vice president. The Democrats renominated Bryan, but the money issue that had made Bryan strong in 1896 was weak in 1900. McKinley won 292 electoral votes to Bryan's 155.

Following his inauguration in 1901, McKinley left Washington for a speaking tour of the western states. Cheering crowds throughout the journey attested to McKinley's immense popularity. In September 1901, at the Pan-American Exposition in Buffalo, N.Y., he spoke of the possibility of lowering tariffs by reciprocal treaties among countries. The "period of exclusiveness" in trade relations was past, he declared.

On September 6, the day following his address, McKinley held a public reception in the Temple of Music of the exposition. An anarchist, Leon Czolgosz, fired two shots into the president's chest and abdomen. Rushed to a hospital in Buffalo, McKinley lingered for a week before dying in the early morning hours of September 14.

THEODORE ROOSEVELT

Library of Congress, Washington, D.C. (digital file number CPH 3A53299)

**26th President of the United States
(1858–1919; president 1901–09)**

Vice President: Charles W. Fairbanks (1852–1918)

The youngest president of the United States was Theodore Roosevelt. He had been vice president under William McKinley. He came into office in 1901, just before his 43rd birthday, when McKinley was killed by an anarchist. He was elected in his own right in 1904. As president, Roosevelt championed progressive reforms and made the United States a strong presence in international affairs. A man of tremendous energy and high spirits, he was not only a statesman but also a soldier, naturalist, and writer.

Early Life

Theodore Roosevelt was born on Oct. 27, 1858, in New York City. His family was wealthy and socially prominent. Sickly as a boy, Theodore was educated by private tutors. From an early age he displayed a wide-ranging intellectual curiosity, but he was especially interested in natural history. He graduated from Harvard College in 1880. In the same year he married Alice Lee, with whom he had a daughter.

Though physically weak during his youth, Roosevelt later developed a strong physique through exercise. He became a lifelong advocate of vigorous physical and mental activity, advising everyone to lead "the strenuous life."

Political Career

Roosevelt studied briefly at Columbia Law School but soon turned to writing and politics as a career. In 1881, when he was only 23 years old, he was elected as a Republican to the New York legislature. In spite of his youth he quickly earned respect for his opposition to corrupt, party-machine politics. In 1884, overcome by grief by the deaths of both his mother and his wife on the same day, he left politics to spend two years on his cattle ranch in the Badlands of the Dakota Territory. He threw himself into the rough life of the frontier, rounding up cattle, hunting, and sometimes serving as deputy sheriff.

In 1886 Roosevelt married his childhood playmate, Edith Carow, in London and settled down to a new life at Sagamore Hill, an estate near Oyster Bay on Long Island, New York. They had five children.

Roosevelt began writing a history, *The Winning of the West*. But when President Benjamin Harrison offered him the position of civil service commissioner in 1889, he moved to Washington and for six years worked for civil service reform. In 1895 he took the post of police commissioner in New York City. In this position he tried to put an end to graft and corruption in the police force, though his efforts were opposed by politicians and newspapers alike.

First Lady Edith Roosevelt (1861–1948)

Born Edith Kermit Carow in Connecticut, Edith Roosevelt knew her future husband, Theodore Roosevelt, from her early childhood. Edith grew up near the Roosevelt home in New York City, and she and Theodore were playmates. After Theodore's first wife died in 1884, he rekindled a teenage romance with Edith. The two married in 1886. In the White House, Edith made her mark by directing renovations that clearly separated the family's living space from the working areas of the house. Among other changes, she and the president arranged for the construction of a new West Wing to house the presidential offices. Edith also changed the job of first lady by hiring a social secretary, who would thereafter remain a valued part of the White House staff.

Library of Congress, Washington, D.C. (neg. no. LC-USZ62-25803)

Theodore Roosevelt Timeline

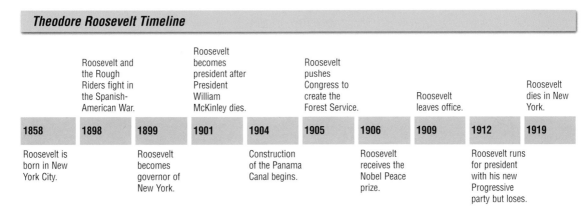

1858	1898	1899	1901	1904	1905	1906	1909	1912	1919

1898 — Roosevelt and the Rough Riders fight in the Spanish-American War.

1901 — Roosevelt becomes president after President William McKinley dies.

1905 — Roosevelt pushes Congress to create the Forest Service.

1909 — Roosevelt leaves office.

1919 — Roosevelt dies in New York.

1858 — Roosevelt is born in New York City.

1899 — Roosevelt becomes governor of New York.

1904 — Construction of the Panama Canal begins.

1906 — Roosevelt receives the Nobel Peace prize.

1912 — Roosevelt runs for president with his new Progressive party but loses.

After two years Roosevelt resigned to become assistant secretary of the Navy under President William McKinley. As war with Spain neared, Roosevelt, on his own authority, quietly ordered preparations. When war was declared he organized the 1st Volunteer Cavalry regiment. They were called Rough Riders because many of them were cowboys. Roosevelt was acclaimed a national hero when he led the daring charge on Kettle Hill (wrongly called the charge on San Juan Hill) in Cuba.

Roosevelt came home to be elected governor of New York in 1898. He became an energetic reformer, removing corrupt officials and enacting legislation to regulate corporations and the civil service. Fearing him as a candidate for the presidency, the Republican bosses succeeded in putting him in the post with the most unpromising future—that of vice president of the United States when McKinley was reelected in 1900. In 1901, however, McKinley was assassinated, elevating Roosevelt to the presidency. In 1904, with Charles W. Fairbanks as vice president, he overwhelmingly defeated the Democratic contender Alton B. Parker to win a full term.

Presidency

From what he called the presidency's "bully pulpit," Roosevelt gave speeches about the country's role in world politics, the need for economic reforms, and the impact of political corruption. At home he worked for peaceful relations between businesses and workers—a program he called the Square Deal. In foreign affairs Roosevelt's policy was to "speak softly and carry a big stick." By this he meant that the United States should deal fairly with other countries but also be ready to protect its interests.

Domestic affairs. In an early example of his Square Deal policies, Roosevelt intervened in a Pennsylvania coal strike in 1902 when it threatened to cut off heating fuel for homes, schools, and hospitals. He pressured the mine owners to enter negotiations with the workers. He also threatened to call out troops to operate the mines in the interest of the public. The combination of tactics worked to end the strike and gain a modest pay hike for the miners.

Roosevelt also attacked industrial monopolies, popularly known as "trusts." He was not concerned with breaking up the monopolies so much as with correcting their evils. To this end he asked Congress in 1903 to create a Department of Commerce and Labor and a Bureau of Corporations. They were authorized to investigate business combinations and to warn them against practices harmful to the public.

Railroad mergers had produced huge monopolies. In 1903 Roosevelt brought suit under the Sherman Antitrust Act of 1890 for the dissolution of a railroad conglomerate, the Northern Securities Company. The United States won the suit. Roosevelt continued this policy of "trust-busting" by beginning suits against the

In the Spanish-American War Roosevelt recruited the 1st Volunteer Cavalry regiment, the Rough Riders, and led them in battle in Cuba. He won fame for his heroism.

Major World Events During Theodore Roosevelt's Administration

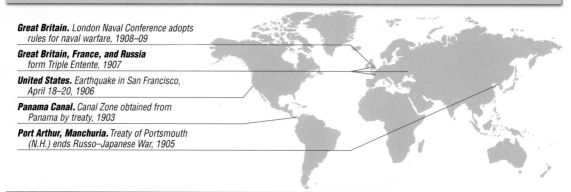

Great Britain. London Naval Conference adopts
  rules for naval warfare, 1908–09

Great Britain, France, and Russia
  form Triple Entente, 1907

United States. Earthquake in San Francisco,
  April 18–20, 1906

Panama Canal. Canal Zone obtained from
  Panama by treaty, 1903

Port Arthur, Manchuria. Treaty of Portsmouth
  (N.H.) ends Russo–Japanese War, 1905

United States Steel Corporation, the Standard Oil Company, and other large corporations.

Roosevelt's boldest actions came in the area of conservation. During his years in the Dakota Territory, he had become increasingly concerned about preserving its great forests and its wildlife. As president he set aside some 194 million acres (78.5 million hectares) of public land as national forests, thereby making them off-limits to commercial exploitation of lumber, minerals, and waterpower. In 1905 Congress created the Forest Service to oversee the national forests.

Foreign affairs. Several times during Roosevelt's first years in office, European powers threatened to intervene in Latin America. In 1903, for example, Great Britain, Germany, and Italy declared a blockade of the ports of Venezuela for the purpose of collecting debts. They proposed to seize the customhouses and pay themselves out of the taxes as they collected them.

Roosevelt protested that such actions were a violation of the Monroe Doctrine, which President James Monroe first announced in 1823. This policy stated that the

United States would not permit any European country to interfere in events on the two American continents. Roosevelt expanded the Monroe Doctrine to say that the United States would make sure that Latin American countries fulfilled their agreements with other countries. This policy statement became known as the Roosevelt Corollary to the Monroe Doctrine. He acted on the policy by forcing the Dominican Republic to pay debts owed to European countries.

Roosevelt resorted to "big-stick" diplomacy most famously in 1903, when he helped Panama to secede from Colombia. The Hay-Pauncefote Treaty of 1900–01 had cleared the way for an American canal across the Isthmus of Panama. It was followed in 1903 by a treaty with Colombia granting the right to build the canal. The Colombian Senate rejected the treaty. Especially alarmed by Colombia's action were members of the French Panama Canal Company who would lose 40 million dollars if they did not sell their rights to the United States before their franchise expired in 1904. Using a revolutionist, Philippe Bunau-Varilla, as their

A cartoon from 1905 shows President Roosevelt using his "New Diplomacy"—characterized by the phrase "speak softly and carry a big stick"—to police the world.
The Granger Collection, New York

agent, they planned a rebellion to free the state of Panama from Colombia.

Roosevelt ordered U.S. naval vessels to keep any hostile forces off the isthmus and to prevent the Colombian troops at Colón from proceeding to Panama City. The president's explanation was that he wanted to avoid bloodshed and that the United States was bound by treaty to keep the isthmian railroad open. Secretary of State John Hay formally recognized the Republic of Panama, and a few days later the new republic gave the United States control of a 10-mile-wide strip across the isthmus. Construction began at once on the Panama Canal. Roosevelt considered the construction of the canal his greatest accomplishment as president.

Roosevelt showed the soft-spoken, sophisticated side of his diplomacy in dealing with major powers outside the Western Hemisphere. In Asia he was alarmed by Russian expansionism and by rising Japanese power. In September 1905 Roosevelt brought about a peace conference between Russia and Japan, which were then at war. The conference was held in Portsmouth, N.H. For this service he was awarded the Nobel Peace prize. In 1908 the United States and Japan agreed to respect each other's territorial possessions in the Pacific and to support Chinese independence and the "open-door policy."

American prestige was further helped by strengthening the Army and Navy. Every year Roosevelt pushed Congress for bigger appropriations for the Army and Navy. By the end of his presidency he had built the U.S. Navy into a major sea power and reorganized the Army along efficient, modern lines.

Later Years

Roosevelt declined to consider a third term and secured the Republican nomination for his friend William H. Taft. He was only 50 years old when he left the White House. Immediately after Taft's inauguration he embarked on a 10-month hunting trip in Africa and then toured Europe.

On his return to Sagamore Hill, Roosevelt wrote magazine articles and another book, *African Game Trails*. But he could not avoid being drawn back into politics. He believed that Taft had failed to carry on his policies and that he was needed to preserve the progressive movement that he had helped to start. His friends urged him to be a candidate for president in 1912, but Taft defeated him for the Republican nomination.

Roosevelt's followers then organized the Progressive party. They held another convention and nominated Roosevelt for president and Senator Hiram W. Johnson for vice president. The party was nicknamed Bull Moose because Roosevelt, when asked how he felt, once replied that he was "fit as a bull moose." The campaign was bitter, and Roosevelt's attacks on the "stand pat" Republicans were more venomous than those on the Democrats. Both he and Taft were soundly defeated by the Democrat Woodrow Wilson.

After this defeat Roosevelt wrote his autobiography and led an expedition into the rain forest of Brazil, where he contracted a near-fatal illness. When World War I began in 1914, Roosevelt followed it with great interest. He soon decided that Wilson "had no policy whatever" and said so in a letter to the author Rudyard Kipling. Roosevelt led rallies for "preparedness," urging Congress to complete the arming of the country. He refused the Progressive party nomination for president in 1916 and supported Charles Evans Hughes, the Republican nominee. Wilson was reelected.

When the United States declared war against Germany in 1917, Roosevelt hurried to Washington to offer his services. To his disappointment and resentment Wilson refused his offer to lead a division to France. Although he could not go to war, his four sons served in combat. By 1918 Roosevelt's support of the war and his harsh attacks on Wilson had made him the odds-on favorite for the 1920 Republican nomination. However, he died at Oyster Bay on Jan. 6, 1919.

WILLIAM HOWARD TAFT

Library of Congress, Washington, D.C. (neg. no. LC-USZ62-103185)

27th President of the United States
(1857–1930; president 1909–13)

Vice President: James Sherman (1855–1912)

prosecuting attorney (1881–82), collector of internal revenue (1882–83), judge of the Cincinnati Superior Court (1887–90), solicitor general of the United States (1890–92), and judge of the federal circuit court (1892–1900). By now he was dreaming of an appointment to the U.S. Supreme Court, his greatest ambition.

In 1886 Taft married Helen (Nellie) Herron, daughter of a Cincinnati attorney. Nellie's father gave them a lot on Walnut Hills, and they built a house overlooking the Ohio River. They had three children.

Philippines Governor and Secretary of War

In 1900 President William McKinley made Taft chairman of the Second Philippine Commission. His task was to form a civil government in a country disrupted by the Spanish-American War of 1898. In 1901 he became the first civilian governor of the Philippines. Taft became very fond of the Philippine people and soon endeared himself to them. Twice he refused to leave the islands when offered appointment to the Supreme Court by President Theodore Roosevelt.

In 1904 Taft agreed to return to Washington to serve as secretary of war. As Roosevelt's "troubleshooter," Taft traveled almost as much as his chief. He visited the Canal Zone many times to supervise construction of the Panama Canal. In 1905, while the Russo-Japanese War was being waged, Roosevelt sent Taft on a trip to the Far East. He visited the Japanese royal family and let it be known that the United States was determined to maintain peace in the Pacific. In 1906 he rushed to Cuba to stop a threatened revolution.

The only person to hold the two highest offices in the United States was William Howard Taft. He was elected the 27th president of the United States in 1908 and later served as chief justice of the U.S. Supreme Court. Taft was well suited for these posts through his long years of experience. He had been in public office almost continuously since 1881.

Early Life

William Howard Taft was born on Sept. 15, 1857, into a wealthy and socially prominent family of Cincinnati, Ohio. His parents were Alphonso Taft and Louisa Maria Torrey. His father was a successful lawyer and judge who served as secretary of war and attorney general under President Ulysses S. Grant.

Taft graduated second in his class at Yale University in 1878 and received a degree from the Cincinnati Law School in 1880. He practiced law very little. His father's prominence and his own friendly personality won him a succession of political appointments—assistant

---

First Lady Helen Taft (1861–1943)

Helen Taft was born Helen Herron in Cincinnati, Ohio. Educated in local private schools, young Helen showed an ambition to make her mark beyond southern Ohio. In the late 1870s, after meeting law student William Howard Taft, she tied that ambition to his career. Following their marriage in 1886, Helen made a determined effort to position her husband for the presidency, even though he would have preferred a judicial appointment. As first lady Helen was a key political adviser to her husband. She also made a lasting contribution to the city of Washington, D.C. An admirer of cherry blossoms from her family's travels in Japan, she arranged for the planting of the famous cherry trees along Washington's Tidal Basin.

Library of Congress, Washington, D.C. (neg. no. LC-USZ62-25804)

William Howard Taft Timeline

	Taft receives a law degree.		President Theodore Roosevelt appoints Taft secretary of war.		Taft and Roosevelt lose the presidential election to Woodrow Wilson.		Taft resigns from the Court.	
1857	**1880**	**1901**	**1904**	**1908**	**1912**	**1921**	**1930**	**1930**
Taft is born in Cincinnati, Ohio.		Taft becomes governor of the Philippines.		Taft is elected president.		Taft becomes chief justice of the U.S. Supreme Court.		Taft dies in Washington, D.C.

Presidency

As the presidential election of 1908 drew near, Roosevelt began to think of a successor who would continue his progressive reforms. He threw his support to Taft, who won the Republican nomination and easily defeated Democrat William Jennings Bryan in the general election. In 1909, with James S. Sherman as vice president, he began a term that was doomed to trouble.

Unlike the dazzling Roosevelt, Taft was unable to popularize his accomplishments. Moreover, his administration was overshadowed by quarrels within the Republican party and by the final break with his old friend Roosevelt. The party under Roosevelt was beginning to split into two factions. The conservative Stalwarts were popularly regarded as the champions of Wall Street and of the "money interests." At the opposite extreme were the younger Republicans, most of them from the West and Midwest. They wanted to go further than Roosevelt in the reform of big business and the trusts. They also called for more aggressive social legislation. Known as the Insurgents, they later became the Progressives. The Progressive party's popular nickname of Bull Moose was derived from Roosevelt's colorful description of his own strength and vigor.

Taft's lack of political insight soon became apparent in his indifference toward the growing division between conservatives and progressives within Republican ranks. He actually encouraged the split by failing to appoint any progressives to his Cabinet. The first task before the new administration was a revision of the tariff. The West wanted lower rates; the East, with its manufacturing economy, wanted full protection. Nelson W. Aldrich, a Stalwart from Rhode Island and leader of the Senate, wrote the bill to suit himself, raising the duties on some 600 items. The Payne-Aldrich Tariff of 1909 was a victory for the Stalwarts. It seemed a clear violation of the party platform that had promised to revise the tariff downward. The Insurgents charged that Taft had abandoned Roosevelt's policies.

Conservation became a political issue soon after the tariff bill was enacted. Roosevelt had been an ardent supporter of the conservation of natural resources. Although Taft also backed conservation, his opponents charged that the new secretary of the interior, Richard A. Ballinger, was favoring the coal, mining, and timber interests that were exploiting the public lands of the West.

A dispute involving Ballinger and Gifford Pinchot, the forester of the United States, became an open scandal, forcing Taft to intervene. He upheld Ballinger, Pinchot's superior, and dismissed Pinchot. The Insurgents attacked Taft as an agent of big business and as a traitor to the cause of conservation. The incident also widened the gap between Taft and Roosevelt, who was a close friend of Pinchot.

In 1910 the Insurgents combined with the Democrats to change the rules of procedure in the House of Representatives. Under the old rules the Insurgents were regularly suppressed by the Speaker of the House, Stalwart Joseph G. Cannon. He refused recognition to Insurgents when they rose to speak unless they had previously obtained his consent. He appointed all

As secretary of war, Taft traveled to Japan in 1905 on a goodwill mission with Alice Roosevelt, President Theodore Roosevelt's daughter. Here they leave the Resting Palace in Yokohama.

Major World Events During Taft's Administration

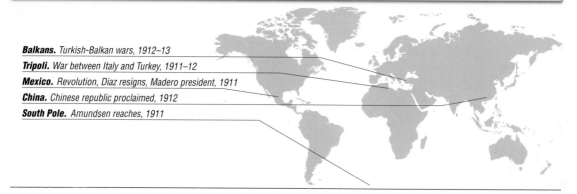

Balkans. Turkish-Balkan wars, 1912–13
Tripoli. War between Italy and Turkey, 1911–12
Mexico. Revolution, Diaz resigns, Madero president, 1911
China. Chinese republic proclaimed, 1912
South Pole. Amundsen reaches, 1911

committees and was the leading member of the committee on rules, which controlled the course of legislation. Under the new rules the speaker was ineligible for membership on the rules committee, and the House selected its own committees. Taft's refusal to support the Insurgents in this controversy added to his unpopularity. In the fall election of 1910 the Democrats won a majority in the House.

In spite of all these reverses, Taft's record as a progressive was as great as Roosevelt's. Twice as many suits were brought against trusts in his administration as in Roosevelt's. The Mann-Elkins Act gave the Interstate Commerce Commission (ICC) jurisdiction over telephone and telegraph lines, authorized it to suspend rate increases until satisfied that they were reasonable, and created a Commerce Court to hear appeals from the ICC. The 16th Amendment, authorizing a graduated federal income tax, was adopted. Alaska was made a territory in 1912, and Arizona and New Mexico were admitted to the Union.

Progressive Republicans made every effort to prevent Taft's renomination in 1912. They persuaded Roosevelt to run again. He found most of his old associates lined up with Taft, and though he made a good fight, a majority of the delegates to the convention were pledged to Taft. Roosevelt's supporters organized the Progressive party, nominated Roosevelt, and entered the campaign. The Democratic nominee was Woodrow Wilson. The split in the Republican party allowed the Democrats to win the election with a minority of the popular vote.

Later Years

Soon after leaving the presidency Taft became a professor of constitutional law at Yale University. As the bitterness of the fight of 1912 faded, the ex-president's opinions on public affairs were welcomed and respected. His views on the use of arbitration to prevent war reflected the spirit of the time.

During World War I Taft devoted his influence to the promotion of an international league to enforce peace. President Wilson endorsed the movement and in 1917 made its proposal the center of his own policy. The League of Nations, established by the Treaty of Versailles in 1919, owed much to Taft's support. In 1918 Taft was

made one of the two joint chairmen of the new National War Labor Board.

The last public service of the ex-president began in 1921 when President Warren G. Harding named him to the post he had longed for throughout his career—that of chief justice of the U.S. Supreme Court. Taft was happier in this position than he had been as president. He improved the Court's efficiency and helped bring about the Judiciary Act of 1925, which gave the Court more choice about which cases to hear. Although generally conservative in his judicial philosophy, he pleasantly surprised progressives with the liberality of some of his decisions. On Feb. 3, 1930, he resigned because of a heart ailment. He died in Washington on March 8.

Fulfilling a long-standing ambition, Taft served as chief justice of the U.S. Supreme Court from 1921 until his death in 1930.

WOODROW WILSON

Library of Congress, Washington, D.C. (neg. no. LC-USZ62-13028)

**28th President of the United States
(1856–1924; president 1913–21)**

Vice President: Thomas R. Marshall (1854–1925)

The president who led the United States through the hard years of World War I was Woodrow Wilson. He was a brilliant student and teacher as well as a statesman. He had been a college professor, president of Princeton University, and the author of books on American government. He had also been governor of New Jersey. Wilson worked out his political beliefs in the classroom. Then he entered politics to put his theories of government into practice.

Early Life and Family

Thomas Woodrow Wilson was born on Dec. 28, 1856, in Staunton, Va. In childhood he was called Tommy. His parents were Joseph Ruggles Wilson, a Presbyterian minister, and Janet Woodrow. The family moved to Augusta, Ga., when Tommy was a year old.

As a child Tommy was taught by his father. He developed strong interests in politics and literature. In 1873 he entered Davidson College in North Carolina, but he did poorly there and left after a year. In 1875 he

enrolled at Princeton University, then known as the College of New Jersey. There he was much more successful and gained a confidence in himself that he never lost. He studied the art of public speaking and was active in the college debating society. In his senior year he published a brilliant essay on cabinet government in the United States. He dropped the name Thomas and signed himself "Woodrow Wilson."

After graduating from Princeton in 1879, Wilson studied law at the University of Virginia. He earned his law degree in 1882 and began to practice law in Atlanta, Ga. After two unsuccessful years he gave up his law career and entered Johns Hopkins University in Baltimore, Md., where he studied history and political science. He received his doctor of philosophy degree in 1886.

In 1885 Wilson married Ellen Louise Axson, the daughter of a minister from Georgia. They had three daughters. The marriage was warm and happy, and Ellen's death in August 1914 left Wilson lonely and depressed. Soon, however, he met Edith Bolling Galt, whom he married in December 1915.

College Professor and President

At age 29 Wilson started on his career as an educator. He was associate professor of history at Bryn Mawr College in Pennsylvania (1885–88) and then professor of history and political economy at Wesleyan University in Connecticut (1888–90). In 1890 he returned as professor of jurisprudence and political economy to the College of

---

First Ladies Ellen Wilson (1860–1914) and Edith Wilson (1872–1961)

Woodrow Wilson's first wife was born Ellen Louise Axson in Savannah, Ga. She studied painting in New York City before marrying Wilson in 1885. Ellen served only 17 months as first lady, and for much of the time she was ill. Nevertheless, she endeared herself to the public through her devotion to social issues, especially her efforts to improve housing for African Americans in Washington. A year after Ellen's death in 1914 Woodrow married Edith Bolling Galt, a wealthy widow from Virginia. Although little interested in politics, Edith fulfilled many of her husband's administrative duties when he was disabled by illness during his second term.

Library of Congress, Washington, D.C. (top, neg. no. LC-USZ62-25806); (bottom, neg. no. LC-USZ62-25808)

Woodrow Wilson Timeline

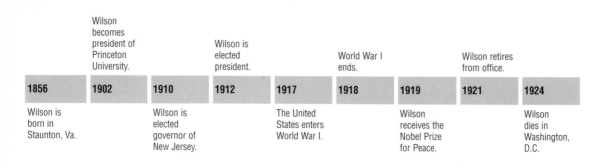

1856	1902	1910	1912	1917	1918	1919	1921	1924

Wilson becomes president of Princeton University. (1902)

Wilson is elected president. (1912)

World War I ends. (1918)

Wilson retires from office. (1921)

Wilson is born in Staunton, Va. (1856)

Wilson is elected governor of New Jersey. (1910)

The United States enters World War I. (1917)

Wilson receives the Nobel Prize for Peace. (1919)

Wilson dies in Washington, D.C. (1924)

New Jersey. In the next 20 years he was to see it grow into the great Princeton University. Year after year Princeton students elected him their most popular professor.

For eight years (1902–10) Wilson was president of the university. In this role he launched his first reform crusade—to build a university that would produce leaders and statesmen. Wilson upgraded the university both financially and intellectually, and he attempted far-reaching reforms of both undergraduate and graduate education. Several of his policies were adopted, but opposition from faculty conservatives and wealthy alumni forced him to abandon several of his plans for restructuring the university.

These were busy years for Wilson. In addition to his teaching and administrative duties he published several books, including *Congressional Government* (1885), *The State* (1889), *Division and Reunion* (1893), *George Washington* (1896), *A History of the American People* (1902), and *Constitutional Government in the United States* (1908).

He wrote many essays and book reviews and was in great demand as a lecturer.

Governor of New Jersey

The Princeton reform battle attracted wide publicity and led to Wilson's election as governor of New Jersey in 1910. In this position he showed his independence and his capacity for getting things done. New Jersey was run by political bosses who thought they could use Wilson as a respectable front. Wilson, however, sidestepped the Democratic party machine and appealed directly to the voters for support of his program. In a little over a year he put through a public utility control act, a corrupt political practices act, a workmen's compensation act, and a direct primary act.

These bold reforms attracted national attention to the college president turned politician. In 1912 Wilson won the Democratic party's nomination for president of the United States. In the general election he faced President William Howard Taft of the Republican party and

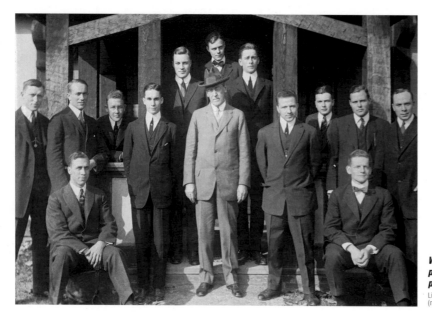

Wilson, who was a professor and president of Princeton University, poses with some of his students.

Library of Congress, Washington, D.C.
(neg. no. LC-DIG-HEC-02139)

Major World Events During Wilson's Administration

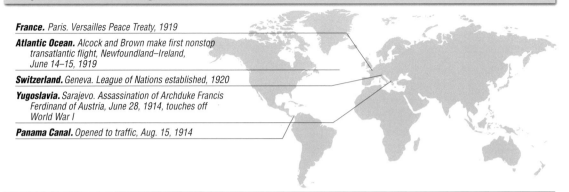

France. *Paris. Versailles Peace Treaty, 1919*

Atlantic Ocean. *Alcock and Brown make first nonstop transatlantic flight, Newfoundland–Ireland, June 14–15, 1919*

Switzerland. *Geneva. League of Nations established, 1920*

Yugoslavia. *Sarajevo. Assassination of Archduke Francis Ferdinand of Austria, June 28, 1914, touches off World War I*

Panama Canal. *Opened to traffic, Aug. 15, 1914*

former president Theodore Roosevelt of the new Progressive party. Taft and Roosevelt split the Republican vote, allowing Wilson to win with only 42 percent of the popular vote.

Presidency

Wilson called his philosophy of government the "New Freedom." Convinced that strong executive leadership was necessary for progress, he went further than any other president in forcing his wishes on Congress. He kept Congress in session continually from April 1913 to October 1914, something that had never before happened. He also broke with previous presidential practice by addressing Congress in person from time to time.

Wilson's approach led to a mass of progressive legislation unequaled in any administration up to that time. The Underwood-Simmons Tariff lowered duties on imports for the first time in 40 years. To offset the loss in revenue from the tariff reduction, an income tax was introduced as authorized by the newly adopted 16th Amendment to the Constitution. Another law established the Federal Reserve System, which remains the most powerful government agency in economic affairs. For the first time in U.S. history, finance and credits were placed under government direction. The Federal Trade Commission (FTC) was created to oversee unfair business practices. The Clayton Act, designed to strengthen the Sherman Antitrust Act, defined the methods of competition that the FTC was empowered to forbid.

Wilson followed those legislative accomplishments with a second wave of reform measures in 1916. He pushed through Congress laws to create an agency to regulate overseas shipping and to make the first government loans to farmers. Other measures prohibited child labor, raised income and inheritance taxes, and set an eight-hour workday for railroad workers.

Diplomacy in Latin America. Foreign affairs troubled Wilson from his first days in the White House. Latin America was the first trouble spot. American businesses were investing heavily in the mines, railroads, and other resources of the region. Wilson announced soon after his inauguration that he would

abandon "dollar diplomacy." This meant that investors could no longer expect the U.S. government to protect their interests. Nevertheless, Wilson permitted U.S. intervention to restore order in Nicaragua, Haiti, and the Dominican Republic.

In 1914 U.S. Marines seized the port of Veracruz, Mexico, after Mexican police arrested several American sailors. Mediation by the "ABC powers" (Argentina, Brazil, and Chile) averted war. In March 1916 a Mexican rebel, Francisco (Pancho) Villa, raided Columbus, N.M., killing 17 Americans. With the permission of Mexico's president, the United States sent an expedition into Mexico under Gen. John J. Pershing. They failed to catch Villa and were withdrawn in January 1917.

World War I. In the summer of 1914 Europe plunged into war. Wilson called upon the United States to be neutral "even in spirit," but few Americans were able to remain impartial. For two years the president made every effort to avoid war. Even after the unarmed British liner *Lusitania* was sunk by a German submarine with a loss of almost 1,200 lives, including more than 120 Americans, he argued: "There is such a thing as a man being too proud to fight."

President Wilson attends the 1915 baseball World Series.

Encyclopaedia Britannica, Inc.

Wilson (carrying flag) marches in a Liberty Loan parade in October 1917, during World War I. The parade encouraged the public to buy Liberty Bonds in support of the U.S. war effort.

Hulton Archive/Getty Images

In 1916 Wilson was reelected, partly because he had kept the country out of the war. He defeated the Republican candidate Charles Evans Hughes by an electoral vote of 277 to 254. After the election Wilson tried to end the war by active mediation. The Germans, however, resumed unrestricted submarine warfare. On April 2, 1917, the president asked Congress for a declaration of war.

In the next 18 months the United States built up its armed forces to 5 million men and women by conscription, 2 million of whom shipped overseas to France. A vast propaganda machine was created under the title of the Committee on Public Information. The words of Wilson reached the German people by radio for the first time in history. Leaflets were scattered from airplanes, shot from guns and rockets, and smuggled behind enemy lines. Wilson said that this was a "war to end war." He spoke of "peace without victory" and without revenge.

On Jan. 8, 1918, Wilson announced his Fourteen Points as the basis for a peace settlement. They were more than peace terms; they were terms for a better world. Among them was the creation of a League of Nations, an international organization dedicated to maintaining world peace.

Battle for the peace treaty. The war came to an end on Nov. 11, 1918. The German proposals for peace came in the midst of the Congressional elections. Wilson appealed to the people to support his policies by returning a Democratic majority to both houses. The party was defeated, however, and with a Republican majority in control he was no longer able to lead Congress.

Against the advice of those close to him, Wilson decided to attend the peace conference in Paris and fight for his Fourteen Points in person. He took with him few advisers, and none from the Republican party. On December 13 he arrived in Europe. Wherever he went he was given a tremendous ovation.

The peace conference dragged on week after week. David Lloyd George of Great Britain, Vittorio Orlando of Italy, and Georges Clemenceau of France all were experienced and shrewd diplomats and each was determined to have his own way. The endless arguing and the official receptions and banquets frayed Wilson's nerves. The Treaty of Versailles, signed in June 1919, left out many of his ideas, but it did include the Covenant (constitution) of the League of Nations.

Wilson returned from the peace conference weary and in failing health, in no shape to face the biggest fight of his career. On July 10, 1919, he laid the treaty before a hostile Senate. The senators were especially opposed to the League of Nations, but Wilson refused to compromise his dream. In search of popular support that would overwhelm the Senate, he toured the country in defense of the League. Exhausted, he collapsed in Pueblo, Colo., late in September. He returned to Washington, D.C., where on Oct. 2, 1919, he suffered a massive stroke that left him partially paralyzed.

This was the worst crisis of presidential disability in U.S. history, and it was handled badly. No one seriously suggested that Wilson resign. His wife, Edith, controlled access to him and made some decisions for him. With Edith guiding his hand, he placed a wobbly signature on major bills. Although he gradually recovered from the worst effects of the stroke, Wilson never again fully functioned as president.

Wilson was awarded the 1919 Nobel Prize for Peace for his advocacy of the League of Nations. However, the Treaty of Versailles went down to defeat in the Senate, and the United States never joined the League. Wilson was unable to participate in the 1920 presidential campaign, and the Democratic candidate, James M. Cox, was overwhelmingly defeated by the Republican Warren G. Harding. Wilson died on Feb. 3, 1924.

WARREN G. HARDING

Library of Congress, Washington, D.C. (neg. no. LC-USZ62-91485)

**29th President of the United States
(1865–1923; president 1921–23)**

Vice President: Calvin Coolidge (1872–1933)

"Back to normalcy" was the campaign slogan of Warren G. Harding, 29th president of the United States. War-weary American voters of 1920 liked the idea so much that they elected this Ohio newspaper publisher by the greatest popular vote margin to that time. Harding's popularity with the public carried over into his administration. After his death, however, his presidency was revealed to be the most corrupt in the country's history.

Early Life

Born in Corsica, Ohio, on Nov. 2, 1865, Warren Gamaliel Harding was the eldest child of George Tryon and Phoebe Dickerson Harding. His father worked as a farmer and later as a doctor. After graduating from Ohio Central College in 1882, Harding tried his hand at several vocations before buying a struggling weekly newspaper in Marion, Ohio, in 1884.

In 1891 Harding married Florence Kling DeWolfe, divorced daughter of a Marion banker. Her business ability and ambition proved instrumental in

transforming the *Marion Star* into a successful daily paper. The Hardings had no children.

Political Career

As the *Star* prospered, Harding turned to politics. A strong supporter of the Republican party, he was elected an Ohio state senator in 1898 and lieutenant governor in 1903. In 1910 he was defeated in his bid for the governorship, but four years later he was elected to the U.S. Senate.

Harding was a popular senator. On most issues he aligned himself with conservative Republicans. After World War I he stood firm against U.S. membership in the League of Nations, which conservatives believed would limit national sovereignty.

In 1920 Americans were upset by the restrictions, sacrifices, and disappointments of the war years. Business, though enjoying high profits, wanted relief from war regulations and high taxes. Labor held that its wartime gains had been wiped out by the mounting cost of living. A business decline in the spring of 1920 brought unemployment and the collapse of farm prosperity. The people blamed their troubles on President Woodrow Wilson and the Democrats.

Republican senators felt that Wilson had extended the power of the presidency at the expense of the legislative branch. They wanted one of their own in office. Although Harding had never gained much voter support, he felt his plea for a "return to normalcy" for the country would make him a favorable candidate. At the Republican National Convention in Chicago, neither of the chief

---

First Lady Florence Harding (1860–1924)

Energetic, strong-willed, and popular, Florence Harding was an important influence on her husband's business and political careers. Born Florence Mabel Kling in Marion, Ohio, she attended the Cincinnati Conservatory of Music before marrying Henry DeWolfe at age 19. She was a divorced mother of one when she married Warren G. Harding in 1891. Soon after their marriage Florence began working at Warren's newspaper, the *Marion Star*, where she oversaw circulation, advertising, and home delivery. When Warren ran for president, she helped to manage the campaign's dealings with the press. As first lady she was a firm believer in making the White House more accessible. She opened the mansion to public tours and invited thousands of guests to garden parties and other gatherings.

Warren G. Harding Timeline

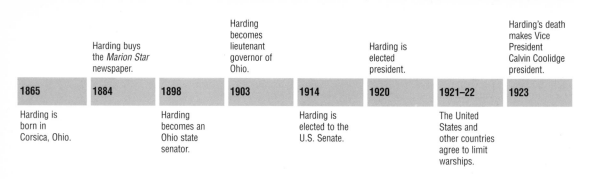

1865	1884	1898	1903	1914	1920	1921–22	1923

Harding buys the *Marion Star* newspaper. (1884)

Harding becomes lieutenant governor of Ohio. (1903)

Harding is elected president. (1920)

Harding's death makes Vice President Calvin Coolidge president. (1923)

Harding is born in Corsica, Ohio. (1865)

Harding becomes an Ohio state senator. (1898)

Harding is elected to the U.S. Senate. (1914)

The United States and other countries agree to limit warships. (1921–22)

candidates could gain a majority. Leaders met and selected Harding as their compromise candidate. Governor Calvin Coolidge of Massachusetts was selected as the vice-presidential candidate. The Democrats nominated Governor James M. Cox of Ohio for president. On Nov. 2, 1920, Harding was elected.

Presidency

At the start of his presidency Harding called a special session of Congress and recommended a conservative program. It included the creation of a federal budget system, higher tariffs, tax reductions for business, restriction of immigration, and aid to veterans and farmers. A cooperative Congress quickly passed a joint resolution declaring World War I officially ended. Other legislation included the Fordney-McCumber Act of 1922, which set the highest tariffs in history, and an immigration bill that sharply reduced the number of immigrants allowed to enter the United States.

The most important achievement of the Harding presidency was the Washington Naval Disarmament

A 1924 cartoon shows Washington officials racing down an oil-slicked road to the White House, trying desperately to outpace the Teapot Dome scandal of President Harding's administration.

The Granger Collection, New York

Conference, which the United States hosted in 1921–22. The conference succeeded in getting the world's major powers to limit expansion of their navies.

Harding's Cabinet was a mixture of distinguished leaders and personal or political friends. He had great and unquestioning confidence in them all. The chief accomplishments of his term reflected the leadership of Charles Evans Hughes, secretary of state; Andrew Mellon, secretary of the treasury; and Herbert Hoover, secretary of commerce.

Harding's faith in other Cabinet appointees proved misplaced, however. Later it would be revealed that a group of high-ranking officials known as the Ohio Gang had taken part in a variety of dishonest activities. Attorney General Harry Daugherty sold illegal liquor permits and pardons. Charles Forbes, director of the Veterans' Bureau, illegally sold government medical supplies to private contractors. The most serious example of wrongdoing in Harding's administration was the Teapot Dome scandal. Albert B. Fall, secretary of the interior, persuaded Harding to transfer authority over two of the country's most important oil reserves from the Navy Department to the Department of the Interior. Fall then leased drilling rights in the Elk Hills, Calif., and Teapot Dome, Wyo., reserves to private oil companies, in return receiving hundreds of thousands of dollars in gifts and loans.

Death

By the spring of 1923 Harding was visibly upset by the behavior of his trusted associates. He sought escape from Washington, D.C. in mid-June by taking a cross-country tour with his wife and a party of 65. Exhausted, he became ill in Seattle and was taken to San Francisco. On August 2 he died there from either a heart attack or stroke. Vice President Coolidge became president.

Harding had been a popular president, and he was deeply mourned. Soon after his death, however, investigations revealed the corruption of his administration to the public. Harding was never personally implicated in the scandals, but he had known of some of the illegal activities and failed to bring them to light. By the mid-1920s the public began to regard Harding as a man who did not measure up to the responsibilities of his office.

CALVIN COOLIDGE

Popperfoto/Getty Images

**30th President of the United States
(1872–1933; president 1923–29)**

Vice President: Charles G. Dawes (1865–1951)

The sixth U.S. vice president to become president at the death of the chief executive was Calvin Coolidge. He took the oath of office as the 30th president at 2:47 AM, on Aug. 3, 1923, a few hours after President Warren G. Harding died. Elected to a second term in 1924, Coolidge was a popular president. A Republican, he served in a time of speedy industrial and business growth, high profits, and rising stock market prices, called the period of "Coolidge prosperity." In this day of quick riches and free spending Coolidge stood for the sound Yankee virtues of economy, caution, and self-respect.

Early Life

John Calvin Coolidge was born on July 4, 1872, in Plymouth, Vt., the son of John Calvin Coolidge and Victoria Moor Coolidge. He was named John Calvin for his father but dropped the John when he graduated from college. His father was a farmer, storekeeper, and occasional political officeholder. As Calvin grew up he learned to do farm chores. He helped to fill the woodbox, drive the cattle to pasture, drop seed potatoes at planting time, and drive the horse-drawn mowing machine and rake at harvest. His boyhood was saddened by the illness of his mother and her death when he was 12 years old.

Coolidge attended Black River Academy in Ludlow, Vt., before he entered Amherst College in Massachusetts. He graduated cum laude from Amherst in 1895. He learned law in the old-fashioned way, studying in a law firm at Northampton, Mass., and began practicing law in 1897. In 1905 Coolidge married Grace Anna Goodhue of Burlington, Vt. They had two sons, John and Calvin.

Political Career

Coolidge took his first steps in politics in these years by working on ward and city committees. He was the opposite of the popular picture of the back-slapping politician. He was quiet, sincere, and rather shy, but he was able to attract and hold the confidence of voters and political leaders alike. He was elected and reelected to one office after another. He served as state representative, mayor of Northampton, state senator and president of the state Senate, and lieutenant governor. Always he stood for economy, conservatism, and party regularity.

In 1918 Coolidge was elected governor of Massachusetts. The following year he came into nationwide prominence during a strike by Boston police, who had formed a labor union to press their demands for better pay and working conditions. He let the mayor

---

First Lady Grace Coolidge (1879–1957)

Born Grace Anna Goodhue in Burlington, Vt., Grace Coolidge earned a degree from the University of Vermont in 1902. She then moved to Northampton, Mass., to teach at the Clarke Institute for the Deaf. There she met Calvin Coolidge, whom she married in 1905. Her outgoing personality contrasted sharply with that of her tight-lipped spouse. Calvin's election as vice president in 1920 took the family to Washington, D.C., where Grace became a favorite for her wit, charm, and fondness for animals. She was active in many causes, including the Red Cross. As first lady she focused on refurbishing the family quarters of the White House. After Calvin's death she devoted herself to the needs of the hearing-impaired.

Calvin Coolidge Timeline

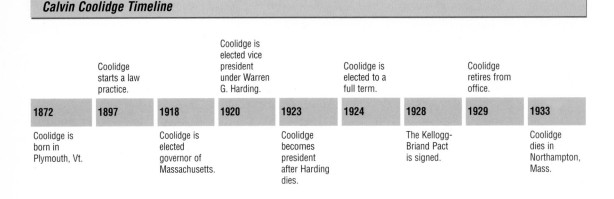

	Coolidge starts a law practice.		Coolidge is elected vice president under Warren G. Harding.		Coolidge is elected to a full term.		Coolidge retires from office.	
1872	**1897**	**1918**	**1920**	**1923**	**1924**	**1928**	**1929**	**1933**
Coolidge is born in Plymouth, Vt.		Coolidge is elected governor of Massachusetts.		Coolidge becomes president after Harding dies.		The Kellogg-Briand Pact is signed.		Coolidge dies in Northampton, Mass.

handle the problem until the police left their posts and disorder arose. Then he summoned the state guard to keep order. To a protest by a labor leader he replied: "There is no right to strike against the public safety by anybody, anywhere, anytime."

At the Republican National Convention the next year Coolidge was nominated as Warren G. Harding's vice-presidential running mate. The Republicans easily won the election. As vice president, Coolidge was modest and silent. He presided over the Senate and sat in Cabinet meetings at President Harding's invitation.

Presidency

Harding's unexpected death in August 1923 brought Coolidge into the presidency at a critical time. Scandals in the Harding Administration were becoming public. Enormous graft in the Veterans' Bureau and other offices

President-Elect Coolidge and his wife Grace leave the White House before his inauguration on March 4, 1925. Coolidge holds the Bible upon which he will take the oath of office.

Hulton Archive/Getty Images

had been revealed. The Senate opened an investigation of private leases on naval oil reserves at Teapot Dome, Wyo., and Elk Hills, Calif. They had been granted by Albert B. Fall, Harding's secretary of the interior. Following a resolution by Congress, Coolidge appointed lawyers to prosecute those involved in the oil scandal. Fall was convicted and imprisoned. Secretary of the Navy Edwin Denby and Attorney General Harry Daugherty resigned under pressure.

Coolidge's handling of the scandals restored the public's faith in the presidency. In 1924 he was nominated for a second term, with Charles G. Dawes of Illinois as the vice-presidential nominee. The Democrats nominated John W. Davis of West Virginia for the presidency and Gov. Charles W. Bryan of Nebraska for the vice presidency. Insurgent Republicans put a Progressive party ticket into the field, headed by Sen. Robert M. La Follette of Wisconsin and Sen. Burton K. Wheeler of Montana. Running on the slogan "Keep Cool with Coolidge," Coolidge and Dawes won a landslide victory. They received 382 electoral votes to 136 for Davis and only 13 for La Follette.

Legislative program. In his messages to Congress President Coolidge called for tax reduction, immigration restriction, extension of the civil service, reorganization of government departments, and adherence to the World Court. Congress was frequently uncooperative. A farm-bloc minority of progressive Republicans held the balance of power. Coolidge vetoed their McNary-Haugen bill, which was designed to support farm prices by government subsidies. He also vetoed a bill for a bonus, in the form of insurance, for World War I veterans. Congress passed this bill over his veto.

Key to the conservative focus of the Coolidge presidency was Andrew Mellon, secretary of the treasury. Under the leadership of Coolidge and Mellon, Congress sharply reduced income taxes and estate taxes. The national debt was reduced by about a billion dollars a year.

Coolidge prosperity. Business rather than politics made the big news of the era. Industry flourished. Big business became bigger through both growth and consolidation. The 1920s saw 7,000 mergers in industry and mining and the same trend in utilities,

Major World Events During Coolidge's Administration

North Pole. *Byrd's polar flight, 1926*

Soviet Union. *Stalin becomes dictator, 1928*

Tokyo. *Earthquake, 1923*

Atlantic Ocean. *Lindbergh's first nonstop transatlantic flight, 1927*

Paris. *Kellogg-Briand treaty to outlaw war, 1928–29*

World. *First globe-girdling flight, 1924*

Keystone/Getty Images

President Coolidge signs the Kellogg-Briand Pact in a ceremony staged at the White House in January 1929. The pact, which renounced war, had been signed by representatives of the United States and 14 other countries in Paris in August 1928. It was ratified by the U.S. Congress in July 1929.

merchandising, and banking. Advertising reached a new peak, helping to move the huge quantities of merchandise turned out by the factories. Chain stores, mail-order houses, and installment buying were expanding features of retail trade. Nearly every town had its real-estate boom.

The stock market rocketed upward, attracting investors and margin buyers from all ranks of society. Corporations found it easy to issue new securities. Credit was overexpanded. Cheap money flowed into foreign bonds and a variety of domestic projects, including 4 million dollars' worth of brokers' loans. When conservative bankers and economists were concerned over the extent of these loans, Coolidge stated that their increase showed a natural expansion of business. He had great faith in the continued march of prosperity.

The so-called Coolidge prosperity did not reach everyone. Farmers continued to suffer from falling prices and the decline in foreign purchase of their products. Farm mortgage foreclosures increased.

The labor picture was uneven. Jobholders enjoyed a rising standard of living and a shorter workweek. Some large firms offered workers such services as low-cost cafeterias, free medical care, profit-sharing plans, and vacations with pay. The number of unemployed, however, fluctuated between 1.5 and 2 million. Unions lost ground in numbers and influence.

Foreign affairs. Reflecting its focus on internal economic growth, the Coolidge Administration showed little interest in events outside the country's borders. The administration's chief international triumph dealt with the Kellogg-Briand multinational treaty. Frank B. Kellogg, secretary of state, threw American influence behind the move to renounce war as an instrument of international policy. Representatives of 15 countries signed the Kellogg-Briand Pact in Paris on Aug. 27, 1928. Other countries signed later. Coolidge backed a naval limitation conference in Geneva in 1927, but it reached no agreement. The Senate voted to join the World Court in 1926. It added so many reservations, however, that the resolution was not accepted by the other members of the Court.

Certain frictions with other countries arose. The immigration bill of 1924 caused ill feeling by including the Japanese with other Asian immigrants whose entry was barred because they were ineligible for citizenship. Trouble with Mexico over oil and land laws was a threat to the property of Americans. The appointment of Dwight W. Morrow as ambassador to Mexico helped to restore harmony. Coolidge was criticized when U.S. Marines were killed and wounded after he sent them to Nicaragua to protect American interests during an uprising.

Retirement

Coolidge's popularity remained unshaken, but in 1927 he issued a historical statement: "I do not choose to run for president in 1928." In March 1929 he was succeeded by Herbert Hoover and retired to Northampton, where he wrote his autobiography and magazine and newspaper articles. He died of a heart attack on Jan. 5, 1933. His *Autobiography* (1929) included little personal reporting, thus perpetuating his taciturn image.

HERBERT HOOVER

Library of Congress, Washington, D.C. (neg. no. LC-USZ62-24155)

**31st President of the United States
(1874–1964; president 1929–33)**

Vice President: Charles Curtis (1860–1936)

Herbert Hoover [signature]

When American voters elected Herbert Hoover as the 31st president in 1928, the United States was enjoying an industrial and financial boom. Within seven months of his taking office, however, the country was swallowed up in a depression that swept the entire world. Hoover's reputation as a humanitarian—earned during and after World War I as he rescued millions of Europeans from starvation—faded when his administration proved unable to stop widespread joblessness, homelessness, and hunger in his own country. Blamed for the hard times, he was defeated in the 1932 election.

Early Life

Herbert Clark Hoover was born in West Branch, Iowa, on Aug. 10, 1874. His parents, Jesse Hoover, a blacksmith and farm implement dealer, and Huldah Minthorn Hoover, died before he was ten years old. The orphaned Herbert moved to Newberg, Ore., to live with an uncle and aunt. Herbert attended the Quaker academy in which his uncle taught.

In 1891 Hoover was one of the first students to enroll at the new Leland Stanford Jr. University (now Stanford University) in Palo Alto, Calif. He graduated in 1895 with a degree in geology.

Engineer and Public Servant

Hoover became a mining engineer, working on a variety of projects that took him to four continents. In 1899 he married Lou Henry, with whom he later had two sons. On their wedding day the couple sailed for China, where Hoover served as chief engineer for the Chinese Imperial Bureau of Mines. When the Boxer Rebellion broke out in 1900, the Hoovers were among 200 foreigners who were besieged in Tianjin for a month. During this period Hoover organized relief for trapped foreigners.

Hoover became a partner in a British engineering firm in 1902. After six years he opened his own engineering firm, with offices in New York City, San Francisco, London, Petrograd (now St. Petersburg), and Paris. He was an exceptional businessman. By 1915 his personal wealth was about 4 million dollars.

When World War I broke out in 1914, Hoover was in London. He drew on his earlier experience in China to help 200,000 stranded American tourists return home. For the next three years Hoover led the Commission for Relief in Belgium, helping to feed some 9 million people whose country had been overrun by the German army.

When the United States entered the war in 1917, President Woodrow Wilson appointed Hoover U.S. food administrator. Fourteen million families pledged themselves to his program for producing and saving

---

First Lady Lou Hoover (1874–1944)

Born Lou Henry in Waterloo, Iowa, Lou Hoover moved to California with her family at age ten. At Stanford University she became one of the first women in the United States to earn a geology degree. While there she met Herbert Hoover, whom she married in 1899. While Herbert worked in London, Lou collaborated with him on an award-winning translation of a 16th-century mining text originally written in Latin. During World War I she was active in relief work, first in London and then in Washington, D.C. She also became a leader in the Girl Scouts and the National Amateur Athletic Federation. As first lady Lou delivered formal speeches on national radio, becoming the first president's wife to use that medium.

Herbert Hoover Timeline

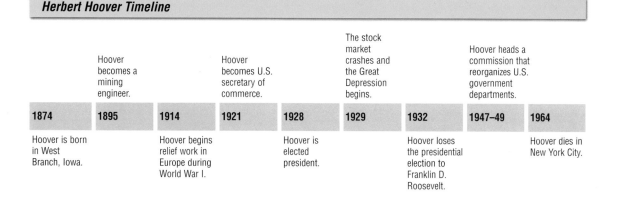

1874	1895	1914	1921	1928	1929	1932	1947–49	1964

1895 Hoover becomes a mining engineer.

1921 Hoover becomes U.S. secretary of commerce.

1929 The stock market crashes and the Great Depression begins.

1947–49 Hoover heads a commission that reorganizes U.S. government departments.

1874 Hoover is born in West Branch, Iowa.

1914 Hoover begins relief work in Europe during World War I.

1928 Hoover is elected president.

1932 Hoover loses the presidential election to Franklin D. Roosevelt.

1964 Hoover dies in New York City.

food for delivery to soldiers at the front. After the war Hoover was named head of the American Relief Administration, which sent shiploads of food and other crucial supplies to war-ravaged Europe.

Political Career

From 1921 to 1928 Hoover served as secretary of commerce in the administrations of Presidents Warren G. Harding and Calvin Coolidge. To the displeasure of conservatives, he greatly expanded the activities of the department. He promoted labor rights and government regulation of such new industries as radio broadcasting and commercial aviation. He also spearheaded efforts that led to construction of Hoover Dam and the St. Lawrence Seaway.

Hoover was nominated for the presidency at the Republican National Convention in Kansas City, Mo., in 1928. Charles Curtis of Kansas received the vice-presidential nomination. The party promised to maintain prosperity, to assist the farmer, and to make stronger attempts to enforce the Prohibition amendment and law in general. Hoover soundly defeated the Democratic nominee, Gov. Alfred E. Smith of New York.

Presidency

When Hoover took office the country was riding the crest of a wave of prosperity. The new president expressed the hope that "we shall soon with the help of God be in sight of the day when poverty will be banished from this nation." His promise of a "New Day" program was soon overwhelmed by the Great Depression.

The stock-market crash of October 1929 is usually regarded as the beginning of the depression, though there had been a slump in industry earlier. Prices of securities had reached their high point in September, as people in all walks of life had begun speculating on a continuously rising market. Their investments were wiped out as stock prices fell. The market collapse was followed by widespread business and bank failures, mortgage foreclosures, and job losses.

Hoover quickly took action. He met with business leaders and received assurances that they would not lay off workers or cut wages. He asked Congress to a appropriate money for public-works projects to create

jobs. He urged state and local governments to join private charities in caring for Americans made destitute by the depression. However, Hoover opposed direct federal relief payments to individuals. Federal relief, he felt, would be subject to political control and graft, while a direct dole would weaken the will of Americans to provide for themselves.

Hoover believed that the economy could best be stimulated by expanding credit. Thus businesses could start activities that would improve trade and employment. His critics called this aid to those at the top the "trickle down" system. They expressed doubt that the unemployed at the bottom could wait for the remedy to work a cure.

In 1932 banks were on the verge of collapse and unemployment was approaching 25 percent. At Hoover's urging, Congress created the Reconstruction Finance Corporation (RFC) to lend money to banks, loan associations, insurance companies, and railroads. The Emergency Relief Act of 1932 provided for RFC loans to states for use in direct relief, though this modest program did little to alleviate suffering or to bring about economic recovery.

Hoover appeals to the country for generous charity during a conference for welfare and relief mobilization in Washington, D.C., in 1932.

AP

Major World Events During Hoover's Administration

London. London Naval Conference, 1930

Germany. War debt and reparations settlements: Young plan, 1929; debt moratorium, 1931; Lausanne Conference, 1932.

Germany. Hitler made chancellor, 1933

Spain. Spanish republic founded, 1931

Japan-Manchuria. Japan occupies Manchuria, 1931

Peru-Chile. Tacna-Arica settlement, 1929

Hoover made some critical mistakes in his handling of the Depression. In 1930, for example, he signed into law the Smoot-Hawley Tariff Act. It raised many import duties so high that foreign countries could not sell goods in the United States. As a result, those countries could not—or would not—purchase American goods at a time when the need for sales abroad had never been greater.

Hoover's position on the Soldiers' Bonus Act made him unpopular with veterans' groups. This bill, which promised bonuses for wartime service, was passed over his veto. In 1932 he aroused resentment by ordering out of Washington the Bonus Army, a group of unemployed former soldiers who had come to demand immediate payment of the bonus. He authorized Gen. Douglas MacArthur to evict the soldiers. MacArthur greatly exceeded Hoover's orders in using military force, making the president appear heartless and cruel.

By 1932 Hoover was blaming the depression on events in Europe. He took international leadership in efforts to

While serving as honorary chairman of the Famine Emergency Committee, Hoover poses with children in Poland in 1946. In this role he coordinated the food supply in more than 20 countries.

The Granger Collection, New York

prevent ruin when banks failed in Austria and Germany and their economies collapsed. However, his efforts failed to save the sagging foreign economies.

Hoover sought international cooperation in other matters. In 1930 he called the London Naval Conference, where countries agreed to limit the size and number of their warships. In 1932 he sent a delegation to the League of Nations disarmament conference. He was organizing a world economic conference when his term ended.

Defeat and Retirement

The depression continued to deepen as the election campaign of 1932 got under way. There were more huge business failures, some of them scandalous, involving banks and utilities companies. An estimated 12 to 13 million people were unemployed. The American people blamed Hoover for the calamity. The homeless began calling their shantytowns "Hoovervilles."

Nevertheless, Hoover was renominated by the Republicans. The Democrats selected Gov. Franklin D. Roosevelt of New York. Hoover was crushingly defeated.

No administration had begun more happily than Hoover's. None ended in such despair. More and more banks closed. States declared bank "holidays" to save the remainder. Hoover tried to find a basis on which the president-elect would cooperate with him, but Roosevelt refused to become involved in the president's policies. When he left the White House on March 4, 1933, Hoover was a defeated and embittered man.

In retirement Hoover moved with his wife first to Palo Alto, Calif., and then to New York City. He made little comment on public affairs for two years. Then in books, articles, and speeches he criticized Roosevelt's New Deal as socialistic. After 1939 he differed with the administration's policies on World War II.

In 1946, as honorary chairman of the Famine Emergency Committee, Hoover flew to Europe, Asia, and South America to survey food needs and supplies. His last major activity was heading the Hoover Commission, under Presidents Harry Truman and Dwight D. Eisenhower, which aimed at making federal agencies more efficient. Hoover died in New York City on Oct. 20, 1964.

FRANKLIN D. ROOSEVELT

Evening Standard—Hulton Archive/Getty Images

32nd President of the United States (1882–1945; president 1933–45)

Vice Presidents: John Nance Garner (1868–1967; vice president 1933–41); Henry A. Wallace (1888–1965; vice president 1941–45); Harry S. Truman (1884–1972; vice president 1945)

The only U.S. president elected to the office four times was Franklin D. Roosevelt. In his 12 years in office, Roosevelt was both hated and loved. His opponents criticized him for the way he greatly expanded the powers of the federal government. Most people, however, hailed him for his efforts to lead the United States through two of the greatest crises of the 20th century: the Great Depression and World War II.

Early Life

Franklin Delano Roosevelt was born on Jan. 30, 1882, in Hyde Park, N.Y. His father, James Roosevelt, was a wealthy landowner and railroad vice president. He had been a diplomat under President Grover Cleveland. His mother was Sara Delano Roosevelt.

Franklin was tutored at home until he was 14 years old, when he entered Groton Preparatory School in

Groton, Mass. In 1900 he entered Harvard University, where he studied history, economics, languages, and science. At Harvard Franklin came under the influence of President Theodore Roosevelt, who was his distant cousin. The president's liberal ideas and strong leadership helped Franklin decide on a career in public service.

During his Harvard days Roosevelt fell in love with Eleanor Roosevelt, Theodore Roosevelt's niece. Franklin and Eleanor married on March 17, 1905. They had six children. Eleanor would become a valued adviser in future years.

After graduating from Harvard, Roosevelt attended Columbia University Law School in New York City. He completed his work in 1907 and began to practice with a leading New York law firm. He soon found, however, that he was not much interested in the legal profession.

Early Years in Politics

Encouraged by his cousin Theodore, Roosevelt looked to start a career in politics. In 1910 he was elected as a Democrat to the New York state senate. Brave and independent, he quickly won statewide and even some national attention for his stand against Tammany Hall, the powerful New York City Democratic organization.

In 1912 Roosevelt strongly supported New Jersey Governor Woodrow Wilson for the Democratic presidential nomination. After Wilson won the presidency, he rewarded Roosevelt for his efforts by appointing him assistant secretary of the Navy. In the years before the United States entered World War I, Roosevelt worked for a larger and more efficient Navy.

First Lady Eleanor Roosevelt (1884–1962)

A great humanitarian, Eleanor Roosevelt was, in her time, one of the world's most widely admired and powerful women. Born Anna Eleanor Roosevelt in New York City, she grew up in a wealthy family that attached great value to community service. She married Franklin Roosevelt, her distant cousin, in 1905. Eleanor had the distinction of being first lady longer than any other presidential wife—slightly more than 12 years. Her defense of the rights of minorities, youth, women, and the poor during her tenure helped to shed light on groups that previously had been alienated from the political process. After her husband's death, as a delegate to the United Nations, she helped write the Universal Declaration of Human Rights (1948).

Library of Congress, Washington, D.C. (neg. no. LC-USZ62-25812)

Franklin D. Roosevelt Timeline

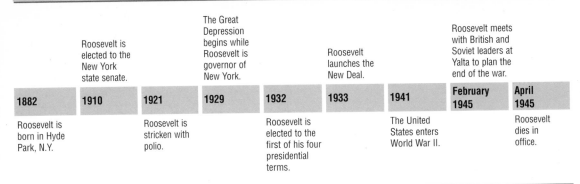

1882	1910	1921	1929	1932	1933	1941	February 1945	April 1945

Roosevelt is elected to the New York state senate. (1910)

The Great Depression begins while Roosevelt is governor of New York. (1929)

Roosevelt launches the New Deal. (1933)

Roosevelt meets with British and Soviet leaders at Yalta to plan the end of the war. (February 1945)

Roosevelt is born in Hyde Park, N.Y. (1882)

Roosevelt is stricken with polio. (1921)

Roosevelt is elected to the first of his four presidential terms. (1932)

The United States enters World War II. (1941)

Roosevelt dies in office. (April 1945)

During the war he helped lead the Navy to victory over German sea forces.

In 1920 the Democrats nominated Roosevelt for vice president on a ticket with presidential candidate Governor James M. Cox of Ohio. In nationwide tours Roosevelt and Cox spoke for full entry of the United States into the League of Nations. However, it was impossible to halt a war-weary country's revolt against Democratic policies. The Republicans, headed by Warren G. Harding, won by a landslide. Roosevelt returned to his legal work in New York City.

Paralysis to Presidency

In August 1921, while vacationing in Canada, Roosevelt's life was transformed when he was stricken with polio. The disease left him paralyzed from the waist down. In later years he could walk a little but only by using a cane, with his legs encased in steel braces, and usually with someone's help.

Roosevelt chats with two Georgia farmers in 1932, the year he was elected president. Help for struggling farmers was a priority of Roosevelt's New Deal program.

H. William Tetlow—Hulton Archive/Getty Images

Roosevelt returned to politics in 1924. At the Democratic convention he nominated New York Governor Alfred E. Smith for president, and he repeated his nomination of Smith at the 1928 convention. Smith, in turn, urged Roosevelt to run for governor of New York. Though Roosevelt was at first reluctant, he eventually agreed and was elected governor in 1928.

Governor Roosevelt continued the progressive policies of Smith, advocating tax relief for farmers, cheaper public utilities for consumers, court reform, and more attention to public health and housing. As the Great Depression deepened, these vigorous relief policies helped earn Roosevelt the Democratic presidential nomination in 1932.

The depression was the only important issue in the campaign. Herbert Hoover, the Republican candidate for reelection, was almost sure to be defeated because millions blamed him for the crisis. Roosevelt promised a "new deal" for those who were suffering, pledging to use the power of the federal government to promote economic recovery. Roosevelt won easily, with about 7 million more popular votes than Hoover and 472 electoral votes to Hoover's 59. His vice president was John Nance Garner of Texas.

The New Deal

During the four months between Roosevelt's election and inauguration, the economy deteriorated even further. By early 1933 most banks had shut down, industrial production had fallen to the lowest level ever recorded, at least 13 million Americans were unemployed, and farmers were in desperate straits. In his inaugural address of March 4, 1933, Roosevelt did much to reassure the public. He promised prompt action and called for courage—"the only thing we have to fear is fear itself."

Roosevelt followed up on his promise with "The Hundred Days"—the first phase of his New Deal program. One part of the program was to promote recovery. Another was to supply relief to the needy. A third part was to furnish permanent reforms, especially in the management of banks and stock exchanges.

Roosevelt's first step was to order all banks closed until Congress could address the banking crisis.

Major World Events During Franklin D. Roosevelt's Administration

Great Britain. *Edward VIII abdicates; George VI is king, 1936*

Germany *attacks Poland, starts World War II, 1939*

France. *Occupied by Germany in World War II, 1940–44*

Spain. *Civil War, 1936–39*

Italy. *Mussolini seizes Ethiopia, 1936*

Soviet Union *signs nonaggression pact with Germany, 1939*

AP

Roosevelt spoke directly to the American people through informal radio broadcasts that became known as "fireside chats." He used the broadcasts to explain his policies and to reassure the public during the dark days of the Great Depression and World War II.

Congress met in special session on March 9 and rushed through a bill that allowed only banks in sound condition to reopen. The "bank holiday," as Roosevelt called it, and the emergency legislation restored public confidence in banks.

Two key but controversial measures of the early New Deal were the Agricultural Adjustment Act (AAA) and the National Industrial Recovery Act (NIRA). The AAA authorized the government to pay farmers for reducing their production. It was designed to cut down crop surpluses, which had hurt farmers by keeping down the value of their products. When the Supreme Court annulled the AAA in 1936, Congress passed a new law that paid farmers for saving and improving their soils.

The NIRA had two parts. It set aside billions of dollars for public-works projects and authorized the Public Works Administration (PWA) to spend it. It also set up

the National Recovery Administration (NRA), which established and administered fair-practice codes for industry. At first the business community backed the NRA, but support dwindled as the codes became more complex and difficult to enforce. In 1935 the Supreme Court declared the NRA to be unconstitutional.

Another major recovery measure was the Tennessee Valley Authority (TVA). This government agency was established in 1933 to control floods, improve navigation, and generate electrical power along the Tennessee River and its tributaries.

The Hundred Days also included relief and reform measures. The Civilian Conservation Corps (CCC) employed hundreds of thousands of young men in the national forests and other government properties. The Federal Emergency Relief Administration (FERA) made grants to the states for relief activities. The Federal Deposit Insurance Corporation (FDIC) was created to insure bank deposits against loss in the event of a bank failure.

By 1934 the measures passed during The Hundred Days had produced some recovery. Yet Roosevelt knew he had to do more. In 1935 he asked Congress to pass additional New Deal policies—sometimes called the Second New Deal. A key measure of the Second New Deal was the Social Security Act, which provided unemployment relief and old-age pensions. Another was the Works Progress Administration (WPA), which provided jobs to millions of people on public projects between 1935 and 1941. The Wagner Act (officially the National Labor Relations Act) guaranteed labor the right of collective bargaining.

Reelection to Second Term

In 1936 Roosevelt ran for reelection with most business leaders against him but with most farmers, workers, and the poor on his side. He won an overwhelming victory over Republican Alfred M. Landon of Kansas.

With this public backing for the New Deal, Roosevelt saw only one remaining obstacle to his program: the Supreme Court. During his first term the Court had struck down several key New Deal measures, and a half dozen important New Deal laws were still up for decision. To make the court more supportive of his

British Prime Minister Winston Churchill, President Roosevelt, and Soviet leader Joseph Stalin pose with leading Allied officers at the Yalta Conference in 1945. In their meetings the three leaders discussed the final stages of World War II and the structure of the postwar world.
U.S. Army Photo

program, Roosevelt proposed a plan that would have allowed him to appoint one new justice for every sitting justice aged 70 years or older. Widely viewed as a court-packing scheme, the bill was voted down by Congress.

Still, Roosevelt continued to press New Deal measures. Congress passed laws to protect farmers, expand the TVA, and set a minimum wage and standard workweek. By 1937 the economy had largely recovered, and by 1938 the New Deal was coming to a close.

By 1939 foreign policy was overshadowing domestic policy. Although Roosevelt had so far spent much of his presidency dealing with domestic problems, he was also deeply involved in foreign affairs. He launched the Good Neighbor Policy to improve relations between the United States and Latin America. Under this policy, the United States greatly reduced its intervention in Latin American affairs. He also supported agreements that encouraged trade between the United States and other countries.

For years Roosevelt worked to awaken the United States to the dangers of war. He tried to halt the aggressive policies of dictators in Japan, Italy, and Germany. Congress and the public, however, wanted the United States to stay out of international affairs.

World War II

On Sept. 1, 1939, Nazi Germany invaded Poland, beginning World War II in Europe. For 27 months the United States was officially neutral, but in reality it was on the side of Great Britain, France, and Poland from the start. In a special session called by Roosevelt, Congress agreed to send shells, guns, and planes to the British and French. When France fell to the Germans in the early summer of 1940, Roosevelt convinced Congress to increase aid to Great Britain and to strengthen the U.S. armed forces.

This was the summer of a presidential campaign. Roosevelt was pitted against Wendell Willkie, the Republican candidate. Never before had the country elected a president to a third term, but to many people

the crisis demanded an experienced leader. Roosevelt won the election with 55 percent of the popular vote and 449 electoral votes to 82 for Willkie.

Soon after the election Roosevelt promised that the United States would be "the arsenal of democracy." The Lend-Lease Act of 1941 allowed the United States to accept noncash payment for military and other aid to Great Britain and its allies. In August 1941 Roosevelt met British Prime Minister Winston Churchill at sea and drew up the Atlantic Charter. In this document the leaders pledged their countries to the goal of defeating the Nazis and defending democracy.

On Dec. 7, 1941, Japan bombed the U.S. naval base at Pearl Harbor. The surprise attack brought the United States into the war against Japan, Germany, and Italy. Roosevelt decided to increase the size of the armed forces to 11 million soldiers and called on industry to produce enormous quantities of aircraft, tanks, and guns.

Roosevelt worked with Churchill to plan the Allied war effort at several conferences. Later Soviet leader Joseph Stalin joined them for meetings in Tehran, Iran, in 1943 and at Yalta in the Soviet Union in 1945. Roosevelt and other world leaders also began planning the United Nations, a new organization to maintain world peace.

Declining Health and Death

Roosevelt had been in declining health for more than a year before the Yalta Conference. When he ran for reelection in 1944, his political opponents had tried to make much of his condition. But Roosevelt campaigned actively and defeated the Republican candidate, Gov. Thomas E. Dewey of New York.

By the time of his return from Yalta, however, Roosevelt was very weak. Early in April 1945 he traveled to his cottage in Warm Springs, Ga., to rest. On the afternoon of April 12 he suffered a cerebral hemorrhage, and he died a few hours later. That evening Vice President Harry S. Truman was sworn in as president.

HARRY S. TRUMAN

Library of Congress, Washington D.C. (neg. no. LC-USZ62-117122)

33rd President of the United States
(1884–1972; president 1945–53)

Vice President: Alben W. Barkley (1877–1956)

Harry Truman [signature]

Upon the death of President Franklin D. Roosevelt in 1945, Vice President Harry S. Truman became the 33rd president of the United States. Truman led the country through the final stages of World War II, making the difficult decision to use the atomic bomb against Japan. After the war he strongly opposed the spread of Communism in Europe and Asia.

Early Life and Career

Truman was born on May 8, 1884, in Lamar, Mo. He was the son of John Anderson Truman, a cattle trader and farmer, and Martha Young Truman. He was named Harry for his mother's brother, Harry Young. He was given the middle initial "S" (but no name) for his grandfathers, Anderson Shipp Truman and Solomon Young.

Shortly after Harry's birth, the Truman family moved to Independence, Mo., near Kansas City. After graduating from high school in 1901, Harry sought an

appointment to the U.S. Military Academy at West Point, N.Y., but was rejected because of poor eyesight. Having no money to pay his way through college, he took a job in a Kansas City drugstore. Later he worked as a bank clerk. Five years after leaving high school, Truman was tired of city life. He returned to his father's farm and worked there for the next ten years.

When the United States entered World War I in 1917, Truman immediately volunteered. He went overseas in 1918 and commanded an artillery unit in France. Returning to the United States in 1919, Truman married Elizabeth (Bess) Wallace, whom he had known since childhood. They had one daughter.

After his marriage, Truman invested all his savings in a Kansas City haberdashery that he opened with an Army friend. The business was successful for two years but then failed during a depression in 1922.

Political Career

Following the failure of his business, Truman decided to seek a job in politics. While in the Army, Truman had been a close friend of James Pendergast, nephew of Thomas Pendergast, the Democratic political boss of Kansas City. This friendship led to Truman's appointment as overseer of highways for Jackson County. After serving one year in that office Truman was elected county judge in 1922, again with Pendergast support. He was not required to be a lawyer to hold this job, but Truman felt that he would help his career if he studied law. So he enrolled in the Kansas City Law School and attended night classes for two years.

First Lady Bess Truman (1885–1982)

Born Elizabeth Virginia Wallace, Bess Truman came from one of the wealthiest and most prominent families in Independence, Mo. She met Harry Truman when they both were in elementary school. Later she attended Miss Barstow's Finishing School for Girls in Kansas City, Mo. Bess and Harry married in 1919, and she became first lady in 1945. Private by nature, she refused to hold press conferences, and, after finally agreeing to answer questions in writing, she often did so with a firm "no comment." Although she did not take an active public role as first lady, she often acted privately as one of the president's chief advisers. After he left office President Truman claimed that Bess had been a "full partner in all my transactions."

Harris & Ewing Collection/Library of Congress, Washington, D.C. (neg. no. LC-USZ62-25813)

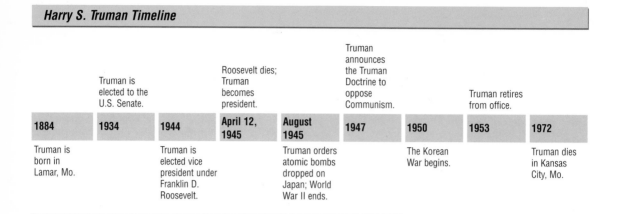

Harry S. Truman Timeline

1884	1934	1944	April 12, 1945	August 1945	1947	1950	1953	1972
	Truman is elected to the U.S. Senate.		Roosevelt dies; Truman becomes president.		Truman announces the Truman Doctrine to oppose Communism.		Truman retires from office.	
Truman is born in Lamar, Mo.		Truman is elected vice president under Franklin D. Roosevelt.		Truman orders atomic bombs dropped on Japan; World War II ends.		The Korean War begins.		Truman dies in Kansas City, Mo.

In 1924 Truman was defeated for reelection, but two years later he was elected presiding judge of the county court. He served two four-year terms in this job, which included the supervision of many county expenditures. He built a reputation for efficiency and honesty in contrast to the bad reputation of many of his political associates. In 1934 Truman was selected as the Pendergast candidate for U.S. senator. He won the seat and was reelected in 1940.

In the early 1940s Truman gained national recognition for leading an investigation into fraud and waste in the

From 1919 to 1922 Truman (left) was a partner in the Truman and Jacobson haberdashery in Kansas City. When the business failed, Truman went into politics.

U.S. military. During this period the United States was preparing for involvement in World War II. While taking care not to harm the war effort, the Committee Investigating the National Defense Program, commonly called the Truman Committee, probed into many agencies and industries that produced war materials. It brought to light and helped to correct many cases of mismanagement, waste, and negligence. This work earned Truman the respect of his Senate colleagues and the public.

At the Democratic National Convention in 1944, a lively contest developed between several candidates for the vice-presidential nomination. Most conspicuous were Henry A. Wallace, who had the support of the liberal wing of the Democratic party, and James Byrnes, who represented the conservative wing. The deadlock was broken by naming Truman as the compromise candidate. Truman at first refused to take the nomination because he wanted to remain in the Senate. But President Roosevelt was insistent, and Truman finally agreed.

Presidency

Roosevelt and Truman won the election and took office on Jan. 20, 1945. As vice president, Truman had little to do with shaping policy at home or abroad. Roosevelt seldom consulted with him. As a result, when Roosevelt suddenly died less than three months into his term, Truman was not fully prepared to become president. Presidential aides and others did their best to help him, however, and Truman learned quickly.

World War II. Truman began his presidency with great energy. He helped arrange Germany's unconditional surrender on May 8, 1945, which ended World War II in Europe. In July he traveled to Potsdam, Germany, for a meeting with Allied leaders to discuss the fate of postwar Germany.

Two weeks after becoming president, Truman learned of the top-secret project to develop an atomic bomb. While in Potsdam he was told of a successful atomic bomb test at Los Alamos, N.M. Truman consulted with his aides to decide whether the bomb should be used against Japan. An invasion of Japan was being planned. They estimated that if the bomb worked it would save

AP

Major World Events During Truman's Administration

England. *King George VI dies, Elizabeth II queen, 1952*
France. *Germans surrender to Allies at Reims, 1945*
Germany. *Berlin airlift emphasizes Cold War, 1948–49*
Japan. *Japanese surrender at Tokyo Bay, 1945*
Korea. *North Korea invades South Korea, 1950*
India. *Gandhi assassinated, 1948*

AP

Truman accepts the Democratic presidential nomination at the 1948 Democratic National Convention in Philadelphia.

up to 500,000 American lives. Truman warned Japan that if it did not surrender, the bomb would be used. Japan refused to yield. In August 1945 Truman authorized the dropping of atomic bombs on the cities of Hiroshima and Nagasaki, killing more than 100,000 men, women, and children. This remains perhaps the most controversial decision ever taken by a U.S. president. On August 14 Japan surrendered.

During the early months of the Truman Administration, an international conference in San Francisco, Calif., had

written a charter for a new peace organization, the United Nations. Truman was strongly in favor of the United States becoming a key member of this organization. On July 28, 1945, the U.S. Senate approved the United Nations charter. In December 1945 the Senate and House of Representatives voted for membership in the United Nations.

Truman Doctrine and Marshall Plan. In the postwar period Truman faced a new threat—the Soviet Union's desire to extend Communism into Europe and beyond. In 1947 Truman called for economic aid to Greece and Turkey to help those countries resist Communist takeover. With this decision he introduced the Truman Doctrine, which asserted that the United States would oppose Communist aggression anywhere in the world. The U.S.-Soviet rivalry known as the Cold War had begun.

Later in 1947 Truman backed Secretary of State George C. Marshall's bold strategy to combat Communism. The Marshall Plan, officially called the European Recovery Program, provided billions of dollars to rebuild devastated European economies. The plan was successful in preventing the spread of Communism into western Europe.

Election and the Fair Deal. As the presidential election of 1948 approached, Truman faced opposition from not only the Republicans but also other Democrats. A group of Southern Democrats, enraged by Truman's civil rights program, revolted and held a "Dixiecrat" convention in Birmingham, Ala. They nominated Senator Strom Thurmond of South Carolina as the States' Rights candidate for president. Another threat to Truman arose from the formation of a Progressive party, with Henry A. Wallace as its presidential candidate.

All political indications pointed to a Republican landslide. Truman, however, refused to believe the public opinion polls. In a one-man campaign he traveled more than 30,000 miles (48,000 kilometers) and made some 300 speeches. He repeatedly criticized what he called the "do-nothing Republican Congress." To most people's surprise, Truman comfortably won reelection against Republican Thomas E. Dewey. Alben Barkley of Kentucky became vice president.

Truman speaks at the closing session of the San Francisco Conference, an international meeting that established the United Nations in 1945.
AP

Energized by his victory, Truman presented his program for domestic reform in 1949. The Fair Deal included proposals for expanded public housing, increased aid to education, a higher minimum wage, federal protection for civil rights, and national health insurance. Despite Democratic majorities in the House and Senate, most Fair Deal proposals either failed to gain legislative approval or passed in much weakened form. Truman succeeded, however, in laying the groundwork for the domestic agenda for decades to come.

Cold War. In part, the Fair Deal fell victim to rising Cold War tensions that absorbed the country's attention and resources. In 1949 Chinese Communists finally won their long civil war, seizing control of the mainland. The Soviet Union successfully tested a nuclear bomb. In 1949 Truman led the United States into a collective security agreement with non-Communist European countries— the North Atlantic Treaty Organization (NATO)—to resist Soviet expansionism. By the end of the decade, the United States and Soviet Union would be involved in a dangerous arms race.

In June 1950 the Soviet-supported Communist government of North Korea invaded South Korea, setting off the Korean War. This was a great personal blow to President Truman. He had often said he wanted more than anything else to be regarded by historians as a president who brought peace to the world. Truman ordered U.S. military forces to join other United Nations troops in turning back the invasion. When Chinese troops rushed in to back the North Koreans, Gen. Douglas MacArthur, commander of the United Nations forces, wanted to strike directly at China. President Truman insisted on confining the fight to Korea. In a courageous move, he removed MacArthur from

command. The war, however, dragged on inconclusively past the end of Truman's presidency.

Retirement

The inability of the United States to win a clear-cut victory in Korea contributed to the belief of many Americans that the United States was losing the Cold War. Meanwhile, in the late 1940s and early '50s, charges swirled that Communists had infiltrated the U.S. government. Despite Truman's strongly anti-Communist foreign policy, some accused him and some of his top advisers of being "soft on Communism." His popularity began to plummet.

Truman chose not to seek reelection in 1952, and the Democratic presidential nomination went to Gov. Adlai E. Stevenson of Illinois. The candidate for the Republican party was Gen. Dwight D. Eisenhower. President Truman made three whistle-stop tours on behalf of Stevenson. Eisenhower was overwhelmingly elected.

Eisenhower was inaugurated on Jan. 20, 1953, and Truman retired to his home in Independence, Mo. His life in retirement was active. Friends raised funds to build the Harry S. Truman Library in Independence, which Truman helped to develop. Although he had left office with low public approval, his standing among U.S. presidents rose in later years. He began to be appreciated as a president who had, in Truman's own words, "done his damnedest." A common man thrust into leadership at a critical time in the country's history, Truman had risen to the challenge and performed far better than nearly everyone had expected.

Truman remained in good health until the mid-1960s, when he declined rapidly. On Christmas Day 1972, he lapsed into unconsciousness. He died the next morning.

DWIGHT D. EISENHOWER

Library of Congress, Washington, D.C. (neg. no. LC-USZ62-104631)

**34th President of the United States
(1890–1969; president 1953–61)**

Vice President: Richard M. Nixon (1913–94)

In World War II Gen. Dwight D. Eisenhower became one of the most successful commanders in history. Later he became the first head of the armies of the North Atlantic Treaty Organization (NATO). Turning to politics in 1952, Eisenhower proved to be a successful commander in that field also. He was overwhelmingly elected the 34th president of the United States and the first Republican president in 20 years. Although Eisenhower had many critics, he was a very popular president. His two terms in office were a time of peace and general prosperity in the United States.

Early Life

Dwight David Eisenhower was born on Oct. 14, 1890, in Denison, Tex. His parents were David and Ida Elizabeth (Stover) Eisenhower. He spent most of his childhood in Abilene, Kan. During his school days Dwight was usually called Ike by his friends. The nickname stayed with him throughout his life. Ike enjoyed sports more

than his studies. After graduating from Abilene High School in 1909, he worked in a creamery to help pay a brother's expenses at law school.

In 1911 Eisenhower entered the U.S. Military Academy at West Point, N.Y. He excelled in football but injured a knee in his second year at the academy and was forced to stop playing. In 1915 he graduated and was assigned to Fort Sam Houston, Tex. In nearby San Antonio he met Mamie Geneva Doud, whom he married in 1916. They had two sons.

Military Service

During World War I Eisenhower commanded a training center for tank crews. For this work he was awarded the Distinguished Service Medal, his highest Army decoration. The war ended just before he was to sail for France.

After the war Eisenhower had assignments in the United States, the Panama Canal Zone, and Europe. In 1933 he became an aide to Army Chief of Staff Gen. Douglas MacArthur. Two years later MacArthur took Eisenhower with him to the Philippines to help organize and train the Philippine army. He returned to the United States in 1940, shortly after Germany's invasion of Poland sparked the European phase of World War II. The United States entered World War II after the Japanese attack on Pearl Harbor in December 1941.

In June 1942 Army Chief of Staff Gen. George C. Marshall selected Eisenhower over 366 senior officers to be commander of U.S. troops in Europe. Eisenhower's rapid advancement was due not only to his knowledge

First Lady Mamie Eisenhower (1896–1979)

Immensely popular with crowds and comfortable with prominent people, Mamie Eisenhower relished her duties as first lady. Born Mamie Geneva Doud in Boone, Iowa, she had a pampered youth and briefly attended finishing school. Her family spent winters in San Antonio, Tex., where she met Dwight D. Eisenhower, then a young lieutenant. They married in 1916. In the White House Mamie was known for gracious entertaining. The diplomacy of the postwar years and the development of air travel enabled the Eisenhowers to entertain an unprecedented number of heads of state and leaders of foreign governments. White House employees reported that Mamie supervised them closely, always on the lookout for lapses.

Harris & Ewing Collection/Library of Congress, Washington, D.C. (neg. no. LC-USZ62-25814)

Dwight D. Eisenhower Timeline

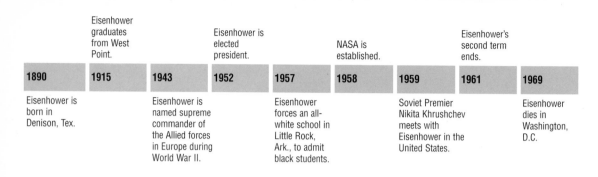

	Eisenhower graduates from West Point.		Eisenhower is elected president.		NASA is established.		Eisenhower's second term ends.	
1890	**1915**	**1943**	**1952**	**1957**	**1958**	**1959**	**1961**	**1969**
Eisenhower is born in Denison, Tex.		Eisenhower is named supreme commander of the Allied forces in Europe during World War II.		Eisenhower forces an all-white school in Little Rock, Ark., to admit black students.		Soviet Premier Nikita Khrushchev meets with Eisenhower in the United States.		Eisenhower dies in Washington, D.C.

of military strategy and talent for organization but also to his ability to persuade and get along with others. On Nov. 8, 1942, he led U.S. forces in an invasion of North Africa, the first major Allied offensive of the war. In 1943 he launched successful attacks on Tunisia, Sicily, and Italy.

In December 1943 Eisenhower was appointed supreme commander of the Allied forces that were to invade France. His forces landed in Normandy on June 6, 1944, in the greatest amphibious operation in history. By the spring of 1945 the Allies had driven through the heart of Germany. The Nazis surrendered on May 8.

General Eisenhower gives orders to U.S. paratroopers in England as they prepare to invade Normandy in June 1944.

Library of Congress, Washington, D.C. (neg. no. LC-USZ62-25600)

Meanwhile, in December 1944, Eisenhower had received the highest U.S. military rank, five-star general.

Late in 1945 Eisenhower returned to Washington, D.C., to succeed General Marshall as Army chief of staff. In 1948 he retired from the Army to become president of Columbia University in New York City, but his career as an academic was brief. In 1950 he was named the first head of the armies of the North Atlantic Treaty Organization (NATO).

Nomination and Election

During his Army career Eisenhower had taken no part in politics and there was some uncertainty as to which party he favored. Early in 1952, however, he revealed publicly that he had always been a Republican. Encouraged by party leaders, he opened a vigorous campaign for the Republican presidential nomination with a speech in Abilene, Kan., on June 4, 1952. At the Republican convention in Chicago he won the nomination with Senator Richard Nixon of California as his running mate.

Eisenhower's leadership and great personal charm united all factions of the Republican party behind his candidacy. Throughout the campaign he called for a firm, middle-of-the-road policy in both foreign and domestic affairs. On Nov. 4, 1952, Eisenhower was elected president by a landslide over Democrat Adlai E. Stevenson.

Presidency

Immediately after taking office on Jan. 20, 1953, President Eisenhower made clear his intentions to work for world peace. He pledged the United States to a constant search for an honorable settlement of international problems.

First term. Foreign affairs drew much of Eisenhower's attention. Shortly after taking office he visited Korea to explore possibilities for ending the Korean War. He succeeded in negotiating a truce in July 1953. However, the continuation of the Cold War—the rivalry between the Soviet Union and the United States—was a grave problem for the president. In an effort to ease Cold War tensions, Eisenhower met with the leaders of Great Britain, France, and the Soviet Union in Geneva,

Major World Events During Eisenhower's Administration

Soviet Union. *Stalin dies, 1953; first artificial Earth satellites (Sputniks I and II) launched, 1957*

France. *De Gaulle becomes premier, 1958*

Egypt. *United Arab Republic formed by merger of Egypt and Syria, 1958*

Africa. *Among former colonies to gain independence are Nigeria, Somalia, and the Congo, 1960*

Nepal. *Mount Everest climbed first time, 1953*

Vietnam. *Truce ends eight years of warfare, 1954*

Peter Stackpole—Time Life Pictures/Getty Images

Delegates at the 1952 Republican convention in Chicago show their support for Eisenhower. The phrase "I Like Ike" became one of the most famous campaign slogans in U.S. history.

Switzerland, in July 1955. Nevertheless, hostile feelings continued between the Soviet Union and the West.

In domestic affairs Eisenhower was generally conservative. He called for reduced taxes, balanced budgets, a decrease in government control over the economy, and the return of certain federal responsibilities to the states. However, he continued most of the social reforms begun under the Democratic presidents who came before him, Franklin D. Roosevelt and Harry S. Truman. The minimum wage was increased and the social security system was broadened. In 1953 the Department of Health, Education, and Welfare was created.

An important domestic issue in the early 1950s was the work of Republican Senator Joseph McCarthy of Wisconsin, who was investigating charges of Communist influence in the U.S. government. Privately Eisenhower expressed his distaste for the senator. At times, however, he seemed to encourage McCarthy's attacks. With Eisenhower's approval, Congress passed a law designed to outlaw the American Communist Party. Late in 1954 the Senate condemned McCarthy for his conduct.

Reelection and second term. A heart attack in September 1955 and an operation for an intestinal disorder in June 1956 raised questions about whether Eisenhower would seek another term. But he recovered quickly, and the Republican convention unanimously endorsed the Eisenhower-Nixon ticket on the first ballot. The Democrats again selected Adlai E. Stevenson. Eisenhower's great personal popularity turned the election into an overwhelming victory.

The election campaign had been complicated by a crisis in the Middle East over Egypt's seizure of the Suez Canal. Great Britain, France, and Israel responded by attacking Egypt, which was supported by the Soviet Union. The crisis prompted Eisenhower to issue a policy that came to be called the Eisenhower Doctrine. He pledged to send military and economic aid to any Middle Eastern country requesting assistance against Communist aggression. Congress adopted the Eisenhower Doctrine in March 1957.

At home Eisenhower's biggest challenge was the integration of schools. In 1954 the U.S. Supreme Court had ruled that racial segregation in public schools was unconstitutional. In September 1957 Governor Orval E. Faubus of Arkansas used the National Guard to prevent the admission of nine black students to a high school in Little Rock. The president tried to settle the problem through negotiation. When this failed, he sent federal troops to Little Rock to enforce the court order calling for integration.

Eisenhower and his wife, Mamie, wave as they leave Pennsylvania Station in New York City aboard the "Eisenhower Special" during the 1952 presidential campaign.
AP

In October 1957 the Soviet Union launched the first artificial Earth satellite, Sputnik I. Stunned by this achievement, many Americans blamed Eisenhower for failing to develop a space program. The president took steps to boost space research, and in January 1958 the United States put its own satellite, Explorer I, into orbit. The National Aeronautics and Space Administration (NASA) was established in July of that year.

The administration again was criticized for an economic recession that struck in the fall of 1957 and lasted through the following summer. For fear of fueling inflation, Eisenhower refused to lower taxes or increase federal spending to ease the slump.

Eisenhower continued to emphasize the achievement of world peace as one of the prime objectives of his administration's foreign policy. Following the death of Secretary of State John Foster Dulles in 1959, the president assumed a more vigorous and personal role in foreign policy. He undertook a series of goodwill tours, traveling more than 300,000 miles (480,000 kilometers) to some 27 countries in his last two years of office.

To improve relations with the Soviet Union, Eisenhower invited Premier Nikita S. Khrushchev to visit the United States. Khrushchev toured parts of the country in September 1959 and held private talks with Eisenhower at Camp David, Md. They agreed that outstanding issues between countries should be handled by peaceful means and that general disarmament was the most important question of the day. President Eisenhower was invited to pay a state visit to the Soviet Union the following year. In addition, a summit meeting between the Western powers and the Soviet Union was planned for Paris in May 1960.

A new era of personal diplomacy seemed at hand. On May 1, 1960, however, the Soviets shot down a U.S. spy plane inside the Soviet Union. Khrushchev bitterly attacked the United States and President Eisenhower, calling the incident "aggressive provocation aimed at wrecking the summit conference." At the opening session in Paris, the belligerent attitude of Khrushchev wrecked any hope of continuing the conference. The Soviet leader also withdrew his invitation to President Eisenhower to visit the Soviet Union in June. Eisenhower admitted that the flights had gone on for four years and accepted much of the blame for the ill-timed incident.

A further display of Cold War tensions came during the last weeks of the Eisenhower Administration, when the United States broke diplomatic relations with Cuba in January 1961. For two years the country had been led by the Communist regime of Fidel Castro.

Retirement

In 1960 John F. Kennedy, a Democrat, was elected Eisenhower's successor. When Eisenhower left office, Congress restored his rank as general of the army. He retired to his farm in Gettysburg, Pa., and devoted much of his time to writing his memoirs. In 1962 he dedicated the Eisenhower Presidential Library in Abilene, Kan., which houses the bulk of his personal and state papers. After a long period of illness and a hospital confinement of almost a year, Eisenhower died of heart failure on March 28, 1969, in Washington, D.C.

JOHN F. KENNEDY

Time Life Pictures/Getty Images

**35th President of the United States
(1917–63; president 1961–63)**

Vice President: Lyndon B. Johnson (1908–73)

In November 1960, at the age of 43, John F. Kennedy became the youngest person ever elected president of the United States. Theodore Roosevelt had become president at 42 when President William McKinley was assassinated, but he was not elected at that age. Kennedy was an immensely popular president, and his assassination in 1963 was a shock to the country and the world.

Early Life

John Fitzgerald Kennedy was born on May 29, 1917, in Brookline, Mass., a suburb of Boston. He was the second of nine children born to Joseph and Rose Kennedy. Politics was a part of his heritage. Both of his grandfathers had been prominent in state politics. His father, a wealthy banker and businessman, held government posts during President Franklin D. Roosevelt's administration.

John excelled in school and in sports. He attended public schools in Brookline and then private schools in New York and Connecticut. In 1935–36 he studied at the London School of Economics, and in 1940 he graduated with honors from Harvard University.

A few months before the United States entered World War II in December 1941, Kennedy attempted to enlist in the U.S. Army. He was rejected because of an old back injury. After several months of exercise, however, he was accepted by the Navy. In 1943 a Japanese destroyer sank the torpedo boat that he was commanding in the South Pacific near the Solomon Islands. Although he was seriously hurt and stranded far behind enemy lines, he led his crew to safety. For his heroism, Kennedy was awarded the Navy and Marine Corps Medal, the Purple Heart, and a citation.

Political Career

After his discharge from the Navy, Kennedy worked for a short time as a newspaper correspondent. Soon he decided to follow the family tradition of public service. In 1946 he was elected to the U.S. Congress as a Democratic representative from Massachusetts. Kennedy served three terms in the House of Representatives, supporting liberal causes such as better working conditions, public housing, and social security for the aged.

In 1952 Kennedy was elected to the U.S. Senate. His victory over the popular incumbent, Republican senator Henry Cabot Lodge, Jr., was particularly impressive because across the rest of the country Republican candidates were swept into office along with the landslide of votes for the new Republican president,

---

First Lady Jacqueline Kennedy (1929–94)

Jacqueline Kennedy endeared herself to the American public with her graciousness, elegance, and beauty. Born Jacqueline Lee Bouvier, she graduated from George Washington University in 1951 and married John F. Kennedy in 1953. As first lady Jacqueline impressed foreign leaders with her broad culture and ease in speaking Spanish and French. Parents named their daughters after her, and women copied her suits, hairstyle, and pillbox hat. Her most enduring contribution was her work to restore the White House to its original Federal style. After John's assassination Jacqueline moved to New York City. In 1968 she married Aristotle Onassis, a wealthy Greek shipping magnate. After his death in 1975 she returned to New York and became a book editor.

White House photo/Library of Congress, Washington, D.C. (neg. no. LC-USZ62-25815)

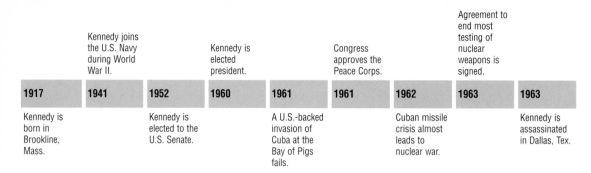

John F. Kennedy Timeline

1917	1941	1952	1960	1961	1961	1962	1963	1963

Kennedy joins the U.S. Navy during World War II. (1941)

Kennedy is elected president. (1960)

Congress approves the Peace Corps. (1961)

Agreement to end most testing of nuclear weapons is signed. (1963)

Kennedy is born in Brookline, Mass. (1917)

Kennedy is elected to the U.S. Senate. (1952)

A U.S.-backed invasion of Cuba at the Bay of Pigs fails. (1961)

Cuban missile crisis almost leads to nuclear war. (1962)

Kennedy is assassinated in Dallas, Tex. (1963)

Dwight D. Eisenhower. As a senator Kennedy became increasingly liberal in his political outlook. Among other causes, he fought for labor reform and civil rights legislation.

Kennedy enhanced his appeal by marrying Jacqueline Lee Bouvier in September 1953. Twelve years younger than Kennedy and from a socially prominent family, the beautiful "Jackie" was the perfect complement to the handsome politician. The glamorous couple had two children.

Beginning in 1954 Kennedy underwent a series of operations to treat his chronic back injury. While recuperating, he worked on the book *Profiles in Courage*, a series of portraits of eight great U.S. senators. Published in 1956, the book became a best-seller and was awarded a Pulitzer prize in 1957.

Nomination and Election

Kennedy was nearly nominated vice president on the Democratic ticket in 1956. Despite his defeat, the campaign made Kennedy one of the best-known political figures in the country. Already his campaign for the 1960 presidential nomination had begun. In 1958 he was reelected to the Senate by a margin of some 874,000 votes, the largest ever in Massachusetts politics. At the 1960 Democratic convention in Los Angeles he received his party's nomination on the first ballot. He chose Senator Lyndon B. Johnson of Texas as his running mate.

After a campaign managed by his brother Robert and aided financially by his father, Kennedy narrowly defeated his Republican opponent, Vice President Richard Nixon. He was the youngest person and the first Roman Catholic elected president. In his inaugural address he called on Americans to help make the country a better place: "Ask not what your country can do for you, ask what you can do for your country."

Presidency

As Kennedy took office, Cold War tensions between Communist and Western countries were increasing. The new president pledged strong efforts to halt the spread of Communism.

The administration's first brush with foreign affairs was a disaster. Kennedy approved a plan drawn up

Hulton Archive/Getty Images

President Kennedy consults with his younger brothers Robert, the attorney general (left), and Edward (or Ted), a U.S. senator (center). The oldest Kennedy son, Joseph, was killed in action in World War II.

during the Eisenhower Administration to land an invasion force of anti-Communist Cuban rebels on their homeland. Kennedy's military advisers had told him that the invasion would spark an uprising against the Cuban leader, Fidel Castro. But the Bay of Pigs invasion—named after the site of the main landing—was a fiasco. Every member of the invasion force was either killed or captured. The incident embarrassed Kennedy and worsened relations between the United States and the Soviet Union.

Continued tensions led to a serious crisis in October 1962. Through aerial photographs, the United States discovered that the Soviet Union was building nuclear missile bases in Cuba. Viewing this as a threat to the United States, Kennedy ordered U.S. warships to form a blockade to prevent Soviet ships from reaching Cuba. For 13 days nuclear war seemed near. At the end of October, however, Soviet Premier Nikita Khrushchev agreed to remove the weapons from the island. By the end of November the missiles had been shipped back to the Soviet Union and the United States had lifted the blockade.

Major World Events During Kennedy's Administration

The Soviet Union *launches first man into space, 1961*

France, Algeria *end seven-year-old conflict, Algeria wins independence, 1962*

Republic of the Congo. *United Nations troops end secession of Katanga Province, 1963*

Cuba. *War between United States and Soviet Union narrowly averted during Cuban missile crisis, 1962*

Cuba *defeats rebel invaders, 1961*

Southeast Asia. *Communists win much of Laos. United States increases military aid to South Vietnam, 1962*

Kennedy's greatest foreign triumph was the Nuclear Test-Ban Treaty. The agreement banned nuclear tests in the atmosphere, in outer space, and underwater but permitted underground testing. Representatives of the United States, the Soviet Union, and Great Britain signed the agreement in 1963. Kennedy called the treaty a "victory for mankind."

Yet Kennedy's commitment to combat the spread of Communism led him to escalate U.S. involvement in Vietnam. As Communist forces threatened South Vietnam at the beginning of the Vietnam War, Kennedy sent military advisers, financial assistance, and supplies to aid the anti-Communist resistance.

Kennedy called his domestic program the New Frontier. His policies were designed to reduce

Kennedy and his wife, Jacqueline, ride in the backseat of an open limousine as the presidential motorcade moves through downtown Dallas on Nov. 22, 1963. Moments later the president was assassinated.

AP

unemployment, provide medical care for the aged, reduce federal income taxes, and protect the civil rights of African Americans. Kennedy's legislative program received little support in the Congress, however. It approved several of his proposals, including greater Social Security benefits, a higher minimum wage, and the Peace Corps, a volunteer service to help other countries in their development efforts. But his two most cherished projects, massive income tax cuts and a sweeping civil rights measure, were not passed until after his death.

Assassination

In November 1963, looking forward to the 1964 presidential election, Kennedy made a political visit to Texas. A large and enthusiastic crowd greeted the presidential party when it arrived at the Dallas airport on November 22. He and his wife were riding slowly through the city in an open limousine when shots rang out. The president, shot in the neck and head, slumped over into his wife's lap. He died shortly after he was brought to the hospital. Within hours Vice President Johnson was sworn in as president.

Dallas police arrested Lee Harvey Oswald for the slaying. Although a mass of circumstantial evidence pointed to Oswald as the killer, the 24-year-old professed Marxist and Castro sympathizer never came to trial. On November 24, as Oswald was being led across the basement of the City Hall for transfer to another prison, Jack Ruby, a Dallas nightclub owner with connections to organized crime, broke through a cordon of police and shot Oswald.

President Johnson created a commission to investigate and report on the facts relating to the tragedy. The chief justice of the Supreme Court, Earl Warren, was appointed chairman. The Warren Commission found that the shots that killed President Kennedy were fired by Oswald. The commission also reported that it had found no evidence that either Oswald or Ruby was part of any conspiracy, domestic or foreign, to assassinate Kennedy. Despite these findings, conspiracy theories have persisted. Kennedy's assassination, the most notorious political murder of the 20th century, remains a source of bafflement, controversy, and speculation.

LYNDON B. JOHNSON

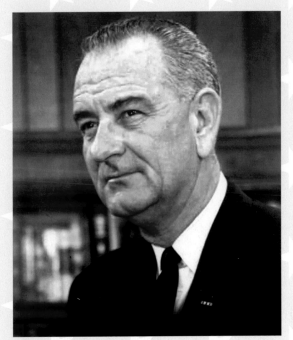

**36th President of the United States
(1908–73; president 1963–69)**

Vice President: Hubert H. Humphrey (1911–78)

At 2:38 PM on Nov. 22, 1963, Lyndon B. Johnson took the oath of office as 36th president of the United States. Less than two hours earlier, President John F. Kennedy had died in a Dallas, Tex., hospital from an assassin's bullets. Vice President Johnson then immediately became president. In 1964 voters elected him to a full term. During his administration Johnson introduced important social legislation, including a historic civil rights bill. He faced harsh criticism, however, for greatly expanding U.S. involvement in the Vietnam War.

Early Life

Lyndon Baines Johnson was born on Aug. 27, 1908, on a farm near Stonewall, Tex. He was the eldest child of Sam Ealy Johnson, Jr., a businessman and member of the state legislature, and Rebekah Baines Johnson, daughter of a state legislator.

After finishing high school in 1924, Johnson spent three years in a series of odd jobs before enrolling at the Southwest Texas State Teachers College in San Marcos, Tex. While studying there he taught Mexican American children in the small southern Texas town of Cotulla. The extreme poverty of his students made a profound impression on him.

Career in Congress

After graduating from college in 1930, Johnson won praise as a teacher of debate and public speaking at a Houston high school. That same year he worked on the Congressional campaign of Democrat Richard Kleberg, one of the owners of the famous King Ranch. After winning the election, Kleberg took Johnson to Washington, D.C., as his assistant.

In 1934 Johnson married Claudia Alta Taylor, known from childhood as Lady Bird. Daughter of a wealthy Texas rancher, she provided great support to her husband in his political career. The couple had two daughters.

Johnson's political career took off with the help of Sam Rayburn, a family friend and powerful Democratic congressman. In 1935 Rayburn got Johnson his first important public job, as director of the National Youth Administration in Texas. Two years later Johnson, a Democrat, was elected to the U.S. House of Representatives. His victory on an all-out New Deal platform attracted the attention of President Franklin D. Roosevelt, who made Johnson his protégé.

The day following the Japanese attack on Pearl Harbor on Dec. 7, 1941, Johnson became the first member of

---

First Lady Lady Bird Johnson (1912–2007)

Lady Bird Johnson was an environmentalist noted for her emphasis on beautification. Born Claudia Alta Taylor, she was nicknamed Lady Bird in childhood on the suggestion of a family nursemaid. Unusually bright, she graduated from high school at 15 and attended the University of Texas at Austin, earning degrees in history and journalism. She married Lyndon B. Johnson in 1934. Lady Bird was an astute businesswoman who built up the family fortune while her husband occupied himself in public office. With an inheritance from her parents she bought a radio station in Austin, which she then managed. As first lady she promoted an environmental program, called "beautification," that encouraged people to make their surroundings more attractive, whether they were wide-open spaces or crowded urban neighborhoods.

Lyndon B. Johnson Timeline

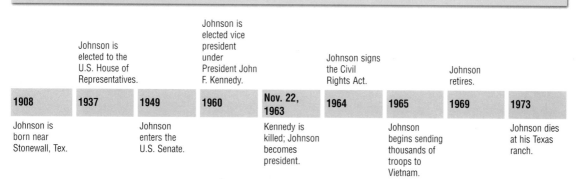

1908	1937	1949	1960	Nov. 22, 1963	1964	1965	1969	1973
	Johnson is elected to the U.S. House of Representatives.		Johnson is elected vice president under President John F. Kennedy.		Johnson signs the Civil Rights Act.		Johnson retires.	
Johnson is born near Stonewall, Tex.		Johnson enters the U.S. Senate.		Kennedy is killed; Johnson becomes president.		Johnson begins sending thousands of troops to Vietnam.		Johnson dies at his Texas ranch.

Congress to enter active duty in World War II. A lieutenant commander in the Navy, he was stationed in New Zealand and Australia. General Douglas MacArthur awarded him the Silver Star for gallantry in action on a flight over enemy territory.

Johnson served five successive full terms in the House. In 1948 he was elected to the U.S. Senate. Here Johnson quickly established himself as one of the most effective and persuasive party leaders in memory. In 1953 he became minority leader in a Republican Senate, and in 1955 he was made Senate majority leader. He followed a policy of compromise that resulted in unusual cooperation between Republican and Democratic senators. His greatest accomplishment was to obtain passage of the first civil rights bill since 1875. He experienced a severe heart attack in 1955, but within several months he was back at work.

Presidency

Johnson was a candidate for the Democratic presidential nomination in 1960, but he accepted second place on the ticket with John F. Kennedy. Johnson's influence in the South helped Kennedy to a narrow victory over the Republican candidate, Richard M. Nixon. On Nov. 22, 1963, Kennedy was assassinated in Dallas, plunging Johnson into the office that he had sought three years earlier.

The new president took firm command of the government, reassuring a worried world of the continuity of U.S. policy and leadership. Addressing Congress on November 27, Johnson urged the passage of legislation that Kennedy had proposed. He placed greatest importance on Kennedy's civil rights bill, which became the focus of his efforts during the first months of his presidency. In February 1964 the House of Representatives passed an even stronger bill than the one that Kennedy had proposed. The measure was finally passed by the Senate in June, after a bitter fight by Southern opponents. The Civil Rights Act was the most far-reaching bill of its kind in the country's history.

The Civil Rights Act set the tone for Johnson's domestic program, which he called the Great Society. It was the most impressive body of social legislation since Franklin D. Roosevelt's New Deal of the 1930s. It

Cecil Stoughton/Lyndon B. Johnson Library

Jacqueline Kennedy (right) and Lady Bird Johnson stand by President Johnson as he takes the oath of office aboard Air Force One after the assassination of John F. Kennedy on Nov. 22, 1963.

included measures to fight the "war on poverty," including legislation establishing the Job Corps for the unemployed. The Voting Rights Act of 1965 outlawed the literacy tests and other devices used to prevent African Americans from voting. Medicare and Medicaid were developed to provide health benefits for the elderly and the poor, respectively. Other laws addressed problems in education, housing and urban development, transportation, conservation, and immigration.

In the presidential election of 1964, Johnson faced Barry Goldwater, a conservative Republican senator from Arizona. Senator Hubert H. Humphrey of Minnesota was Johnson's running mate. Johnson won easily, receiving more than 61 percent of the popular

Major World Events During Lyndon B. Johnson's Administration

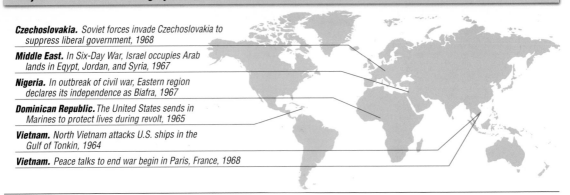

Czechoslovakia. Soviet forces invade Czechoslovakia to suppress liberal government, 1968

Middle East. In Six-Day War, Israel occupies Arab lands in Egypt, Jordan, and Syria, 1967

Nigeria. In outbreak of civil war, Eastern region declares its independence as Biafra, 1967

Dominican Republic. The United States sends in Marines to protect lives during revolt, 1965

Vietnam. North Vietnam attacks U.S. ships in the Gulf of Tonkin, 1964

Vietnam. Peace talks to end war begin in Paris, France, 1968

vote. He saw his victory as a sign of support for the Great Society program. After the election, Congress passed almost all the president's bills.

The success of Johnson's domestic program was tempered by events in Vietnam. In early August 1964 North Vietnamese gunboats allegedly attacked U.S. destroyers in the Gulf of Tonkin near the coast of North Vietnam. Johnson responded by ordering retaliatory attacks.

During the presidential campaign Johnson had pledged not to widen U.S. military involvement in the Vietnam War. Over the next several years, however, he sent hundreds of thousands of U.S. troops into the conflict and expanded their mission. In March 1965 he ordered a series of massive bombing raids on North Vietnam.

Criticism of Johnson's policies in Vietnam grew as the U.S. role in the fighting intensified. With no end to the combat in sight, the president's public support declined

Johnson (right) talks with civil rights leaders Roy Wilkins, James Farmer, Martin Luther King, Jr., and Whitney Young in the Oval Office of the White House in January 1964. Later that year Johnson signed the historic Civil Rights Act into law.

AP

steeply. American casualties reached nearly 500 a week by the end of 1967. Moreover, the enormous financial cost of the war took money away from Johnson's cherished Great Society programs. Beginning in 1965 the war provoked protests among students, civil rights leaders, and others. As his popularity sank to new lows in 1967, Johnson was confronted by demonstrations almost everywhere he went.

Meanwhile, the country's poor grew increasingly frustrated with the slow progress of Johnson's Great Society reforms. Vast numbers of African Americans still suffered from unemployment, run-down schools, and lack of adequate medical care, and many were malnourished or hungry. Beginning in the mid-1960s riots erupted in several cities, including Los Angeles, Detroit, and Washington, D.C. The unrest further damaged Johnson's reputation.

Last Days

On March 31, 1968, Johnson startled television viewers with a national address in which he announced that he had just ordered major reductions in the bombing of North Vietnam and that he was requesting peace talks. He also declared that he would neither seek nor accept his party's renomination for the presidency.

The Democratic presidential nominee in 1968 was Vice President Humphrey. Burdened by his association with Johnson's unpopular Vietnam policies, Humphrey tried to distance himself from the president by calling for an unconditional end to the bombing in North Vietnam. Meanwhile, negotiations had begun with the North Vietnamese. In October, one week before the election, Johnson announced a complete cessation of the bombing, to be followed by direct peace talks. But it was too late for Humphrey, who narrowly lost the election to Richard M. Nixon.

After attending Nixon's inauguration in January 1969, Johnson retired to his Texas ranch. There he wrote his memoirs, *The Vantage Point* (1971), and helped establish both a library to house his presidential papers and the Lyndon Baines Johnson School of Public Affairs at the University of Texas at Austin. On Jan. 22, 1973, just a few days before the end of the Vietnam War, Johnson suffered a fatal heart attack at his ranch.

RICHARD M. NIXON

U.S. Department of Defense

**37th President of the United States
(1913–94; president 1969–74)**

**Vice Presidents: Spiro T. Agnew (1918–96; vice president 1969–73)
Gerald R. Ford (1913–2006; vice president 1973–74)**

[signature: Richard Nixon]

The first U.S. president to resign from office was Richard M. Nixon. A former congressman and vice president, he was elected the 37th president in 1968. He was resoundingly reelected four years later. Midway through his second term, however, he was forced to step down in disgrace because of his involvement in the political scandal known as Watergate.

Early Life

Richard Milhous Nixon was born in Yorba Linda, Calif., on Jan. 9, 1913. His father, Frank Nixon, was a service station owner and grocer with a strong interest in politics. His mother, Hannah Milhous Nixon, strongly influenced him with her devotion to Quakerism.

At age 17 Nixon entered Whittier College, a Quaker institution that his mother had attended. He graduated in 1934 and won a scholarship to Duke University in Durham, N.C. After graduating from Duke in 1937, he returned to Whittier to practice law. In a theater group

he met Thelma Catherine (Pat) Ryan, a high school teacher and amateur actress. They married in 1940 and had two children.

In 1942, after a brief stint in the Office of Price Administration in Washington, D.C., Nixon joined the U.S. Navy. He served in World War II as an aviation ground officer in the Pacific, rising to the rank of lieutenant commander.

Congressional Career

After the war a Republican citizen's committee in Whittier recruited Nixon as a candidate for Congress. Running on a strong anti-Communist platform, Nixon won his first political election. As a congressman he was assigned to the House Un-American Activities Committee, which was investigating suspected Communist influence in the United States. Nixon played a major role in the prosecution of Alger Hiss, a former State Department official accused of spying for the Soviet Union. The Hiss case made Nixon nationally famous as a strong opponent of Communism.

In 1950, while the Hiss case was still in the courts, Nixon decided to run for the Senate. In his campaign he attacked his opponent for being "soft" toward Communists. Nixon won the election and, at age 38, became the Senate's youngest member. As a senator Nixon hammered hard at three main issues—the war in Korea, Communism in government, and the high cost of the Democratic party's programs.

Vice Presidency and Defeat

At their 1952 national convention the Republicans chose Nixon as Dwight D. Eisenhower's vice-presidential

---

First Lady Pat Nixon (1912–93)

Born Thelma Catherine Patricia Ryan, in Ely, Nev., Pat Nixon grew up on a farm in California. After a year at Fullerton Junior College, she was paid to drive an elderly couple to New York City. She stayed there for two years, working as a secretary and then as a hospital X-ray technician. She used her savings to attend the University of Southern California. After graduating in 1937 she became a teacher. Three years later she married Richard Nixon. As first lady Pat took up the cause of volunteerism, urging people to donate their time and services to hospitals, schools, day care centers, and nursing homes. She also traveled thousands of miles, speaking to school groups and representing her husband on visits to foreign countries.

Richard M. Nixon Timeline

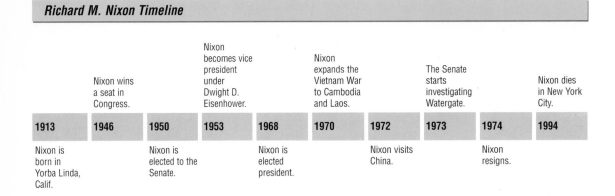

1913	1946	1950	1953	1968	1970	1972	1973	1974	1994

Nixon wins a seat in Congress. (1946)

Nixon becomes vice president under Dwight D. Eisenhower. (1953)

Nixon expands the Vietnam War to Cambodia and Laos. (1970)

The Senate starts investigating Watergate. (1973)

Nixon dies in New York City. (1994)

Nixon is born in Yorba Linda, Calif. (1913)

Nixon is elected to the Senate. (1950)

Nixon is elected president. (1968)

Nixon visits China. (1972)

Nixon resigns. (1974)

running mate. The Republicans won easily and were reelected in 1956. As vice president, Nixon campaigned for Republican candidates but otherwise did not take on significant responsibilities. Nevertheless, he helped to make the role of vice president more prominent. In 1955–57 Eisenhower suffered a series of serious illnesses. Three times during this period Nixon assumed the president's duties, chairing Cabinet sessions and meetings of the National Security Council. He also made a series of goodwill tours that took him to every continent.

In 1960 the Republican party chose its seasoned vice president to run for the country's highest office. Nixon narrowly lost the presidential race to Democrat John F. Kennedy. Nixon's supporters blamed his defeat on irregularities in both the Texas and Illinois votes. Another factor was his poor appearance in a series of televised debates with Kennedy.

Two years later Nixon unsuccessfully ran for governor in his native California. Disillusioned by these defeats, he announced that he was retiring from politics to practice law in New York City. Nevertheless, he continued to campaign for Republican candidates around the country.

Presidency

The Republicans rewarded Nixon for his efforts by nominating him for the presidency in 1968. For his running mate Nixon chose Spiro T. Agnew, the governor of Maryland. On Nov. 5, 1968, Nixon's long and loyal support of his party was repaid when he defeated Vice President Hubert H. Humphrey to become the 37th U.S. president.

First term. Upon taking office, Nixon turned his attention primarily to foreign affairs. The most pressing foreign policy issue was the ongoing Vietnam War. In 1969 Nixon began a phased withdrawal of U.S. troops. Under his policy of "Vietnamization," combat roles were transferred to South Vietnamese troops. At the same time, however, he resumed the bombing of North Vietnam, which President Lyndon B. Johnson had stopped in October 1968. He also expanded the war to neighboring Cambodia and Laos, inciting widespread protests in the United States.

AP

President Nixon and his wife, Pat, tour the Great Wall of China in February 1972. Nixon's trip to China was the first by a sitting U.S. president.

Despite the continuing conflict, Nixon sought to negotiate with the Communist countries that were supporting North Vietnam. His most significant achievement in foreign affairs may have been the establishment of direct relations with China after a 21-year break. Nixon's visit to China in February–March 1972 was the first by a U.S. president while in office. In May 1972 Nixon visited the Soviet Union and signed a number of treaties, the most important of which limited the manufacture of nuclear weapons.

The most important domestic problem that Nixon faced in his first term was the economy. The country faced high inflation and increasing unemployment. Nixon responded by devaluing the dollar and imposing unprecedented peacetime controls on wages and prices. These policies produced only temporary improvements in the economy.

Nixon's administration undertook a number of important reforms in welfare policy, civil rights, law enforcement, the environment, and other areas. It increased funding for many federal civil rights agencies, in particular the Equal Employment Opportunity

Major World Events During Nixon's Administration

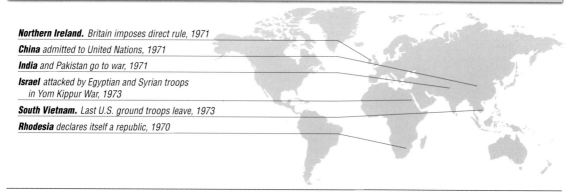

Northern Ireland. *Britain imposes direct rule, 1971*

China *admitted to United Nations, 1971*

India *and Pakistan go to war, 1971*

Israel *attacked by Egyptian and Syrian troops in Yom Kippur War, 1973*

South Vietnam. *Last U.S. ground troops leave, 1973*

Rhodesia *declares itself a republic, 1970*

Commission (EEOC). It also proposed legislation that created the Occupational Safety and Health Administration (OSHA) and the Environmental Protection Agency (EPA).

Second term. Nixon was nominated for a second term in 1972. He defeated his Democratic challenger, the liberal senator George McGovern, in one of the largest landslide victories in the history of U.S. presidential elections. Nixon received 520 electoral votes to McGovern's 17.

Assisted by National Security Adviser Henry A. Kissinger, Nixon concluded a peace agreement with North Vietnam in January 1973. In March Nixon welcomed home the last U.S. ground troops and prisoners of war from Vietnam.

Nixon boards a helicopter to leave the White House en route to his home in California on Aug. 9, 1974, the day after announcing his resignation to the American people.

This achievement was soon overshadowed, however, by political scandals. In October 1973 Vice President Agnew resigned from office and was convicted in federal court on a felony charge of income tax evasion. Nixon chose Representative Gerald R. Ford of Michigan to succeed Agnew.

The predominant issue of Nixon's second term was the unfolding of the Watergate scandal. In June 1972 five men hired by the Republican party's Committee to Reelect the President had been arrested while breaking into the Democratic party's national headquarters at the Watergate apartment-office complex in Washington, D.C. Early in 1973 the men were tried for burglary and wiretapping; five pleaded guilty and two were convicted by a jury. Soon afterward a special Senate committee was established to probe allegations that White House officials had attempted to cover up administration involvement in the affair.

When the committee learned that all of Nixon's conversations in his White House office had been recorded, it ordered him to turn over the tapes as evidence. At first Nixon refused, but eventually he was forced to comply. The tapes documented the president's personal order to cover up the Watergate break-in.

Meanwhile, the House Judiciary Committee had already voted to recommend Nixon's impeachment. With his Congressional support destroyed, Nixon chose to resign. Vice President Ford succeeded him on Aug. 9, 1974. Within a month President Ford granted Nixon a full pardon for all crimes he may have committed during his administration.

Retirement

Nixon retired with his wife to the seclusion of his estate in San Clemente, Calif. He spent the next 20 years trying to rehabilitate his domestic reputation, though he never lost the admiration of foreign leaders. He became a respected elder statesman in foreign affairs. He revisited China in 1976 and 1989 and made several visits to Russia, the last early in 1994. He also wrote *RN: The Memoirs of Richard Nixon* (1978) and several books on international affairs. Nixon died in a New York City hospital on April 22, 1994, four days after suffering a severe stroke.

GERALD R. FORD

Courtesy, Gerald R. Ford Library; photograph, David Hume Kennedy

**38th President of the United States
(1913–2006; president 1974–77)**

Vice President: Nelson A. Rockefeller (1908–79)

Gerald R. Ford (signature)

Gerald R. Ford was the only president of the United States who was never elected either president or vice president. He had been appointed vice president by President Richard M. Nixon in 1973 to replace Spiro T. Agnew, who had resigned in disgrace. Ford became president in 1974 when Nixon also resigned over the Watergate scandal.

Early Life

Ford was born Leslie Lynch King, Jr., on July 14, 1913, in Omaha, Neb. His parents were Leslie Lynch King, Sr., a wool trader, and Dorothy Gardner King. When the boy was less than two years old, his parents divorced. His mother took him to Grand Rapids, Mich., where she married Gerald Rudolph Ford. He adopted the boy and gave him his name.

The younger Ford attended the University of Michigan, where he was a star football player. When Ford graduated with a liberal arts degree in 1935, he refused offers from the Green Bay Packers and the Detroit Lions to play professional football. He decided instead to coach football and boxing at Yale University. In 1938 he began to take law courses, and three years later he received his degree from Yale Law School.

Ford practiced law for a short time before joining the U.S. Navy in 1942, during World War II. He served in the South Pacific as an aviation operations officer. After the war he returned to Grand Rapids and his law practice. He also began to take an active interest in politics. Through friends Ford met Elizabeth Bloomer Warren, known as Betty. They married in 1948 and had four children.

Congress and Vice Presidency

A Republican, Ford was elected to the U.S. Congress in 1948. He served in the House of Representatives for 25 years, becoming minority leader in 1965. Ford was a moderate in domestic affairs, a conservative in fiscal policy, and an internationalist in foreign affairs. Well-liked among his colleagues from both parties, he developed a reputation for openness and honesty.

Ford often said that his ambition was to become speaker of the House, but in the early 1970s it was unlikely that Republicans would soon be controlling the House. Ford was thinking about ending his political career and perhaps returning to law practice, but then came a new opportunity.

On Oct. 10, 1973, Vice President Agnew resigned after pleading no contest on a felony charge of federal income tax evasion. Under the 25th Amendment to the Constitution, passed in 1967, President Nixon had

---

First Lady Betty Ford (born 1918)

Born Elizabeth Anne Bloomer in Chicago, Ill., Betty Ford grew up in Grand Rapids, Mich. A dancer, she came under the influence of the legendary modern dancer and teacher Martha Graham while attending Bennington College in Vermont. After college she modeled clothes and danced in Graham's troupe in New York City.

She was divorced when she married Gerald Ford in 1948. As first lady she was noted for her strong opinions on public issues, some of which disagreed with her husband, and her candor regarding her health and other intimate matters. After leaving the White House, Betty entered a treatment center in California to end her addiction to prescription drugs. Later she founded the Betty Ford Center to help others recover from drug and alcohol dependence.

Gerald R. Ford Timeline

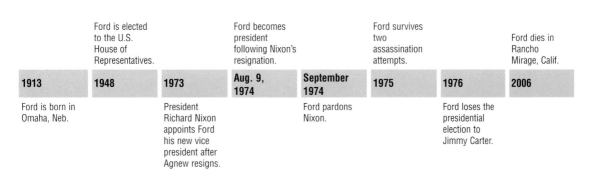

1913	1948	1973	Aug. 9, 1974	September 1974	1975	1976	2006
	Ford is elected to the U.S. House of Representatives.		Ford becomes president following Nixon's resignation.		Ford survives two assassination attempts.		Ford dies in Rancho Mirage, Calif.
Ford is born in Omaha, Neb.		President Richard Nixon appoints Ford his new vice president after Agnew resigns.		Ford pardons Nixon.		Ford loses the presidential election to Jimmy Carter.	

the power to fill the vacancy, subject to confirmation by a majority vote in both houses of Congress. He chose Ford, the only Republican whom the Democratic leadership of Congress would approve. With his nomination confirmed, Ford took office on Dec. 6, 1973.

During his eight months as vice president, Ford flew more than 100,000 miles (160,000 kilometers) and made more than 500 appearances to rally his party. The Republicans were agonized, along with other Americans, by the Watergate scandal. Former Nixon aides and associates were being indicted, tried, and sentenced to prison terms. Nixon was resisting subpoenas for evidence, and the House of Representatives was weighing impeachment. Ford supported Nixon, but he also urged him to cooperate with the special Watergate prosecutor.

Presidency

In President Nixon's resignation speech on Aug. 8, 1974, he said that the leadership of the country would be in good hands with Ford. On the following day Ford took the oath of office and became president. In a brief address, he called on the country to bind up the wounds of Watergate. "Our long national nightmare is over," he said. He appointed Nelson A. Rockefeller, former governor of New York, as vice president.

At the beginning of his presidency Ford tried to turn the attention of the country from Watergate. Two acts intended as conciliatory, however, caused much dissension and hurt his chances for reelection. On Sept. 8, 1974, Ford granted "a full, free, and absolute pardon" to Nixon for all crimes that he had committed or might have committed as president. Because the pardon precluded federal prosecution of Nixon, many people criticized it as violating the principle of equal justice under the law. Many people also opposed Ford's plan to give conditional amnesty to those who had evaded military service during the Vietnam War.

The Vietnam conflict came to an end during Ford's first year in office. When South Vietnam fell to the North in April 1975, Ford ordered the evacuation of remaining U.S. personnel from South Vietnam. The simultaneous evacuation of some 237,000 Vietnamese

University of Michigan Sports Publicity/AP

Ford was a center on the University of Michigan's undefeated championship football teams of 1932 and 1933. He was voted the team's most valuable player in 1934.

orphans and refugees and their resettlement in the United States were widely criticized. The next month, after Cambodia seized the U.S. merchant ship *Mayaguez*, Ford declared the event an "act of piracy" and sent U.S. Marines to rescue the ship and its crew. They succeeded, but the rescue operation resulted in the deaths of 41 people.

At home Ford confronted a combination of inflation and high unemployment. His administration tried to cope with the high rate of inflation by slowing down the economy. His WIN (Whip Inflation Now) program relied upon several voluntary measures to hold down prices and wages. By the end of 1974, however, it became apparent that decreasing industrial production and

Major World Events During Ford's Administration

India suspends constitutional rights, 1976

Middle East. Palestine Liberation Organization recognized by United Nations, 1974

Spain. Juan Carlos becomes king, 1975

Egypt abrogates its 1971 friendship treaty with the Soviet Union, 1976

Ethiopia. Haile Selassie deposed as emperor, 1974

Papua New Guinea gains independence, 1975

Sitting in the Oval Office of the White House, President Ford delivers a proclamation to the country granting former president Nixon a controversial pardon on Sept. 8, 1974.

AP

business activity, accompanied by rapidly rising unemployment, were as serious as inflation. Ford's WIN campaign was abandoned for alternate measures that would bring the country out of its most severe recession since World War II.

The president's economic proposals were generally cautious. He agreed to tax cuts, and he released some funds for housing and other construction to stimulate the economy. He advocated holding down government spending, particularly for social programs. Ford worked to restore health to the private sector of the economy and through it to the country as a whole.

Ford's economic program received a mixed reception—largely because of its failure to create more jobs. The overwhelmingly Democratic Congress strongly opposed his policies, especially in the areas of tax legislation, public works programs, and energy policy. During the first two years of his presidency Ford vetoed nearly 60 bills. Congress was able to override only about one of every five of the vetoes.

In September 1975 Ford was the target of two assassination attempts. In the first instance, in Sacramento, Calif., Secret Service agents stopped the would-be assassin before shots were fired. Two weeks

later a woman fired a shot at Ford in San Francisco, Calif., but missed by several feet.

Defeat and Retirement

Ford announced his candidacy for election in July 1975. He won the Republican nomination despite a serious challenge from Ronald Reagan, a former governor of California. Ford chose Bob Dole, a conservative senator from Kansas, as his vice-presidential running mate.

By late 1975 Ford's cautious economic policies seemed to be bringing steady improvement to the economy. Unemployment remained high, however, and it was largely on this issue that Ford lost the 1976 election to the Democratic nominee, Jimmy Carter. Ford was the first incumbent since Herbert Hoover to be defeated for the presidency.

After leaving the White House, Ford happily retired from public life. In 1980 he was asked to run for vice president alongside presidential candidate Ronald Reagan, but he refused. He golfed and skied at his leisure and ultimately joined the boards of directors of several corporations. His autobiography, *A Time to Heal*, was published in 1979. Ford died on Dec. 26, 2006, in Rancho Mirage, Calif.

JIMMY CARTER

Library of Congress, Washington, D.C. (digital. id. cph 3b52090)

39th President of the United States
(born 1924; president 1977–81)

Vice President: Walter F. Mondale (born 1928)

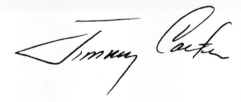

Elected president of the United States in 1976, Jimmy Carter emphasized morality in government and social welfare. However, his perceived inability to deal successfully with serious problems at home and abroad led to an overwhelming defeat in his bid for reelection. After leaving office he embarked on a career of diplomacy and advocacy, for which he was awarded the Nobel prize for peace in 2002.

Early Life

James Earl Carter, Jr., was born on Oct. 1, 1924, in Plains, a small town in southwestern Georgia. He was the eldest child of Earl Carter, a peanut warehouser and politician, and Lillian Gordy Carter, a registered nurse.

Jimmy was the first member of his family to complete a high school education. He went on to attend Georgia Southwestern College and the Georgia Institute of Technology. In 1946 he graduated from the U.S. Naval Academy in Annapolis, Md. Later that year he married Rosalynn Smith, who came from his hometown. They had four children.

Carter spent seven years in the U.S. Navy, serving submarine duty for five years. He rose to the rank of lieutenant, and a brilliant naval career seemed to be ahead of him. Then, in 1953, his father died. Carter was moved by the outpouring of admiration and affection for his father, who had been a member of the Georgia House of Representatives. He saw that his father had had a great effect on people through his business success, his personal generosity, and his service in local and state politics. Carter decided to resign from the Navy and pursue a life modeled after his father's. He returned to Georgia to manage the family peanut farm.

State Politics

Carter began his political career by serving on the local board of education. He won election as a Democrat to the Georgia state senate in 1962 and was reelected in 1964. As a state senator, Carter developed approaches to issues that he would later use as governor and as a presidential candidate. He advocated comprehensive planning in government, critical examination of budgets, and programs to help the poor and the disadvantaged.

In 1966 Carter announced his candidacy for the U.S. House of Representatives. When the Republican candidate, a political rival for many years, then switched to the race for governor, Carter also changed his plans and became a candidate for the Democratic gubernatorial nomination. He lost the primary election. Depressed by this experience, he found solace in evangelical Christianity, becoming a born-again Baptist.

First Lady Rosalynn Carter (born 1927)

Rosalynn Carter was one of the most politically active of all the first ladies. Born Eleanor Rosalynn Smith in Plains, Ga., she had to work at a young age to help support the family after the death of her father. Later she attended Georgia Southwestern College. In 1946 she married Jimmy Carter, her best friend's older brother. While Jimmy ran the family peanut business, she assisted him with bookkeeping. She also helped him in his political career with her extensive campaigning. As first lady Rosalynn took an unprecedented role in political affairs, attending Cabinet meetings and visiting foreign leaders. She had an especially strong interest in mental health issues, serving as honorary chair of the President's Commission on Mental Health.

White House Photo/Library of Congress, Washington, D.C. (neg. no. LC-USZCN4-117)

Jimmy Carter Timeline

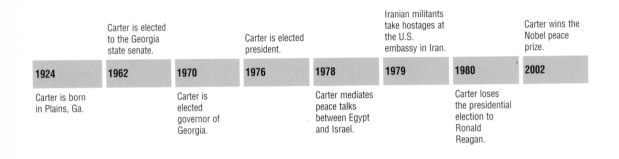

1924	1962	1970	1976	1978	1979	1980	2002
	Carter is elected to the Georgia state senate.		Carter is elected president.		Iranian militants take hostages at the U.S. embassy in Iran.		Carter wins the Nobel peace prize.
Carter is born in Plains, Ga.		Carter is elected governor of Georgia.		Carter mediates peace talks between Egypt and Israel.		Carter loses the presidential election to Ronald Reagan.	

Carter ran again for governor in 1970, and this time he was successful. Although he had not campaigned as a radical innovator, as governor Carter introduced policies that helped change the government and society of Georgia. He appointed many African Americans and women to posts in state government and formed biracial groups to deal with racial tensions. He promoted prison reform and mental health programs. He also reorganized the state government in an effort to make it more efficient.

Nomination and Election

In 1974, just before his term as governor ended, Carter announced his candidacy for the Democratic nomination for president. When he began his national campaign, Carter was not as well known as several other candidates. From the first, however, he demonstrated his ability to win votes. In the aftermath of the Watergate scandal, Carter presented himself as a man of strong principles who could restore the public's faith in their leaders. In the primaries he was strong in both traditionally conservative and liberal states. He ran well in industrial states as well as farm states. By the time the primaries had ended, most of his rivals had withdrawn.

At the Democratic convention in New York City, Carter received the nomination on the first ballot. For his vice-presidential running mate he chose Walter F. Mondale, a liberal U.S. senator from Minnesota. Carter campaigned for efficiency and honesty in government as well as broader social programs, including national health insurance. With the backing of much of the traditional Democratic coalition and with strong support from African Americans and labor unions, Carter won a narrow victory over the incumbent Republican president, Gerald R. Ford.

Presidency

On inauguration day, Carter walked the parade route to the White House with his wife. This was the first of many acts by which he tried to establish the image of a man of the people. Carter adopted an informal style of dress and speech in public appearances and reduced the pomp of the presidency. He sold the presidential yacht, cut back the White House limousine service, and conducted a radio phone-in program.

Carter took office during one of the most severe winters on record, with the country facing the worst shortage of natural gas in its history. This compounded an energy crisis that had started in the early 1970s as a result of overdependence on foreign oil. In April 1977 Carter gave the first of a series of major addresses to the country on energy, which became one of the dominant concerns of his administration. His energy program included an oil tax, conservation, and the use of alternative sources of energy. Congress approved several of Carter's energy proposals, including the deregulation of natural gas prices, but rejected others.

The economy was Carter's other domestic concern. He emphasized cutbacks in spending but also approved some measures to stimulate the economy, such as voluntary wage and price controls. Nevertheless, unemployment stayed high and inflation skyrocketed. Both business leaders and the public blamed Carter for the country's economic problems.

In foreign affairs Carter stressed human rights, publicly criticizing several countries and specific leaders

President Carter oversees a discussion between Israeli Prime Minister Menachem Begin (left) and Egyptian President Anwar el-Sadat (right) at Camp David, the presidential retreat in Maryland, in September 1978.

Karl Schumacher—AFP/Getty Images

Major World Events During Carter's Administration

Panama. *Panama Canal treaty ratified by United States, 1978*

China *and United States restore diplomatic relations, 1979*

Iran. *Ayatollah Khomeini returns from exile to declare the country an Islamic republic, 1979*

Middle East. *Peace treaty signed between Egypt and Israel, 1979*

Iran. *U.S. embassy seized by militants, American hostages taken, 1979*

Afghanistan *invaded by Soviet troops, 1979*

for their repressive policies. He supported several Soviet dissidents, an action that the Soviet Union denounced as interference in its domestic affairs. Some Latin American governments broke off agreements with the United States over the charges of repression.

Carter had several noteworthy foreign-policy achievements. In 1977 he narrowly won Senate approval of two treaties in which the United States agreed to relinquish control of the Panama Canal to Panama at the end of 1999. In 1978 he conducted a summit meeting between Israeli Prime Minister Menachem Begin and Egyptian President Anwar el-Sadat that resulted in a historic peace treaty between the two countries. On Jan. 1, 1979, Carter established full diplomatic relations between the United States and China.

Later in 1979 Carter and Soviet leader Leonid Brezhnev signed a new strategic arms limitation treaty (called SALT II). But renewed tensions between the countries led Carter to remove the treaty from Senate consideration in January 1980, after the Soviet Union invaded Afghanistan. Carter also banned shipments of grain and high-technology goods to the Soviet Union and called for a boycott of the 1980 Olympic Games in Moscow.

Carter's foreign-policy successes were overshadowed by a serious crisis in Iran. On Nov. 4, 1979, Iranian militants seized the U.S. Embassy in Tehran and took more than 50 Americans hostage. Carter tried to negotiate with the militants while avoiding a direct confrontation with the Iranian government. As the crisis wore on, however, his failure to secure the release of the hostages contributed to his reputation for weakness and indecisiveness.

In 1980 Carter was able to fend off a strong challenge from Massachusetts Sen. Edward Kennedy to win the Democratic presidential nomination. But the faltering economy and the hostage crisis had badly eroded the public's confidence in Carter's executive abilities. His loss to Ronald Reagan, the Republican nominee, in the general election was one of the worst ever suffered by an incumbent president. Carter won only 49 of the 538 votes in the electoral college. The day after Reagan's inauguration in January 1981, the hostages were released.

Alex Brandon/AP

Former president Carter and his wife, Rosalynn, help construct a house in Louisiana in 2007 as part of their work for Habitat for Humanity, a volunteer organization that builds affordable housing for the poor.

Retirement

Carter's public image improved after he left the White House. In 1982 he and his wife founded the Carter Center in Atlanta, Ga., to secure human rights, to resolve conflicts, and to combat disease, hunger, and poverty around the world. His volunteer efforts ranged from hands-on help in building low-income housing in the United States to continuing international mediation for human rights and peace. He also monitored controversial elections throughout the world. For his work as a peacemaker and champion of human rights and democracy, both during and after his presidency, Carter was awarded the Nobel peace prize in 2002.

RONALD REAGAN

U.S. Department of Defense

40th President of the United States
(1911–2004; president 1981–89)

Vice President: George Bush (born 1924)

In a stunning electoral landslide, Ronald Reagan was elected the 40th president of the United States in 1980. A former actor known for his folksy charm and confident ease as a public speaker, The Great Communicator, as he was sometimes called, won the votes of divergent groups who had not traditionally supported the Republican party. Strongly conservative, Reagan was a critic of social-welfare programs, an advocate of a strong military, and a zealous opponent of Communism.

Early Life

Ronald Wilson Reagan was born on Feb. 6, 1911, in Tampico, Ill., a small town in the northwestern part of the state. He was the son of John Edward Reagan (called Jack) and Nelle Wilson Reagan. His nickname, Dutch, came from his father's habit of referring to his infant son as his "fat little Dutchman."

Jack Reagan was a struggling shoe salesman who moved his family from one small town to another in Illinois. When Ronald was nine, the family settled in

Dixon, Ill. In high school and college he showed his ability in the three fields that came to dominate his life—sports, drama, and politics. At Eureka College in Eureka, Ill., Reagan played football and was active in the drama society but earned only passing grades. A popular student, he was elected class president in his senior year. He graduated in 1932 with a bachelor's degree in economics and sociology.

Radio, Motion Pictures, and Television

Trying to launch a career in show business, Reagan auditioned for radio station WOC in Davenport, Iowa, by improvising play-by-play commentary for a football game. He was hired to announce the University of Iowa football games for 10 dollars a game, and by the end of 1932 he became a staff announcer.

The next year Reagan was transferred to an affiliated station, WHO, in Des Moines. An announcer there until 1937, he also wrote a sports column for a newspaper. Among his duties was broadcasting Chicago Cubs baseball games from ticker tapes.

While at the Cubs training camp in California in 1937, Reagan took a screen test for the Warner Brothers studio and was signed to a contract. During the following 27 years he appeared in more than 50 movies. In his first movie, *Love Is on the Air*, Reagan played a radio announcer. Throughout his career he most often had supporting roles, frequently as the sidekick of the hero. Among Reagan's best-known movies were *Brother Rat*, *Dark Victory*, *Knute Rockne—All American*, and *King's*

First Lady Nancy Reagan (born 1921)

Nancy Reagan was born Anne Frances Robbins in New York City. Later she took the name of her adoptive father, becoming Nancy Davis. She attended Smith College in Massachusetts, where she majored in drama. After graduating in 1943 she turned to acting. By 1949 she was working in Hollywood, and she eventually made 11 movies. She married Ronald Reagan in 1952. Nancy's conservative political views encouraged her husband's drift to the right. When Ronald won the presidency in 1980, Nancy was considered one of his most trusted advisers. Some people criticized her for her extravagance, characterized by her wealthy, glamorous friends and her expensive, stylish clothing. She improved her image by playing down her contacts with celebrities and associating herself with a serious cause, the antidrug campaign "Just Say No."

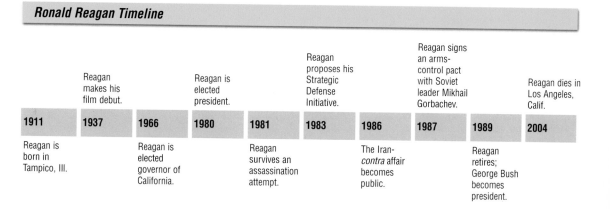

Ronald Reagan Timeline

1911	1937	1966	1980	1981	1983	1986	1987	1989	2004

Reagan makes his film debut. (1937)

Reagan is elected president. (1980)

Reagan proposes his Strategic Defense Initiative. (1983)

Reagan signs an arms-control pact with Soviet leader Mikhail Gorbachev. (1987)

Reagan dies in Los Angeles, Calif. (2004)

Reagan is born in Tampico, Ill. (1911)

Reagan is elected governor of California. (1966)

Reagan survives an assassination attempt. (1981)

The Iran-*contra* affair becomes public. (1986)

Reagan retires; George Bush becomes president. (1989)

Row. While filming *Brother Rat* in 1938, Reagan became engaged to his costar Jane Wyman. Married in 1940, they had a daughter and adopted a son. In 1948 they divorced.

During World War II Reagan was a member of the Army Air Corps, but he was rejected for active duty because of his poor eyesight. He spent the war years narrating training films and was discharged with the rank of captain in 1945.

Reagan served six terms—from 1947 to 1952 and in 1959–60—as president of the Screen Actors Guild, the union of movie actors. He helped achieve better pay, revised tax procedures, and improved working conditions for actors. He also fought against Communist influence in the movie industry. Much to the disgust of guild members, Reagan appeared in 1947 as a cooperative witness before the House Un-American Activities Committee, identifying actors, directors, and writers suspected of Communist sympathies.

In 1952 Reagan married the actress Nancy Davis. They had a daughter and a son. In 1957 Reagan and his wife appeared together in the war movie *Hellcats of the Navy*.

After having performed on several television programs, in 1954 Reagan began an eight-year association with the General Electric Company. He hosted the popular television series *General Electric Theater* and occasionally appeared as an actor in the series. As part of his contract, Reagan also spent several weeks each year speaking to General Electric employees throughout the country. During these talks he frequently defended free enterprise and criticized big government.

Political Commitments

During the 1930s and 1940s Reagan had been a liberal Democrat. He admired Franklin D. Roosevelt and supported President Harry S. Truman for reelection in 1948. But his political opinions gradually grew more conservative. After first supporting Democratic senatorial candidate Helen Douglas in 1950, he switched his allegiance to Republican Richard Nixon midway through the campaign. In the presidential elections of 1952 and 1956 he backed Republican Dwight D.

Everett Collection

A still from the 1938 film Brother Rat *shows Reagan with Jane Wyman, who would become his first wife.*

Eisenhower, and in 1960 he campaigned for Nixon. In 1962 he officially switched his registration to the Republican party. His stirring televised speech on behalf of Republican Barry Goldwater during the 1964 presidential campaign catapulted Reagan onto the national political stage.

With the support of businessmen and other conservative backers Reagan entered the 1966 race for the governorship of California. He defeated his moderate Republican opponent in the primary and then conducted a campaign on such issues as welfare, student dissidents, crime, and "big government." Although registered Democrats outnumbered Republicans by three to two in the state, Reagan won by nearly a million votes. He was reelected in 1970.

Major World Events During Reagan's Administration

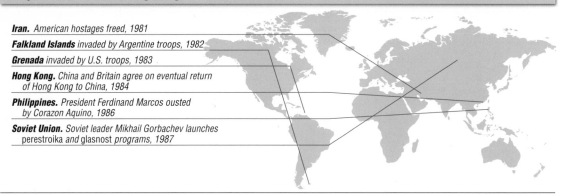

Iran. *American hostages freed, 1981*

Falkland Islands *invaded by Argentine troops, 1982*

Grenada *invaded by U.S. troops, 1983*

Hong Kong. *China and Britain agree on eventual return of Hong Kong to China, 1984*

Philippines. *President Ferdinand Marcos ousted by Corazon Aquino, 1986*

Soviet Union. *Soviet leader Mikhail Gorbachev launches* perestroika *and* glasnost *programs, 1987*

As governor of California, Reagan was not wholly successful in carrying out his conservative programs. During his two terms the state had its largest budget increases in history and spending nearly doubled. Partly because of previous deficits, Reagan increased taxes at a rate greater than the national average, and taxes became more progressive. California voters rejected his proposal to limit state spending and levels of taxation. Reagan did, however, accomplish some of his goals. He vetoed 994 bills passed by the state legislature, and all but one of the vetoes were upheld.

Several of Reagan's accomplishments during his terms as governor were highly regarded, even by his political opponents. He doubled aid to schools and increased spending for mental health by 400 percent. He cooperated with the legislature in reforming the state's welfare system by restricting eligibility and reducing the numbers of people receiving benefits while increasing benefits for the most needy. Reagan signed the most stringent air and water pollution bills in the country and promoted judicial reform.

National Politics

In 1968, while serving his first term as governor of California, Reagan announced his candidacy for president during the Republican convention. As a conservative alternative to Nixon, the front-runner, Reagan received only 14 percent of the delegate votes, and Nixon was nominated.

Reagan's disagreement with the foreign policy of President Gerald R. Ford led him to enter the 1976 race for the Republican nomination. Reagan defeated Ford in several primaries, but he did not enter primaries in enough large states to win a clear majority of the delegates. Reagan lost the nomination to Ford by only 117 delegate votes.

Reagan sought the Republican presidential nomination again in 1980, and this time he prevailed. The Republican platform was tailored to suit Reagan's views. It advocated large tax cuts, decreased government spending for social programs, increased military spending, and a more aggressive foreign policy. Reagan chose George Bush of Texas, who had been his

most successful opponent in the primaries, as his vice-presidential running mate.

After the convention Reagan lost the large lead he had held over President Jimmy Carter, and the candidates were often tied in the polls. Even though Reagan was often criticized for not being specific, his ability as a speaker helped him project a favorable image. His strong performance in a debate with Carter one week before the election was credited with winning over a large number of voters. In the electoral college Reagan defeated Carter by a vote of 489 to 49.

Presidency

The first months of Reagan's presidency were dramatic. Just after his inauguration he announced that Iran had agreed to release the American hostages who had been held captive since November 1979. Then, on March 30,

Standing in front of the Brandenburg Gate in West Berlin, Reagan acknowledges the crowd after delivering a historic speech in 1987 challenging the Soviet Union to tear down the Berlin Wall, which separated West Germany from Soviet-dominated East Germany. At Reagan's left is West German Chancellor Helmut Kohl.

Former Soviet leader Mikhail Gorbachev and his wife, Raisa, visit former president Reagan and his wife, Nancy, at the Reagans' ranch near Santa Barbara, Calif.
Reuters/Landov

1981, a deranged drifter named John W. Hinckley, Jr., fired at Reagan as he left a hotel in Washington, D.C. After surgery to remove a bullet from his left lung, he recuperated quickly and returned to his duties.

From the beginning of his presidency Reagan tried to reduce the role of the federal government. His administration set a new tone, indicated in such themes as "getting the government off the backs of the people" and not letting it spend more than it takes in. He proposed massive tax cuts and increased defense spending as well as significant reductions in spending on social-welfare programs such as education, food stamps, and low-income housing. In 1981 Congress passed most of the president's budget proposals, which succeeded in lowering inflation but produced the largest budget deficits in the country's history. A severe recession in 1982–83 lessened the appeal of so-called Reaganomics, but a strong economic recovery aided his landslide reelection over Democrat Walter F. Mondale in 1984. Reagan received an unprecedented 525 electoral votes to Mondale's 13.

In foreign policy Reagan took a firm stand against the Soviet Union. In 1983 he announced his Strategic Defense Initiative, a space-based missile defense system popularly called Star Wars. The Soviets perceived the system as a threat, but early in Reagan's second term they agreed to resume disarmament talks. Historic summits between Reagan and Soviet leader Mikhail Gorbachev in 1985, 1986, and 1987 resulted in a treaty reducing intermediate-range nuclear weapons.

Reagan's strong anti-Communist stance also dictated U.S. policy in other parts of the world. In 1983 he sent U.S. forces to the Caribbean island country of Grenada to depose a leftist regime. He justified the invasion as necessary to prevent the country from becoming a dangerous Soviet outpost. Elsewhere, Reagan expanded military and economic assistance to governments battling leftist rebellions; conversely, in countries with leftist governments, he supported opposition forces. This policy was applied most often in Latin America. During the 1980s the United States supported military-dominated governments in El Salvador in a civil war with left-wing guerrilla forces. In Nicaragua the United States backed guerrillas known as *contras* in their war against the leftist Sandinista government.

In 1986 Reagan became embroiled in the worst scandal of his political career. Late in the year the public discovered that his administration had secretly sold weapons to Iran in exchange for that country's help in securing the release of American hostages held by terrorists in Lebanon. This violated a U.S. policy that prohibited relations with countries—such as Iran—that supported terrorism. Soon it was revealed that profits from the sale had been illegally diverted to the *contras* in Nicaragua.

Senate hearings on what was called the Iran-*contra* affair began in 1987. Among those indicted were National Security Adviser John M. Poindexter and Lieut. Col. Oliver North. By 1990 six former Reagan officials had been convicted in the affair. Reagan accepted responsibility for the arms-for-hostages deal but denied any knowledge of the diversion of the profits to the *contras*.

Retirement

Neither the political scandals of his administration nor the weight of enormous budget deficits clung to Reagan. He retired on a crest of popularity to his home in California. After years of declining health, Reagan revealed in 1994 that he had been diagnosed with Alzheimer disease. The brain disorder made public appearances difficult for him, but his wife occasionally appeared on his behalf. Reagan died in Los Angeles on June 5, 2004.

GEORGE BUSH

White House Photo

**41st President of the United States
(born 1924; president 1989–93)**

Vice President: Dan Quayle (born 1947)

After serving two terms as vice president under Ronald Reagan, George Bush was elected the 41st president of the United States in 1988. For the first time since Martin Van Buren won in 1836, a sitting vice president succeeded directly to the presidency through an election rather than through the death or resignation of the incumbent. The defining event of Bush's presidency was the Persian Gulf War, in which a multinational force led by the United States forced Iraq to withdraw from Kuwait.

Early Life

George Herbert Walker Bush was born on June 12, 1924, in Milton, Mass., a suburb of Boston. His father, Prescott Sheldon Bush, was a banker who also served as a U.S. senator. His mother was Dorothy Walker Bush. George grew up in Greenwich, Conn., and attended private schools there and in Andover, Mass.

After graduating from Andover's prestigious Phillips Academy in 1942, Bush enlisted in the U.S. Naval Reserve. At age 20 he became the youngest pilot in the Navy. He served from 1942 to 1944 as a torpedo bomber pilot on aircraft carriers in the Pacific during World War II, flying many dangerous missions; in 1944 he was shot down by the Japanese. He received the Distinguished Flying Cross for his service in the war. In 1945, soon after returning home, Bush married Barbara Pierce. They had six children.

Following the family tradition, Bush attended Yale University, graduating in 1948 with a bachelor's degree in economics. He then took his young family to Texas and became a salesman of oil-field supplies. In the early 1950s he cofounded three companies dealing in oil and offshore drilling equipment.

Political Career

In 1959 Bush entered politics as a member of the Republican party in Houston. He ran unsuccessfully for the U.S. Senate in 1964. Two years later he was elected to the U.S. House of Representatives, becoming the first Republican to represent Houston in Congress. In 1970 Bush relinquished his seat in the House to run again for the Senate, but again he lost.

Shortly after his defeat, Bush was appointed by President Richard M. Nixon to serve as U.S. ambassador to the United Nations (UN). In 1973 Nixon named Bush chairman of the Republican National Committee. Bush remained strongly supportive of the president during

---

First Lady Barbara Bush (born 1925)

Barbara Bush was a highly respected first lady noted for her charitable and humanitarian efforts. Born Barbara Pierce in Rye, N.Y., she graduated from a private boarding school in Charleston, S.C., in 1943. She married George Bush in 1945, when she was 19 years old. As her husband's political career advanced, she began to acquire the skills required of a politician's spouse, including public speaking. During George's vice presidency Barbara, motivated by her son Neil's dyslexia, spoke at hundreds of events in a campaign to improve literacy. In 1989 she established the Barbara Bush Foundation for Family Literacy. As first lady she won many admirers with her humorous and self-deprecating style. Throughout her tenure in the White House she consistently ranked among the most-admired women in the United States.

George Bush Timeline

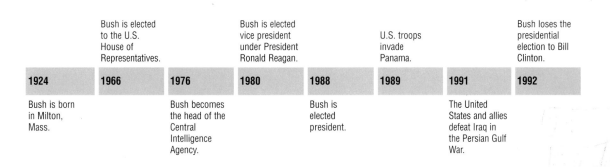

1924	1966	1976	1980	1988	1989	1991	1992

Bush is elected to the U.S. House of Representatives. — 1966

Bush is elected vice president under President Ronald Reagan. — 1980

U.S. troops invade Panama. — 1989

Bush loses the presidential election to Bill Clinton. — 1992

Bush is born in Milton, Mass. — 1924

Bush becomes the head of the Central Intelligence Agency. — 1976

Bush is elected president. — 1988

The United States and allies defeat Iraq in the Persian Gulf War. — 1991

the Watergate scandal until August 1974, when he joined a growing chorus of voices calling on the president to resign.

The next president, Gerald R. Ford, named Bush head of the first U.S. Liaison Office in the capital city of Beijing, China. Bush served there until December 1975, when Ford appointed him head of the Central Intelligence Agency (CIA). In this role Bush took steps to ensure that the agency's activities did not exceed Congressional authorization. In 1977, with Democratic president Jimmy Carter taking office, Bush resigned from the CIA and returned to Texas.

In 1979 Bush announced his candidacy for president. He withdrew from the race in May 1980, however, and became Ronald Reagan's vice-presidential running mate. The Reagan-Bush ticket defeated President Carter and Vice President Walter Mondale by a large margin. Bush won Reagan's loyalty, and the two repeated their success with an even more lopsided win in 1984.

Bush was an early and leading candidate to become the Republican party's presidential candidate in 1988. He won the nomination and chose Senator Dan Quayle of Indiana as his running mate. Bush and Quayle defeated the Democratic ticket of Michael Dukakis and Lloyd Bentsen with 53 percent of the popular vote.

Presidency

From the outset of his presidency, Bush demonstrated far more interest in foreign than domestic policy. In December 1989 Bush sent U.S. troops to Panama to topple that country's dictator, Gen. Manuel Noriega, who had become notorious for his brutality and his involvement in the drug trade. The invasion resulted in hundreds of deaths, mostly of Panamanians, and was denounced by both the Organization of American States and the UN General Assembly. Noriega was brought to the United States to face charges of drug trafficking.

Bush's presidency was a time of momentous world events, including the collapse of Communism in eastern Europe and the Soviet Union and the reunification of Germany. In November 1990 Bush met with Soviet leader Mikhail Gorbachev in Paris and signed a mutual

MPI/Getty Images

As the youngest pilot in the Navy, Bush saw action in the Pacific theater during World War II.

nonaggression pact, a symbolic conclusion to the Cold War. They signed treaties sharply reducing the number of weapons that the two superpowers had stockpiled over the decades of Cold War hostility.

In August 1990 the Persian Gulf region became the focus of international attention when Iraq invaded and occupied neighboring Kuwait. Bush responded forcefully. He helped impose a worldwide UN-approved embargo against Iraq to force its withdrawal and sent U.S. troops to Saudi Arabia to counteract Iraqi pressure and intimidation. Perhaps his most significant diplomatic achievement was his skillful construction of a coalition of western European and Arab states against Iraq. When Iraq failed to withdraw from Kuwait, Bush authorized a U.S.-led air attack that began on Jan. 16,

Major World Events During George Bush's Administration

China. *Troops put down Tiananmen Square rebellion, 1989*

Eastern Europe. *Communism collapses, 1989*

Panama. *United States invades Panama to oust Noriega, 1989*

Germany. *East and West Germany become one nation, 1990*

Iraq. *United Nations coalition war against Iraq, 1991*

Soviet Union. *Disintegration of Soviet Union, 1991*

Somalia. *U.S. troops arrive to aid in famine relief, 1992*

1991. The ensuing Persian Gulf War culminated in a U.S.-led ground invasion into Iraq that decimated the Iraqi army and liberated Kuwait.

On the strength of the victory over Iraq, Bush's approval rating soared to about 90 percent. His popularity soon waned, however, as a result of the struggling economy. An economic recession that began in late 1990 persisted into 1992. In his response to the slump, Bush made no drastic departures from Reagan's policies—except in taxes. His most memorable campaign pledge had been, "Read my lips: no new taxes." In 1990, however, he raised taxes in an attempt to cope with a soaring budget deficit. This move turned many conservative party members and voters against him.

Bush had made campaign pledges to become the "environmental president" and the "education

Consulting a map of the Middle East, President Bush and Defense Secretary Dick Cheney discuss strategy during the Persian Gulf War.

president." He signed the Clean Air Act of 1990, which made automobiles and industries meet tougher pollution control standards, and appointed the first professional conservationist to lead the Environmental Protection Agency. In education policy, he unveiled what he called the "America 2000" program. Among its goals were new national achievement tests in core subjects and the creation of nontraditional schools. Bush signed a bill for the largest expansion ever of the Head Start preschool program. Other major laws passed during Bush's term were the Americans with Disabilities Act, which required businesses, schools, and public institutions to provide accessible facilities for disabled people, and the Civil Rights Act of 1991, which made it easier for workers to seek damages in cases of job discrimination.

Bush's policy reversal on taxation and his inability to turn around the economy ultimately proved to be his downfall. Bush ran a lackluster campaign for reelection in 1992. He faced a fierce early challenge from Patrick Buchanan in the Republican primaries and then lost votes in the general election to third-party candidate Ross Perot. The Democratic candidate, Governor Bill Clinton of Arkansas, won the presidency by taking 43 percent of the vote to Bush's 37 percent. Perot captured an impressive 19 percent of the vote.

In his last weeks in office, Bush intervened in a crisis in the war-torn East African country of Somalia. A civil war between rival clans had led to famine among the country's people. Bush sent U.S. troops to Somalia to assist UN peacekeepers with the distribution of food and medical supplies. The humanitarian effort led to fighting that killed 18 U.S. soldiers in the first year of Clinton's administration.

Retirement

After Clinton's inauguration in January 1993, George and Barbara Bush returned to Houston. Although Bush had little involvement in the Republican party after his presidency, he saw two of his sons rise in politics. George W. Bush, governor of Texas from 1995 to 2000, was elected president of the United States and served two terms. Jeb Bush was governor of Florida from 1999 to 2007.

BILL CLINTON

*42nd President of the United States
(born 1946; president 1993–2001)*

Vice President: Al Gore (born 1948)

Bill Clinton

Emphasizing change and a "new covenant" between citizens and government, Governor Bill Clinton of Arkansas was elected the 42nd president of the United States in 1992. He was the first Democrat to be elected to the country's highest office since 1976. A popular president, Clinton oversaw the country's longest peacetime economic expansion. His presidency was marred by scandal, however. In 1998 he became only the second U.S. president to be impeached.

Early Life

William Jefferson Blythe III was born on Aug. 19, 1946, in Hope, Ark., a small town near the Texas-Oklahoma border. His father, a traveling salesman, died in a car crash three months before Bill was born. A few years later his mother, Virginia Dell Blythe, married Roger Clinton, and Bill eventually took his stepfather's name.

Bill became interested in politics at an early age. During high school he traveled to Washington, D.C., as a member of the American Legion Boys Nation. There he met President John F. Kennedy, an encounter that solidified his political ambitions.

Clinton attended Georgetown University in Washington, D.C., earning a bachelor's degree in international studies in 1968. During his junior and senior years he worked for Democratic Senator J. William Fulbright of Arkansas, chairman of the Senate Foreign Relations Committee, whom Clinton later called his mentor. Then Clinton attended Oxford University in England for two years as a Rhodes scholar. In 1973 he received a law degree from Yale University. Afterward he returned to Arkansas to teach at the University of Arkansas School of Law.

In 1975 Clinton married Hillary Rodham, a fellow graduate of Yale Law School. She became a successful attorney and took an active role in her husband's political career. The couple had one daughter.

Governor of Arkansas

Clinton's first political campaign, for a seat in the U.S. House of Representatives in 1974, was unsuccessful. The close race brought him statewide attention, however, and two years later he was elected attorney general of Arkansas. In 1978 he won the governorship. At age 32, he was the youngest person to be elected governor of any state since 1938.

Clinton lost his bid for reelection in 1980, but he regained the governor's office two years later. He was reelected three more times by substantial margins. A centrist Democrat, Clinton made educational reform and economic growth top priorities of his administration. He introduced the country's first program to test teacher

---

First Lady Hillary Rodham Clinton (born 1947)

Elected to the U.S. Senate in 2000, Hillary Rodham Clinton was the first wife of a sitting president to be elected to public office. Born Hillary Diane Rodham in Chicago, she graduated from Wellesley College in 1969 and Yale Law School in 1973. She married Bill Clinton in 1975. While Bill served as Arkansas governor, Hillary maintained a successful law practice and worked on programs that aided children and the disadvantaged. In the early years of her husband's presidency she was highly visible, chairing a task force on health care reform, but later she played a more traditional role as first lady. She took office as a senator from New York in 2001 and ran for president in 2008, narrowly losing the Democratic nomination to Barack Obama.

Bill Clinton Timeline

	Clinton is elected governor of Arkansas.		Congress passes the North American Free Trade Agreement.		Clinton defeats Bob Dole to win a second term.		The U.S. Senate acquits Clinton.	
1946	**1978**	**1992**	**1993**	**1994**	**1996**	**1998**	**1999**	**2001**
Clinton is born in Hope, Ark.		Clinton defeats George Bush to win his first term as president.		The Democrats lose control of Congress.		The U.S. House of Representatives impeaches Clinton.		Clinton retires as president.

Arnold Sachs—Hulton Archive/Getty Images

As a delegate to the American Legion Boys Nation, the teenage Clinton met President John F. Kennedy in Washington, D.C., in 1963.

competency and encouraged investment in the state by granting tax breaks to industries.

Presidency

Clinton announced his candidacy for president in 1991. Although his campaign was nearly sunk early on by charges of marital infidelity, he secured the Democratic nomination in 1992. He chose Tennessee senator Albert A. Gore, Jr., as his vice-presidential running mate. In November Clinton was elected president over the Republican incumbent, George Bush, and independent candidate Ross Perot.

First term. Clinton's presidency got off to a shaky start. His attempt to fulfill a campaign promise to end discrimination against gays and lesbians in the military was met with criticism from conservatives and some military leaders. In response, Clinton proposed a compromise policy—summed up by the phrase "Don't ask, don't tell"—that failed to satisfy either side of the issue.

Health-care reform, which had been a pillar of Clinton's campaign platform, proved even more troublesome. Clinton appointed his wife to lead a task force charged with developing a plan for providing health insurance to every American. Clinton's conservative opponents in Congress criticized Hillary Rodham Clinton's role in the task force and objected to its eventual proposal. After a year of debate, Clinton abandoned the health care reform effort in September 1994.

Despite these early missteps, Clinton's first term had many successes. Clinton changed the face of the federal government, appointing women and minorities to important posts throughout his administration. In 1993 Congress passed the North American Free Trade Agreement, which removed barriers on trade between the United States, Canada, and Mexico. Congress also enacted some 30 major bills related to education, crime prevention, the environment, and women and family issues.

Controversy was never far from the Clinton White House, however. In January 1994 Attorney General Janet Reno approved an investigation into business dealings by Clinton and his wife with an Arkansas housing development corporation known as Whitewater. Led from August by independent counsel Kenneth Starr, the Whitewater inquiry lasted several years but did not turn up conclusive evidence of wrongdoing by the Clintons.

Tax increases, failed health-care reform, and the Whitewater investigation made the Democratic party vulnerable for defeat in the midterm elections of November 1994. For the first time in 40 years, the Republicans gained control of both houses of Congress. Clinton responded by softening some of his positions and accommodating some Republican proposals. He put forth an aggressive deficit-reduction plan and embraced a massive overhaul of the country's welfare system. However, he continued to oppose Republican efforts to slow government spending on social programs.

In foreign policy Clinton inherited from the Bush Administration military commitments to United Nations peacekeeping missions in Somalia and in Bosnia and Herzegovina. He withdrew U.S. forces from Somalia, a country torn apart by clan fighting, after much public pressure. He kept U.S. peacekeeping forces in Bosnia and

Major World Events During Clinton's Administration

Northern Ireland. Good Friday peace agreement signed, 1998

Yugoslavia. Civil war breaks out over province of Kosovo, 1998

Haiti. President Aristide returns to power, 1994

Korean Peninsula. First summit between leaders of North and South Korea, 2000

Rwanda. Genocide kills more than 800,000 people, 1994

South Africa. First election by universal suffrage, 1994

Brennan Linsley/AP

Clinton leads a group of ethnic Albanian children during his tour of a refugee camp in Macedonia in 1999. The children were among hundreds of thousands of refugees driven out of neighboring Kosovo by a Serbian campaign of ethnic cleansing.

Herzegovina while also sponsoring peace talks aimed at ending the country's ethnic civil war. Clinton took a leading role in the ongoing attempt to resolve the dispute between Palestinians and Israelis in the Middle East. In 1993 he invited Israeli Prime Minister Yitzhak Rabin and Palestinian Leader Yasir Arafat to Washington to sign a historic agreement on Palestinian self-rule. In 1994 a U.S. peace delegation successfully negotiated the return to power of Haiti's president, Jean-Bertrand Aristide, who had been ousted by a military coup in 1991.

No Democrat stepped forward to challenge Clinton for the 1996 Democratic presidential nomination. Former Senate Majority leader Bob Dole emerged from a pack of Republican contenders to face Clinton in the November election. A healthy economy helped Clinton to an easy victory.

Second term. Strong economic growth continued during Clinton's second term, eventually setting a record for the country's longest peacetime expansion. By 1998 the Clinton Administration was overseeing the first balanced budget since 1969 and the largest budget surpluses in the country's history. The vibrant economy also produced historically high levels of home ownership and the lowest unemployment rate in nearly 30 years.

Still, scandal continued to plague Clinton's presidency. In 1998 Kenneth Starr, the Whitewater investigator, switched the focus of his probe to an alleged affair between the president and a White House intern, Monica Lewinsky. Clinton repeatedly denied that the affair had taken place. After strong evidence of the affair surfaced, Clinton apologized to his family and to the American public. On the basis of Starr's 445-page report and supporting evidence, the House of Representatives approved two articles of impeachment against Clinton, charging him with perjury and obstruction of justice in his effort to conceal the affair. He was only the second president in U.S. history to be impeached (the first was Andrew Johnson in 1868). The Senate acquitted him of the charges in 1999. Despite his impeachment, Clinton's job-approval rating remained high.

In the final years of his presidency Clinton was active in foreign affairs. In late 1998 he ordered air strikes against Iraq in response to that country's failure to cooperate fully with United Nations weapons inspectors. In 1999 U.S. forces led the North Atlantic Treaty Organization (NATO) in a bombing campaign against Yugoslavia that was designed to end Serbian attacks against ethnic Albanians in the province of Kosovo. The successful campaign ended after three months with the signing of a peace treaty. In 1998 and 2000 Clinton was hailed as a peacemaker in visits to Ireland and Northern Ireland, and in 2000 he became the first U.S. president to visit Vietnam since the end of the Vietnam War. He spent the last weeks of his presidency in an unsuccessful effort to broker a final peace agreement between the Israelis and the Palestinians.

Later Years

After leaving the White House in 2001, Clinton remained active in political affairs and was a popular speaker on the lecture circuit. He lived in New York, which Hillary Rodham Clinton represented in the Senate. His autobiography, *My Life*, was published in 2004.

GEORGE W. BUSH

Eric Draper/White House Photo

**43rd President of the United States
(born 1946; president 2001–09)**

Vice President: Dick Cheney (born 1941)

The son of former U.S. President George Bush, George W. Bush emerged from his father's shadow to be elected president himself in 2000. With his victory, he took his place alongside John Quincy Adams as the second son of a president also to serve in the office. His presidency was defined by the terrorist attacks of September 2001 and protracted wars in Afghanistan and Iraq.

Early Life

The oldest son of George and Barbara Bush, George Walker Bush was born in New Haven, Conn., on July 6, 1946. He grew up largely in Midland and Houston, Tex. From 1961 to 1964 he attended Phillips Academy in Andover, Mass., the prestigious boarding school from which his father had graduated. An average student, he received a degree in history from Yale University, his father's alma mater, in 1968.

After leaving Yale Bush returned to Texas. Soon he was accepted into the Texas Air National Guard as a pilot trainee, and in 1970 he was certified as a fighter pilot. Despite apparently missing at least eight months of duty between May 1972 and May 1973, Bush was granted an early discharge to attend business school at Harvard University. He earned a master's degree in 1975.

Business and Politics

Bush then returned to Midland, where he started his own oil and gas business. In 1977 he married Laura Welch, a former classmate from junior high school. Four years later they had twin daughters.

After an unsuccessful run for Congress in 1978, Bush devoted himself to building his business. A sharp drop in oil prices in the early 1980s hurt his fledgling company. In 1986 oil prices collapsed and Bush was forced to sell the company to Harken Energy Corporation.

After the sale, Bush spent 18 months in Washington, D.C., working as an adviser and speechwriter in his father's presidential campaign. Following the election Bush settled in Dallas. A lifelong baseball fan, he put together a group of investors to purchase the Texas Rangers baseball team. Bush's position as managing partner of the team made him a prominent figure throughout Texas.

Hoping to carry his newfound business success into the political realm, Bush challenged the popular Democratic incumbent Ann Richards for the governorship of Texas in 1994. Bush won the election with 53 percent of the vote. As governor Bush cut taxes, increased spending for schools, reformed the state welfare system, and took a tough stance against crime.

First Lady Laura Welch Bush (born 1946)

Born Laura Lane Welch in Midland, Tex., Laura Bush earned a bachelor's degree in elementary education from Southern Methodist University in 1968 and then taught in public schools in Dallas and Houston. She received a master's degree in library science from the University of Texas in 1973 and later worked as a librarian in Austin. She married George W. Bush in 1977. While George was governor of Texas Laura worked to improve literacy and raise funds for public libraries. As first lady she traveled solo to Europe, spoke on radio (in the president's place) in support of the Afghan people, and testified before a Senate committee on education. She also organized a national book fair featuring American authors and continued her fundraising for libraries.

George W. Bush Timeline

1946	1994	2000	Sept. 11, 2001	October 2001	2003	2005	2008	2009
	Bush is elected governor of Texas.		Terrorists crash airplanes into the World Trade Center and the Pentagon.		U.S. and allied forces invade Iraq.		A major financial crisis strikes the United States.	
Bush is born in New Haven, Conn.		Bush defeats Al Gore in the presidential election.		The United States attacks Afghanistan and its Taliban government.		Hurricane Katrina devastates New Orleans and the Gulf coast.		The Bush presidency ends.

Throughout his tenure he received international attention for the frequent use of capital punishment in Texas compared to other states.

Nomination and Election

Bush easily won reelection as governor in 1998 with a record 69 percent of the vote. His huge victory and his popularity made him an early front-runner in the 2000 presidential election. Surviving a stiff challenge from Senator John McCain of Arizona, Bush eventually emerged as the Republican candidate to oppose Vice President Al Gore, the Democratic nominee. He selected Dick Cheney, who had served as secretary of defense in his father's administration, as his running mate.

The presidential election of 2000 was one of the closest and most fiercely contested in U.S. history. The popular vote totals put Gore ahead of Bush by some 500,000 votes out of more than 100 million votes cast. In the electoral college, however, the contest was too close for either candidate to claim victory on election day. Eventually the outcome of the election came to hinge on the state of Florida, with both candidates needing its electoral votes to win. Bush held the lead in Florida, but the vote was remarkably tight. For several weeks the election remained unresolved as attorneys for both candidates argued in court, with the Gore team pressing for recounts and the Bush camp seeking to prevent them.

Eventually the U.S. Supreme Court issued a controversial split decision that halted the recounts, preserving Bush's slight lead in Florida and in effect awarding him the state's decisive electoral votes. Bush ended up with 271 electoral votes, one more than the minimum number required to take the presidency; Gore had 266 electoral votes. With his victory Bush became the first president to be elected despite losing the popular vote since 1888, when Benjamin Harrison defeated Grover Cleveland.

Presidency

At the start of his presidency Bush enjoyed Republican majorities in both houses of Congress. He had an early legislative success in June 2001 when Congress passed a 1.35-trillion-dollar tax cut, despite Democratic objections that it unfairly benefited the wealthy. In foreign affairs

Paul J. Richards—AFP/Getty Images

Standing on rubble of the World Trade Center in New York City, President Bush speaks through a megaphone to firefighters and other emergency workers on Sept. 14, 2001, three days after terrorist attacks destroyed the buildings.

the administration opposed international measures to control global warming, withdrew from the 1972 treaty on antiballistic missiles, and rejected the jurisdiction of the new International Criminal Court.

On Sept. 11, 2001, Bush faced a crisis that would transform his presidency. Islamic terrorists hijacked four U.S. airplanes, crashing two of them into the World Trade Center in New York City and a third into the Pentagon building outside Washington, D.C. Both World Trade Center towers collapsed. The fourth plane crashed in a Pennsylvania field after passengers rebelled against the hijackers. Some 3,000 people died in the attacks.

Bush responded by calling for a global war on terrorism. He worked to form an international coalition to combat terrorism using financial, legal, and political means as well as military force. In October 2001 Congress passed the USA Patriot Act, which gave the Federal Bureau of Investigation and other law-enforcement

Major World Events During George W. Bush's Administration

North Korea tests its first nuclear missile, 2006

Georgia. Russia invades South Ossetia region, 2008

Afghanistan. Taliban government falls after U.S.-led attack, 2001

Iraq. Saddam Hussein driven from power by U.S.-led forces, 2003

Sudan. Ethnic conflict escalates in Darfur region, 2003

Indian Ocean. Tsunami kills at least 225,000 people across a dozen countries, 2004

South Africa. African Union holds first summit, 2002

Ed Andrieski/AP

Bush addresses U.S. troops at an Army airfield in Colorado in 2003, the first year of the Iraq War.

agencies wide powers of search and surveillance in pursuing suspected terrorists. The act drew widespread criticism from civil liberties advocates. To coordinate efforts to protect the country against attacks, Bush created the Cabinet-level Office of Homeland Security.

The Bush Administration blamed the September 11 attacks on al-Qaeda, an Islamic extremist group led by Osama bin Laden. On Oct. 7, 2001, Bush launched a military campaign against Afghanistan, whose Taliban government was accused of harboring bin Laden and his followers. By the end of the year al-Qaeda had been routed and the Taliban forced from power.

In September 2002 Bush announced a new national security strategy that emphasized the need to defend against terrorists and "rogue states" that might threaten the country with "weapons of mass destruction"— biological, chemical, or nuclear arms. The strategy declared that the United States would take "preemptive" military action to prevent possible attacks.

Bush signaled his intention to put the new strategy into practice by identifying Iraqi President Saddam Hussein as a security threat. In late 2002 Bush accused the Iraqi government of possessing and developing weapons of mass destruction in violation of United Nations (UN)

resolutions. Saddam's failure to cooperate fully with UN weapons inspectors led Bush to declare an end to diplomacy on March 17, 2003, giving Saddam 48 hours to step down and leave Iraq or face removal by force.

After Saddam refused to leave, Bush ordered an invasion of Iraq. By mid-April a coalition of mainly U.S. and British forces had overthrown Saddam's regime. Iraqi guerrilla attacks continued, however, and coalition forces lost control of many parts of the country. Meanwhile, investigations failed to produce evidence to support the administration's claims that Saddam had been developing weapons of mass destruction on a large scale.

As the Iraq War persisted, the U.S. economy foundered. Financial markets suffered an extended decline and unemployment surged. A string of four consecutive years of budget surpluses ended in 2002, when the combination of military spending, tax cuts, and slow economic growth brought back deficits. A second tax-cut package passed in May 2003 added to the deficit but failed to revive the economy.

In his campaign for reelection in 2004, Bush deemphasized the economy and instead focused on national security, often invoking the September 11 terrorist attacks. The Democratic challenger was Senator John Kerry of Massachusetts. Bush was reelected with 286 electoral votes to Kerry's 251 and a slim majority in the popular vote.

After putting forth an ambitious agenda for his second term, Bush experienced a string of setbacks. His major domestic initiative, his plan to replace Social Security with private retirement savings accounts, collapsed after attracting little support. In 2005 Bush was criticized for the sluggish federal response to the devastation caused by Hurricane Katrina in New Orleans and the Gulf coast. Later that year it was revealed that Bush had secretly authorized the National Security Agency to conduct domestic surveillance without warrants in the aftermath of the September 11 attacks. The Iraq War continued to claim U.S. soldiers, and the Taliban staged a resurgence in Afghanistan. A severe financial crisis during Bush's last months in office caused his popularity to sink to new lows and helped to propel Democrat Barack Obama to a resounding victory in the presidential election of 2008.

BARACK OBAMA

Courtesy of the Office of U.S. Senator Barack Obama

**44th President of the United States
(born 1961; president 2009–)**

Vice President: Joe Biden (born 1942)

In only four years Barack Obama made an improbable rise from the state legislature of Illinois to the highest office of the United States. The first African American to win the presidency, he made history with his resounding victory in the election of 2008. His eloquent message of change and hope inspired voters across the country, even in states that had gone decades without supporting a Democratic presidential candidate.

Early Life and Education

Barack Hussein Obama, Jr., was born on Aug. 4, 1961, in Honolulu, Hawaii. His mother, who was white, came from Kansas; his father, Barack Obama, Sr., was from Kenya. They met while they were both students at the University of Hawaii. When young Barack was two years old, his parents divorced, and his father eventually returned to Kenya to work as an economist. His mother later married a student from Indonesia, and Barack lived in that country between the ages of six and ten. He returned to Hawaii in 1971, living sometimes with his grandparents and sometimes with his mother.

Following high school Obama attended Occidental College in suburban Los Angeles for two years and then transferred to Columbia University in New York City. He received a bachelor's degree in political science in 1983. Obama worked as a business writer and editor in New York before taking a position in 1985 as a community organizer on Chicago's largely impoverished Far South Side. Three years later he entered Harvard Law School, where he was the first African American to serve as president of the Harvard Law Review. He graduated with honors in 1991.

While a summer associate in 1989 at a Chicago law firm, Obama met Chicago native Michelle Robinson, a young lawyer at the firm. The two married in 1992 and had two daughters.

Entry into Politics

After law school Obama moved to Chicago and became active in the Democratic party. He organized Project Vote, a drive that registered tens of thousands of African Americans on voting rolls. He also practiced civil rights law and taught constitutional law at the University of Chicago. In 1996 Obama was elected to the Illinois Senate, where he helped pass legislation that tightened campaign finance regulations, expanded health care to poor families, and reformed criminal justice and welfare laws.

In 2004 Obama was elected to represent Illinois in the U.S. Senate. He handily defeated Republican Alan Keyes, a conservative radio talk-show host and former diplomat, in the first Senate race in which the two leading candidates were African Americans. Obama was

---

First Lady Michelle Obama (born 1964)

Born Michelle LaVaughn Robinson in Chicago, Michelle Obama earned a bachelor's degree at Princeton University before attending Harvard Law School. After graduation she returned to Chicago and took a job at the law firm Sidley Austin LLP, where she specialized in intellectual property law. Seeking a more public-service-oriented career path, she then became an assistant to Chicago Mayor Richard M. Daley. Michelle married Barack Obama in 1992. The next year she founded the Chicago branch of Public Allies, a leadership-training program for young adults. Later she served in a series of administrative positions at the University of Chicago. A skillful speaker, she took a prominent role in her husband's presidential campaign, earning a reputation as "the closer" for her persuasiveness in winning over uncommitted voters.

Evan Agostini/AP

Barack Obama Timeline

1961	1985	1991	1996	July 2004	November 2004	2008

Obama becomes a community organizer in Chicago.

Obama is elected to the Illinois Senate.

Obama is elected to the U.S. Senate.

Obama is born in Honolulu, Hawaii.

Obama graduates from Harvard Law School.

Obama delivers the keynote address at the Democratic National Convention.

Obama is elected president.

President-Elect Barack Obama waves to the crowd at a massive election night rally in Chicago's Grant Park on Nov. 4, 2008. With him are (from left) his daughters, Sasha and Malia, and his wife, Michelle.
Jae C. Hong/AP

only the third African American to be elected to the Senate since the end of Reconstruction in 1877.

While campaigning for the Senate, Obama shot to national prominence by delivering the keynote address at the Democratic National Convention in July 2004. The rousing speech wove a personal narrative of Obama's biography with the theme that all Americans are connected in ways that transcend political, cultural, and geographical differences. After taking office the following year, Obama quickly became a major figure in his party. He received several coveted committee assignments, including a post on the Foreign Relations Committee. As a senator he supported ethics reform in government, championed alternative energy sources, and worked to secure or destroy deadly weapons in Russia and elsewhere.

Nomination and Election

In early 2007 Obama declared himself in the running for the 2008 Democratic presidential nomination. The overwhelming favorite to win the nomination was Senator Hillary Clinton of New York. However, Obama's personal charisma, stirring oratory, and campaign promise to bring change to the established political system resonated with many Democrats, especially young and minority voters.

On Jan. 3, 2008, Obama won a surprise victory in the first major nominating contest, the Iowa caucus. Five days later, however, Obama finished second to Clinton in the New Hampshire primary. A bruising—and sometimes bitter—primary race followed, with both Obama and Clinton claiming important victories. Obama did not secure the nomination until after the final primaries in June. He officially accepted the nomination at the Democratic National Convention in August, becoming the first African American to be nominated for the presidency by either major party. Joe Biden, a senator from Delaware, was his vice-presidential running mate.

Obama's Republican opponent for the presidency was Senator John McCain of Arizona. Key issues in the hard-fought contest were the Iraq War, with Obama calling for a swift withdrawal of most U.S. forces from Iraq, and the domestic problems of health care and taxation. A financial crisis in the weeks leading up to the election made the economy the single most important issue, with polls indicating that the majority of voters believed Obama was better equipped to turn the economy around.

In November 2008 Obama decisively won the presidency, capturing some 53 percent of the popular vote. In addition to being the first African American president, he was also the first sitting U.S. senator to win the office since John F. Kennedy in 1960.

PRESIDENTIAL ELECTION PROCESS

Every four years American voters go to the polls to elect a president. The process of selecting the president, however, begins long before election day. Starting early in an election year, candidates compete in a series of state-by-state contests that determine who wins their party's nomination. Then the nominees face each other in a national election to decide the presidency.

The nomination process starts with the state primaries and caucuses. Each state holds one or the other, though primaries are much more common. The primaries and caucuses select delegates to represent the state at the parties' national conventions. In a primary, voters go to a polling place to cast a secret ballot. In a caucus, people gather at a polling place to hear speeches and take part in debates before casting their vote publicly. The significance of the primaries and caucuses is reflected in the time and money that candidates typically spend campaigning for the earliest contests, particularly the Iowa caucus and the New Hampshire primary. A poor performance in either of those states can drive a candidate from the race, while a good performance can boost a campaign.

The nomination season culminates at the Democratic and Republican national conventions, which are held during the summer prior to the November election. For many years the conventions were tense and often corrupt affairs as delegates and party bosses met behind the scenes and forged deals to decide on a candidate.

In the December following a general election for the presidency, electors in each state gather in their state capitals to cast their ballots. The vote in the electoral college, not the popular vote, decides the election.

Ed Andrieski/AP

After the chaotic Democratic convention of 1968, however, reforms reduced the importance of the conventions relative to the primaries and caucuses. Today, most convention delegates are pledged to support a particular candidate, and they merely ratify the choice of the voters. Nevertheless, the conventions are still considered vital. It is there that the parties draft their platforms, which set out the policies of the party and its presidential candidate. The convention also serves to unify each party after what may have been a bitter contest for the nomination.

After the conventions, the presidential candidates have a few months to campaign before the general election. On election day—the Tuesday following the first Monday in November—voters across the country make their choice for president. However, the final vote comes not from the people but rather from an institution called the electoral college.

The framers of the U.S. Constitution were wary of letting the people choose the president directly. In Article II of the Constitution they vested the election of the president and vice president in the electoral college. Members of the college, called electors, were originally appointed by the legislatures of each of the states. By the end of the Civil War, all the states chose their electors by direct popular vote. Each state is allowed a number of electors equal to the total of its Congressional representation: one for each House member and one for each of its two senators. The District of Columbia has three electors.

When people cast their vote for a candidate in a general election for the presidency, they actually vote for a slate of electors. All states except Maine and Nebraska use a "winner take all" system in which the party of the candidate who receives the most votes is awarded all the state's electors, even if the margin of victory in the state's popular vote is small. Hence it is possible for a candidate to lose the popular vote and still take the election by winning the electoral vote—an unusual scenario that occurred in 1876, 1888, and 2000.

The slates of electors meet in their state capitals on the Monday following the second Wednesday in December to cast their votes for president and vice president. Electors are not bound by the Constitution to vote for the candidates who won the state's popular vote, though some states have laws requiring their electors to do so. Regardless, electors rarely vote for anyone other than their party's candidates.

The electors' votes are delivered to Congress, and the candidates are formally elected when Congress counts the electoral votes on January 6 of the next year. The candidates who receive a majority, or more than half, of the votes become president and vice president. Should no candidate receive a majority, the House of Representatives chooses the president. The formal inauguration of the new president occurs on January 20 in Washington, D.C.

CABINET

Like other heads of state, the president of the United States relies on a group of advisers called the Cabinet. The word cabinet does not appear anywhere in the U.S. Constitution. The framers of the Constitution did, of course, expect that the president would appoint officers to help him. Article II stipulates: "The President . . . may require the Opinion, in writing, of the principal Officer in each of the Executive Departments, upon any Subject relating to the Duties of their respective Offices." But if the president wanted advice, he was expected to go to the Senate for it.

George Washington, however, instead turned to his department heads for counsel. At first he met with them individually. Soon he began to invite some or all of them to more formal meetings. By 1793 the meetings became fairly regular, and his advisers soon became known as the president's Cabinet. Congress created the Departments of State, of the Treasury, and of War in its first session in 1789. The heads of these departments and the attorney general formed the first Cabinet. The Department of the Navy was created in 1798. In 1829 the postmaster general was raised to the rank of a department head. The Department of the Interior was established in 1849. The Department of Justice was created in 1870, and the attorney general became its head. The Department of Agriculture was created in 1862; its chief became a Cabinet officer in 1889. A Department of Commerce and Labor was created in 1903 and was divided into two departments in 1913.

In 1947 a new Cabinet post, the secretary of defense, was created to replace the secretaries of war and the Navy. Congress also created a new Department of the Air Force and converted the War Department to the Department of the Army. Two years later the three branches of the military officially became part of the new Department of Defense. In 1953 the Department of Health, Education, and Welfare was created. Departments of Housing and Urban Development and of Transportation were added in 1965 and 1966, respectively. In 1971 the Post Office Department was reorganized as the U.S. Postal Service, and the postmaster general lost his Cabinet position. A Department of Energy was created in 1977. In 1980 the Department of Health, Education, and Welfare was renamed the Department of Health and Human Services, and a separate Department of Education was created. The Department of Veterans Affairs was added in 1989. In 2002 the Department of Homeland Security was created.

The heads of these 15 executive departments form the Cabinet. At the discretion of the president, other officials, such as the ambassador to the United Nations or the head of the Environmental Protection Agency, can be accorded Cabinet-level rank.

Although the president appoints the department heads, they must be approved by the Senate. The Senate rarely rejects a president's choice. The president may dismiss any Cabinet member by asking for his or her

The Granger Collection, New York

George Washington (right), the first U.S. president, began the custom of consulting regularly with his department heads as a group. His Cabinet in 1793 consisted of (from left) Henry Knox, secretary of war; Thomas Jefferson, secretary of state; Edmund Jennings Randolph, attorney general; and Alexander Hamilton, secretary of the treasury.

resignation. Presidents generally choose Cabinet members from among their political supporters. They have often tried to select people from different parts of the country and to include women and members of ethnic minorities. Some presidents have even selected members of the other major party to make the Cabinet more inclusive.

The Cabinet meets regularly at the White House on days chosen by the president. Special meetings are called in emergencies. The president and the vice president sit across from each other at an oval conference table, and the rest of the Cabinet members sit in an arrangement that reflects the order in which their offices were established. Meetings are informal. No records are kept. Questions are seldom put to a formal vote because the president alone makes the final decision. Abraham Lincoln is reported to have suggested a policy to his Cabinet that every member voted against. Lincoln calmly declared, "Seven nays, one aye. The aye has it." Harry S. Truman expressed the same sentiment with a sign on his desk that said simply, "The buck stops here."

© Albert Bruijn/Shutterstock.com

The north portico and lawn of the White House face Pennsylvania Avenue.

WHITE HOUSE

The official home of the president of the United States is the White House, at 1600 Pennsylvania Avenue N.W. in Washington, D.C. The stately, white stone home is almost as old as the United States. Americans have a deep regard for it as a symbol of the country's history and democracy.

The White House and its landscaped grounds occupy 18 acres (7.2 hectares). The main entrance to the building is through the north portico, which is lined with Ionic columns. The entrance faces Pennsylvania Avenue and Lafayette Square. The south side, with its semicircular portico, overlooks a beautiful park with a broad lawn, flower gardens, and wooded groves.

The White House has more than 130 rooms. The main building contains living quarters for the president and his family as well as various reception rooms, all decorated in styles of the 18th and 19th centuries. The public rooms are on the main floor. They are the State Dining Room, the great East Room, and the three salons named for their predominating color—the Blue, Green, and Red rooms. The living quarters are on the second floor. Guests are housed on both the second and third floors. The family and guests can enjoy the White House's movie theater, swimming pool, tennis court, jogging track, and library. The White House also has its own doctor's and dentist's offices.

The West and East wings of the White House connect with the main building. The president's office, known as the Oval Office, is located in the West Wing. The vice president's office is also in the West Wing. The East Wing holds other offices, including those of the first lady (the president's wife) and her staff.

The history of the White House begins in 1790, when Washington, D.C., was named the new capital of the United States. Two years later a contest was held to choose a design for a presidential residence in the city. The winner of the contest was James Hoban, an Irish-born architect. Pierre-Charles L'Enfant, who planned the city, chose the site for the new building, and the cornerstone was laid in October 1792. The first residents

of the mansion were John Adams, second president of the United States, and his wife, Abigail. Only six rooms were finished when they arrived in November 1800.

Originally called the "President's Palace," the building was officially named the Executive Mansion in 1810. About the same time people started to use the name "White House" because the mansion's white-gray sandstone contrasted strikingly with the red brick of nearby buildings. The name was made official nearly a century later by President Theodore Roosevelt.

During the War of 1812 the building was burned by the British, and President James Madison and his family were forced to flee the city. The architect, Hoban, reconstructed and expanded the house starting in 1815. President James Monroe and his family were the first to occupy the reconstructed mansion, moving there in 1817. He had the south portico built in 1824. Since then nearly every president has made some change in the White House. The north portico was erected in 1829. The first water pipes were installed in 1833, gas lighting in 1848, an elevator in 1881, and electricity in 1891.

During Theodore Roosevelt's presidency at the beginning of the 20th century, the White House was remodeled to create more living space for his large family. The mansion's second-floor rooms were converted from presidential offices to family living quarters. The West Wing was constructed in 1902 to provide more office space. The East Wing was added in 1942. More changes took place from 1948 to 1952, during Harry S. Truman's administration, when engineers feared that the building was in danger of collapsing. The original outside walls were left standing, but the inside was completely rebuilt.

National interest in the White House grew when Jacqueline Kennedy, wife of President John F. Kennedy, conducted a televised tour of the mansion in 1962. Renowned for her beauty and refined taste, she made the White House a center of national culture by displaying items of historical and artistic value throughout its rooms. Today the White House is a major tourist site, attracting more than 1.5 million visitors annually.

Presidential Election Results*

Year	Candidate	Party	Electoral Vote	Popular Vote
1789	George Washington†	—	69	
1792	George Washington†	Federalist	132	
1796	John Adams	Federalist	71	
	Thomas Jefferson	Democratic-Republican	68	
1800	Thomas Jefferson	Democratic-Republican	73‡	
	Aaron Burr	Democratic-Republican	73‡	
	John Adams	Federalist	65	
	C.C. Pinckney	Federalist	64	
	John Jay	Federalist	1	
1804	Thomas Jefferson	Democratic-Republican	162	
	C.C. Pinckney	Federalist	14	
1808	James Madison	Democratic-Republican	122	
	C.C. Pinckney	Federalist	47	
	George Clinton	Independent Republican	6	
1812	James Madison	Democratic-Republican	128	
	DeWitt Clinton	Federalist	89	
1816	James Monroe	Democratic-Republican	183	
	Rufus King	Federalist	34	
1820	James Monroe	Democratic-Republican	231	
	John Quincy Adams	Independent Republican	1	
1824	John Quincy Adams	(no distinct party designations)	84§	108,740
	Andrew Jackson		99	153,544
	W.H. Crawford		41	40,856
	Henry Clay		37	47,531
1828	Andrew Jackson	Democratic	178	647,286
	John Quincy Adams	National Republican	83	508,064
1832	Andrew Jackson	Democratic	219	687,502
	Henry Clay	National Republican	49	530,189
	John Floyd	Nullification	11	—
	William Wirt	Anti-Masonic	7	100,715
1836	Martin Van Buren	Democratic	170	762,678
	William Henry Harrison	Whig	73	550,816
	Hugh L. White	Whig	26	146,107
	Daniel Webster	Whig	14	41,201
	W. P. Mangum	Anti-Jackson	11	—
1840	William Henry Harrison	Whig	234	1,275,016
	Martin Van Buren	Democratic	60	1,129,102
1844	James K. Polk	Democratic	170	1,337,243
	Henry Clay	Whig	105	1,299,062
	James G. Birney	Liberty	—	62,103
1848	Zachary Taylor	Whig	163	1,360,099
	Lewis Cass	Democratic	127	1,220,544
	Martin Van Buren	Free Soil	—	291,501
1852	Franklin Pierce	Democratic	254	1,601,274
	Winfield Scott	Whig	42	1,386,580
	John P. Hale	Free Soil	—	155,210
1856	James Buchanan	Democratic	174	1,838,169
	John C. Frémont	Republican	114	1,341,264
	Millard Fillmore	Know Nothing (American)	8	873,053
1860	Abraham Lincoln	Republican	180	1,866,452
	John C. Breckinridge	Democratic	72	847,953
	John Bell	Constitutional Union	39	590,901
	Stephen Douglas	Democratic	12	1,380,202
1864	Abraham Lincoln	Republican	212	2,213,665
	George B. McClellan	Democratic	21	1,805,237
1868	Ulysses S. Grant	Republican	214	3,012,833
	Horatio Seymour	Democratic	80	2,703,249
1872	Ulysses S. Grant	Republican	286	3,597,132
	Horace Greeley ♦	Democratic	63	2,834,125
1876	Rutherford B. Hayes	Republican	185	4,036,298
	Samuel J. Tilden	Democratic	184	4,300,590
1880	James A. Garfield	Republican	214	4,454,416
	Winfield S. Hancock	Democratic	155	4,444,952
	James B. Weaver	Greenback-Labor	—	305,997
1884	Grover Cleveland	Democratic	219	4,874,986
	James G. Blaine	Republican	182	4,851,981
1888	Benjamin Harrison	Republican	233	5,439,853
	Grover Cleveland	Democratic	168	5,540,309
	Clinton B. Fisk	Prohibition	—	249,819
1892	Grover Cleveland	Democratic	277	5,556,918
	Benjamin Harrison	Republican	145	5,176,108
	James B. Weaver	Populist	22	1,027,329
	John Bidwell	Prohibition	—	270,770
1896	William McKinley	Republican	271	7,104,779
	William Jennings Bryan	Democratic	176	6,502,925
1900	William McKinley	Republican	292	7,207,923
	William Jennings Bryan	Democratic	155	6,358,133

Presidential Election Results* (continued)

Year	Candidate	Party	Electoral Vote	Popular Vote
1904	Theodore Roosevelt	Republican	336	7,623,486
	Alton B. Parker	Democratic	140	5,077,911
	Eugene V. Debs	Socialist	—	402,489
1908	William Howard Taft	Republican	321	7,678,908
	William Jennings Bryan	Democratic	162	6,409,104
	Eugene V. Debs	Socialist	—	420,380
1912	Woodrow Wilson	Democratic	435	6,293,454
	Theodore Roosevelt	Progressive (Bull Moose)	88	4,119,207
	William Howard Taft	Republican	8	3,483,922
	Eugene V. Debs	Socialist	—	900,369
1916	Woodrow Wilson	Democratic	277	9,129,606
	Charles Evans Hughes	Republican	254	8,538,221
	Allan L. Benson	Socialist	—	589,924
1920	Warren G. Harding	Republican	404	16,147,249
	James M. Cox	Democratic	127	9,140,864
	Eugene V. Debs	Socialist	—	897,704
1924	Calvin Coolidge	Republican	382	15,725,016
	John W. Davis	Democratic	136	8,386,503
	Robert M. La Follette	Progressive	13	4,822,856
1928	Herbert Hoover	Republican	444	21,392,190
	Alfred E. Smith	Democratic	87	15,016,443
1932	Franklin D. Roosevelt	Democratic	472	22,821,857
	Herbert Hoover	Republican	59	15,761,841
	Norman Thomas	Socialist	—	884,781
1936	Franklin D. Roosevelt	Democratic	523	27,476,673
	Alfred M. Landon	Republican	8	16,679,583
1940	Franklin D. Roosevelt	Democratic	449	27,243,466
	Wendell L. Willkie	Republican	82	22,304,755
1944	Franklin D. Roosevelt	Democratic	432	25,602,505
	Thomas E. Dewey	Republican	99	22,006,278
1948	Harry S. Truman	Democratic	303	24,105,695
	Thomas E. Dewey	Republican	189	21,969,170
	Strom Thurmond	States' Rights	39	1,169,021
	Henry A. Wallace	Progressive	—	1,156,103
1952	Dwight D. Eisenhower	Republican	442	33,778,963
	Adlai E. Stevenson	Democratic	89	27,314,992
1956	Dwight D. Eisenhower	Republican	457	35,581,003
	Adlai E. Stevenson	Democratic	73	25,738,765
1960	John F. Kennedy	Democratic	303	34,227,096
	Richard M. Nixon	Republican	219	34,107,646
1964	Lyndon B. Johnson	Democratic	486	42,825,463
	Barry M. Goldwater	Republican	52	27,146,969
1968	Richard M. Nixon	Republican	301	31,710,460
	Hubert H. Humphrey	Democratic	191	30,898,055
	George C. Wallace	American Independent	46	9,906,473
1972	Richard M. Nixon	Republican	520	46,740,323
	George S. McGovern	Democratic	17	28,901,598
1976	Jimmy Carter	Democratic	297	40,825,839
	Gerald R. Ford	Republican	240	39,147,770
1980	Ronald Reagan	Republican	489	43,642,639
	Jimmy Carter	Democratic	49	35,480,948
	John B. Anderson	(independent)	—	5,719,437
1984	Ronald Reagan	Republican	525	54,455,075
	Walter F. Mondale	Democratic	13	37,577,185
1988	George Bush	Republican	426	48,886,097
	Michael S. Dukakis	Democratic	111	41,809,074
1992	Bill Clinton	Democratic	370	44,909,889
	George Bush	Republican	168	39,104,545
	Ross Perot	(independent)	—	19,742,267
1996	Bill Clinton	Democratic	379	47,402,357
	Bob Dole	Republican	159	39,198,755
	Ross Perot	Reform	—	8,085,402
2000	George W. Bush	Republican	271	50,456,002
	Al Gore	Democratic	266	50,999,897
	Ralph Nader	Green	—	2,882,955
2004	George W. Bush	Republican	286	62,028,285
	John Kerry	Democratic	251	59,028,109
2008	Barack Obama	Democratic	365	66,000,000¶
	John McCain	Republican	173	58,000,000¶

*Candidates who won no electoral votes or less than 2 percent of the popular vote are excluded.
†Washington was unopposed for president in 1789 and 1792.
‡Because Jefferson and Burr received the same number of electoral votes, the decision was referred to the House of Representatives, which chose Jefferson.
§Because no candidate received a majority of the electoral votes, the decision was made by the House of Representatives.
◆Greeley died shortly after the election in November. His electoral votes went to four minor candidates.
¶Official results were not available at publication time. Totals are rounded to the nearest million.

Presidential Seal

The presidential seal is based on the Great Seal of the United States. A circle of 50 stars, representing the 50 states of the Union, surrounds the presidential coat of arms. The coat of arms consists of an American eagle bearing a shield without support, signifying that the United States should rely on its own virtues. The eagle's head is turned toward the right talon, which holds the olive branch of peace. The left talon holds arrows signifying war. In the eagle's beak is a banner inscribed with the Latin phrase "E Pluribus Unum," meaning "One Out of Many." The 6 red and 7 white stripes on the shield and the array of 13 stars and clouds above the eagle represent the original 13 states.

The design of the seal dates to the presidency of Rutherford B. Hayes (1877–81), who introduced the coat of arms. An executive order issued by President Harry S. Truman in 1945 changed the direction in which the eagle's head is turned from left to right. It also placed a circle of 48 stars around the coat of arms. His successor, Dwight D. Eisenhower, added two stars in 1959 and 1960 to reflect the admission of Hawaii and Alaska to the Union.

Presidential Flag

Before 1916 various flags represented the president. In 1916 President Woodrow Wilson approved a design that included the presidential coat of arms on a blue field with a white star in each of the four corners. President Truman's executive order of 1945 altered the design, calling for 48 stars to surround the coat of arms. As with the presidential seal, President Eisenhower added two stars to the flag to represent Alaska and Hawaii.

FURTHER RESOURCES

Alvarez, R.M., and others, eds. Election Fraud: Detecting and Deterring Electoral Manipulation (Brookings, 2008).

Bardes, B.A., and others. American Government and Politics Today: The Essentials (Thomson Wadsworth, 2008).

Bausum, Ann. Our Country's First Ladies (National Geographic, 2007).

Bendat, Jim. Democracy's Big Day: The Inauguration of Our President (IUniverse.com, 2004).

Benenson, Bob. Elections A to Z, 3rd ed. (CQ Press, 2008).

Buell, E.H., Jr., and Sigelman, Lee. Attack Politics: Negativity in Presidential Campaigns Since 1960 (Univ. Press of Kansas, 2008).

Craughwell, Thomas J. Failures of the Presidents: From the Whiskey Rebellion and War of 1912 to the Bay of Pigs and War in Iraq (Fair Winds, 2008).

DeGregorio, W.A. The Complete Book of U.S. Presidents, 6th ed., updated (Barricade Books, 2005).

Federer, W.J. Treasury of Presidential Quotations (Amerisearch, 2004).

Felchner, M.E., ed. Voting in America, 3 vols. (Praeger, 2008).

Hardesty, Von. Air Force One: The Aircraft That Shaped the Modern Presidency (Creative, 2005).

Harris, Bill. The White House: An Illustrated Tour (Courage Books, 2002).

Hennessey, Jonathan. The United States Constitution: A Graphic Adaptation (Hill, 2008).

Jewell, Elizabeth. U.S. Presidents Factbook (Random, 2005).

Kelly, Martin, and Kelly, Melissa. The Everything American Presidents Book: All You Need to Know About the Leaders Who Shaped U.S. History (Adams Media, 2007).

Klapthor, Margaret Brown, and Black, A.M. The First Ladies of the United States of America, 11th ed. (Scala, 2006).

Lamb, Brian. Who's Buried in Grant's Tomb? A Tour of Presidential Gravesites (Public Affairs, 2004).

McCaffrey, Paul, ed. U.S. Election System (Wilson, 2004).

Moore, Kathryn. The American President: A Complete History (Barnes, 2007).

Morris-Lipsman, Arlene. Presidential Races: The Battle for Power in the United States (Twenty-First Century Books, 2008).

Nelson, Michael, ed. Guide to the Presidency, 4th ed., 2 vols. (CQ Press, 2008).

Platt, Camille Smith. Real Cheesy Facts About U.S. Presidents (Crane Hill, 2006).

Polsby, N.W., and others. Presidential Elections: Strategies and Structures of American Politics (Rowman, 2008).

Purcell, L.E., ed. Vice Presidents: A Biographical Dictionary, 3rd ed. (Facts on File, 2005).

Schroeder, Alan. Presidential Debates: Fifty Years of High-Risk TV, 2nd ed. (Columbia Univ. Press, 2008).

Utter, G.H., and Strickland, Ruth Ann. Campaign and Election Reform: A Reference Handbook, 2nd ed. (ABC-CLIO, 2008).

Waldrup, Carole Chandler. The Vice Presidents: Biographies of the 45 Men Who Have Held the Second Highest Office in the United States (McFarland, 2006).

Watson, R.P., and Eksterowicz, A.J., eds. The Presidential Companion: Readings on the First Ladies, 2nd ed. (Univ. of South Carolina Press, 2006).

INDEX

Page numbers in **bold** indicate main subject references; page numbers in *italics* indicate illustrations.

Page numbers in **bold** indicate main subject references; page numbers in *italics* indicate illustrations.